FINDING YOUR WAY

OTHER BOOKS BY TOMMY TENNEY

GODCHASERS SERIES
The GodChasers
God's Favorite House
The God Catchers
God's Eye View
Prayers of a God Chaser

UNITY SERIES
God's Dream Team
Answering God's Prayer
God's Secret to Greatness

COMPASSION SERIES
Chasing God, Serving Man
Mary's Prayers and Martha's Recipes

FAMILY SERIES
How to Be a God Chaser and a Kid Chaser
On Daddy's Shoulders

DEVOTIONAL BOOKS
The Daily Chase
Experiencing His Presence
Up Where You Belong
Daily Inspiration for Finding Favor with the King

GIFT BOOKS
The Heart of a God Chaser
God Chasers for Kids
God Chasers for Teens
You Are a God Chaser If…

OTHER BOOKS
Trust and Tragedy
Secret Sources of Power
The Ultimate Comeback

ESTHER SERIES
Finding Favor with the King
*Hadassah: One Night with the King
*Hadassah: The Girl Who Became Queen
*Esther (children version)

One Night with the King—Special Movie Edition
The Hadassah Covenant

RUTH SERIES
The Road Home
Finding Your Way

*Fiction titles.

FINDING YOUR WAY

...to things that really matter

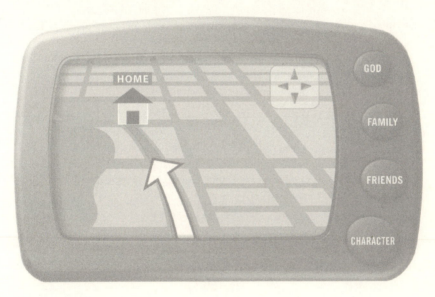

TOMMY TENNEY

NEW YORK   BOSTON   NASHVILLE

Unless otherwise indicated, Scriptures are taken from the King James Version of the Bible.

Scriptures noted *The Message* are taken from *The Message*. Copyright © 1993, 1994, 1995, 1996, 2000, 2001, 2002. Used by permission of NavPress Publishing Group.

Scriptures noted NLT are taken from the *Holy Bible*, New Living Translation, copyright © 1996. Used by permission of Tyndale House Publishers, Inc., Wheaton, Illinois 60189. All rights reserved.

Scriptures noted NASB are taken from the New American Standard Bible®. Copyright © 1960, 1962, 1963, 1968, 1972, 1975, 1977, 1995 by The Lockman Foundation. Used by permission.

Scriptures noted NKJV are taken from the NEW KING JAMES VERSION. Copyright © 1979, 1980, 1982, Thomas Nelson, Inc., Publishers.

Scriptures noted NIV are taken from the HOLY BIBLE: NEW INTERNATIONAL VERSION®. Copyright © 1973, 1978, 1984 by International Bible Society. Used by permission of Zondervan Publishing House. All rights reserved.

Scriptures noted TEV are taken from TODAY'S ENGLISH VERSION. Copyright © American Bible Society 1966, 1971, 1976, 1992.

FaithWords
Hachette Book Group USA
237 Park Avenue
New York, NY 10017

Visit our Web site at www.faithwords.com.
FaithWords is a division of Hachette Book Group USA, Inc. The FaithWords name and logo is a trademark of Hachette Book Group USA, Inc.
Printed in the United States of America
First Edition: January 2008
10 9 8 7 6 5 4 3 2 1

Library of Congress Cataloging-in-Publication Data

Tenney, Tommy.
Finding your way : ...to things that really matter / Tommy Tenney.—1st ed.
        p. cm.
ISBN-13: 978-0-446-57833-2
ISBN-10: 0-446-57833-9
1. Christian life. I. Title.
BV4501.3.T457 2008
248.4—dc22
2007026029

In the class of life, some teachers you choose, others are thrust upon you; but you learn from all.

Thank you to E. W. and Johnnie Ruth Caughron, Doyle and Faith Spears, T. W. and Lucille Barnes, Charles and Barbara Green, T. F. and Thetus Tenney, and G. E. and Mildred Switzer.

If the names sound old, they are. You can often learn better how to get somewhere from someone who has been there.

CONTENTS

INTRODUCTION xiii

1. DESTINATION AND DESTINY 1
GPS vs. "EPS"

2. HOW DID I GET HERE? 5
Famine of the Soul

3. HOW DO I GET BACK ON THE ROAD? 18
The End of Naomi's "Normal"

4. PAST LOSS MAGNIFIES PRESENT PAIN 36
It's Going to Feel Worse Before It Feels Better...

5. STUMBLING ONTO THE RIGHT ROAD 51
Your Personal Crisis May Trigger Another Person's Epiphany

6. THE JOURNEY BACK 65
Muddling Through the Mess

7. COMING HOME TO A PLACE YOU'VE NEVER BEEN 79
"Déjà Vu the First Time"

8. FINDING YOUR WAY TO THINGS THAT REALLY MATTER 92
What's It Really Worth?

9. FAMILY IS NOT A DO-IT-YOURSELF PROJECT 111
But Does It Take a Village?

10. "I FINALLY FOUND IT" 127
Whose Field Is It?

11. THE ROAD TO REDEMPTION 140
Whatever Did She See in Him?

12. SOMETIMES YOU HAVE TO WAIT FOR DIRECTION 155
Traveling in the Dark

13. REVERSE IS A GOOD GEAR TO HAVE 169
I Know It's Around Here Somewhere . . .

14. THE VALUE OF VALUES 183
The Road Map to What Really Matters

ENDNOTES 197

ABOUT THE AUTHOR 217

In the classic fairy tale *Hansel and Gretel,* the youngsters, worried about becoming lost in the woods, leave a trail of breadcrumbs behind them so that they can find their way back home. The animals of the forest, however, eat the crumbs, and they end up lost with no hope of finding their way back.

Today, Hansel and Gretel would not have walked through the forest; they would have driven in an SUV that was fully equipped with a navigation system to ensure they never became lost on their journey.

If only life came with a GPS system. We would never take a wrong turn, and we would never lose our way.

Tommy Tenney's new book *Finding Your Way . . . to things that really matter* provides just such a GPS navigation system for blazing a path to what really matters in your life. It also helps you figure out what to do when you lose your way, and how to get back on the right road.

At some point in everyone's life, we become lost and doubt our current place in the world. Tenney helps you make sense out of it all.

I am sure you will enjoy *Finding Your Way,* and that you will find it an irreplaceable resource as you travel through this beautiful journey we call life.

And you can keep the bread to make sandwiches.

Bishop T. D. Jakes, Sr., Pastor
The Potter's House of Dallas

INTRODUCTION

Many cars now come equipped with GPS (Global Positioning System) technology. Perhaps you've entered the address of your destination on one of these dashboard electronic navigators and easily found your way, even avoided detours.

Do you wish finding your way through life was that easy? Wouldn't it be great if you could just punch in some data and follow the voice from inside the car, with detailed turn-by-turn verbal directions, along with the electronic map displayed on the dashboard?

Fortunately there exists an EPS—Eternal Positioning System. That EPS is the Bible, with its record of people from ancient times. Culture may have changed. Geography may have been altered. But people have always had the same fundamental needs regardless of where they live geographically or chronologically. After essential needs like food and shelter are met, what makes life worth living? What really matters? These stories from antiquity provide clear directions for us, if we take the time to study their lives and apply them to ours today.

I found an ancient road map where two generations journeyed together to a place that reflected what was really valuable: a place of family, friends, and a purpose to their life's work and a connection to the eternal. The lead characters from this historical account include Naomi the mother, Elimelech the father, and their two sons, Mahlon and Chilion; Ruth the Moabite, who left; Orpah, her sister, who stayed;

Boaz of Bethlehem; and an anonymous character whom Jewish rabbi's often call "Ploniy Almoniy" (the Jewish equivalent of "John Doe").

Perhaps you, too, are "finding your way" to things that really matter. May these modern musings of mine on an ancient story guide you to that place of comfort and security.

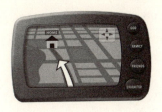

CHAPTER 1

Destination and Destiny

GPS vs. "EPS"

Strange cities and strange places seem to bring out the best or the worst in me. Because I travel so much, my family and I often find ourselves in unfamiliar places. Some years, I've been in over a hundred cities across the United States and twenty different nations. There is no way possible I could know my way around every one of these places.

In fact, I am grateful that we can now rent cars that have GPS (Global Positioning System) navigation devices installed. The Global Positioning System is a network of twenty-four satellites placed into orbit by the U.S. Department of Defense. GPS satellites circle the earth twice a day in a very precise orbit and transmit signal information to earth. GPS was originally intended for military applications, but in the 1980s, the government made the system available for civilian use. GPS works in any weather conditions, anywhere in the world, twenty-four hours a day. The government charges no subscription fees or setup charges to use GPS.

GPS has saved my frazzled nerves many times. It seems as if I have spent half of my life looking for airports (and the other half looking for motels). I'll never forget one particular incident, before the advent of GPS navigation systems.

I had a travel assistant who was infatuated with downloading maps from the Internet. After a late-night meeting, he insisted that he knew exactly how to take us back to the airport to catch the plane. The only problem was that he had downloaded the map to the wrong airport.

When we wound up on some country road miles from where we should be, at a locked gate, at a closed airport, my patience wore very thin.

He said, "Well, I *thought* it was the right airport."

And I said, "And you *thought* you had a job too." The moment was pretty tense, I must admit. My supply of charity and forbearance was being stretched to the limit. Many phone calls later, we wound up at the correct airport, only much too late.

Again, I am thankful for GPS navigation systems.

On some occasions, however, I just knew, "We need to go *this* direction." At those times it was refreshing to suddenly come across a familiar landmark or to stumble onto the right road.

If satellites can be the fixed point from which you can determine your geographical location and destination, what compass would point the right direction for a more spiritual journey? In earthly terms you might need a Global Positioning System. In heavenly terms you would need an Eternal Positioning System, a fixed point from which you can guide the direction of your life.

Personal crisis in looking for direction often creates the opportunity for great adventure. Many of those adventures I did not want and I did not enjoy, but I sure have seen a lot of them.

This book is about what is valuable. It is about moving toward what is of value, and away from what is not. What is on sale is not always valuable. Discerning the difference between the valuable and the not valuable is what we all want today. Who wants to be fooled by "fool's gold"? That is why the phrase "All that glitters is not gold" still resonates. I want to help you separate the glitter from the real gold, the costume jewelry from the real jewels.

This is a book about values. It is *not* about "traditional values." Sometimes tradition assigns values that are correct, and sometimes they are incorrect.

I remember these words from "Tradition," a song in the musical and film *Fiddler on the Roof*:

Who, day and night, must scramble for a living,
Feed a wife and children, say his daily prayers?

Perhaps you remember the scene from the film or stage musical where the generations clash. The perspective of years has changed my opinion of this song. I hated it in my late teens, resented it in my early twenties, disliked it in my thirties, forgot about it in my forties, appreciate it now in my fifties, and fear it will be my anthem in my sixties. Did the song change? No, I did. I gained an appreciation for things I once questioned.

Have you ever said or thought, "They don't value things that we once did"? Perhaps that is true; perhaps they value other, more important things than we did.

My father's generation valued the work ethic, sometimes even at the expense of the family. A new generation is arising that refuses overtime, intentionally simplifies, and has brought to the forefront buzzwords like "quality of life." This generation attaches a different meaning to those words *working* and *buying* than did their fathers and mothers. Quality of life is not defined as necessarily a bigger house, a prestigious branded automobile, and clothes with designer labels prominently displayed on the outside.

Quality of life for them involves such things as paternal pregnancy leave (the father getting time off!), telecommuting (so they can work from home), and flex time (they work different hours in order to prioritize family time).

Instead of suburban flight there is now urban flight, a move back into city centers, so commutes are not so long, and grocery stores and markets are within walking distance. Convenience with a purpose!

Many of us are feeling a very primal urge to sort out what really matters. To return to what is really valuable: family, friends, a purpose to our life's work, and a connection to the eternal. For some this is not even a "return" but more a discovery (or a rediscovery!) of what really matters in life.

Let's discover how your destination can affect your destiny. Where are you going? Do you even really know? Perhaps you need a reliable road map.

The biblical book of Ruth can be our "EPS" to guide us as we each find our way to the things that really matter in life.

CHAPTER 2

How Did I Get Here?

Famine of the Soul

Have you ever arrived somewhere only to discover it's not where you wanted to be? Perhaps you followed someone's vague directions only to wind up in a troubled place.

Now it came to pass...that there was a famine in the land.[1]

You may have already read or heard about the Jewish story known to Christians as Ruth but never imagined how lost Naomi, her mother-in-law, felt when she decided to move to a country she had never seen, to live with people she did not know, all while fleeing a famine.

Have you ever felt lost?

You knew where you were geographically, but you still felt *lost*?

In unfamiliar territory, but not sure how you got there?

Obviously you made a wrong turn somewhere that led you *here*...wherever *here* is.

Things *look* familiar. They just don't *feel* familiar.

You are no longer comfortable where you are. The neighborhood, the street, they *look* the same; they just don't *feel* the same. This *is* your house but it does not feel like *home*.

If this is most definitely where I live, then why do I feel a strange disconnection?

This is my job, but why am I tempted to just walk away?

Growing dissatisfaction leads to a bout of second-guessing: *Should I have turned left or right? Did I marry the right person?*

How did I get here? And why am I sometimes so unhappy—especially when everything tells me I should be happy...the good job, a decent marriage, manageable children?

If you know what city you're in, if you know where you work and you know where your house is; then why do you feel so unsettled? Why do you feel like "this is not home"?

If I'm not lost geographically, maybe I'm just lost emotionally. But if home is where the heart is, then why does my heart hurt?

If home is where the heart is, then why does my heart hurt?

Is *home* the problem, or is it a *heart* problem? Is it possible that the *heart* is not a good compass? I followed my heart (or so I thought), but I'm just not satisfied.

I travel often, and getting lost is an occupational hazard. Finding good places to eat is an occupational challenge. Winding up in places I never intended to be is just part of the process of my life.

Sometimes, I look for a highly touted restaurant only to find that it is "Closed on Monday." And I'm hungry. It's always easy to find junk food (which I *hate*), but at least it satisfies hunger.

What about real life, when the concern is not an empty stomach but a famished soul? When you can't seem to find your way to a place of "soul satisfaction"?

If you just don't feel satisfied with your life and *where it's at*, then maybe you, too, are asking yourself the question, "How did I get here?" You have plenty of food, family, or friends, but still, your heart hurts. That's "famine of the soul." You are surrounded by plenty and still feel empty. You have a home, yet you still feel a little bit *home-*

less—not homeless, as in sleeping under the bridge or on the sidewalk, but disconnected. You have family, but you don't really feel connected to them. You don't know where to tell people you are from. You have lots of acquaintances, but few real friends. That's what I would call "homeless soul."

On some vague and very shallow level, I *do* identify with feeling "homeless." My children also grew up traveling extensively as a by-product of my occupation. In our many travels, we often took them with us when they were young. In fact, when my youngest daughter was about four years old, someone asked her where we lived. She confidently replied, *"At a moten-tel!"* (That's hybridized "childspeak" for *motel* and *hotel*: ergo "moten-tel.")

Then the puzzled adult asked another question, hoping this might provide a translation clue for my daughter's first answer. "What does your daddy do?" My travel-weary four-year-old hotel hound said, *"He vandalizes!"* (Again, this was "childspeak" for "evangelizes"!)

I am sure our vagabond experience does not truly qualify us as "homeless," but you get the point. On some level, we have all felt as if we were not *where we wanted to be,* or perhaps even where we *needed* to be.

Again, have you ever just felt lost?

I don't know what may have caused you to "lose your way," or to feel homeless or perhaps homesick at some level. It is difficult to pinpoint, especially when your head tells you that you are home, but your heart says otherwise. We know something is missing, but we just don't have a clue as to what it is. Our best hope at times seems to be the process of elimination . . . one by one we have to go through the stuff in the closet of life and eliminate the things that don't satisfy until we can get back on track.

I do know some of the various things that have caused me to "lose my way." I've determined how I found myself in some of the places I didn't really want to be, wondering all the while how I got there. Sometimes it was a *bad decision* or sometimes *incorrect information.* Sometimes it's my fault; other times I'm not sure. All I know is, "I feel lost!"

Even *good* people can lose their way. Unknowingly, and often innocently in all the frantic rush to succeed, to stand out, or even merely to survive, we've lost the very things we all innately seek after. And sometimes we even forget why we should even care.

Yet, something instinctive, even "spiritual," rises in our hearts that might best be termed an urge to "go home."

Can You *Really* "Go Home"?

Sometime back, I had to feed an uninvited, overwhelming, and urgent desire to revisit a boyhood home. I even insisted that my wife and children accompany me.

It was a totally unsatisfying visit (even for my family, but especially for me!).[2]

It didn't *feel* right! It was the right house (114 Slack Street, West Monroe, Louisiana), but the house seemed mysteriously smaller than I remembered. And the trees were bigger than I recalled. And then there was the atmosphere—the only way I can describe it is, "It didn't *smell like Mom*." She always had certain flowers and shrubbery that I remembered by scent. Perhaps her forty-year absence from that location had taken its botanical toll. (To this day, whenever I smell the fragrance of a sweet olive bush, I momentarily "go home.")

I know from my conversations with many others that they have felt similar urges. I am not sure how other people would commonly describe these primal longings, or how many would actually act on these feelings. But I *do* know how they feel.

They *know* something is missing; they feel fragmented and fragile. Many people sense that *if they can just go home* and connect with what really matters in life, then everything will be alright.

Have you ever felt like "moving back home"? Perhaps you hoped that a fresh start and renewed "connection" with home would somehow alleviate the pain of feeling so lost and "disconnected."

Anyone who has played baseball—whether in the sandlot behind the house or in an organized league of some kind—knows how important it is to "touch base" before running when someone else is at bat. You can't "move on" or you'll get caught in the proverbial "pinch play." The goal of a "pinch play" is to catch a runner who has moved *too far away from his base* to return to safety; and it is accomplished by the pitcher feigning disinterest or by acting distracted until the right time to "spring the trap."

You feel that deep ache that says, "Touch base again." You know you need to "tag up" before proceeding. You sense a deep need to go back home for a fresh start, but for whatever reason, you haven't "moved back home." You feel caught between *where you need to go* and *where you came from*. There is a connection, you know!

Perhaps you hate the "small town" atmosphere, or the basic ground rules that seem to go along with "life at home." Or perhaps you equate "going home" with "moving in" (as in "back with your parents"). I'm not talking about moving *back*, but rather about moving on.

Something inside you may be urging you to "move on" or "move back" as you read these words. You know in your heart that you would even be willing to accept *less pay* in return for the possibility of more relationship. Are you afraid to make that move?

We're not necessarily talking about a geographical move, although lessons on "going home" that I'm learning from came from a woman who *did* make a geographical move back home. Ironically, though, somebody went back with her who didn't come from a home like hers. Let me tell you her story. This is straight from the pages of history, and the Bible.

The Historical Road Home

Ruth grew up in a terrible home. The daughter of a vicious man known for ruling a sexually decadent tribal family in the ancient Middle East. A tribe with a predilection for ritual child sacrifice.

She met a foreign man from a refugee family that had fled to Ruth's area to escape famine and drought. She was somehow attracted to this man for reasons she was unable to define. As a Middle Eastern princess, she could have had her pick of men. But he innately offered her some sense of belonging that was intangible.

Ruth certainly lived a tragic life. Her father, the obese king of Moab, Eglon, was murdered; and shortly after Ruth married Mahlon, he died unexpectedly, leaving her alone and childless. All she had left was her sister, Orpah (who had married Mahlon's brother, Chilion, who tragically died the same day and the same way as Mahlon), and she had her foreign mother-in-law, Naomi.

Naomi seemed to be the source of the intangible stability to which

Ruth was attracted. Even after the death of Naomi's own husband, her strength in the midst of her pain appealed to Ruth. Behind Naomi's grief, Ruth glimpsed hope.

Everything in Ruth's life looked hopeless . . . except there was something about Naomi—and the way she lived her life—that spoke to the deep, aching place in Ruth's heart.

She discovered that she loved this Jewish woman and her ways more than her own family, her own people, and her own land. After the death of both of her sons, Naomi announced her intention to return home. She hadn't been home for more than a decade. She had fled Bethlehem because of a famine, but now it was time to go home.

All three women, Orpah, Ruth, and Naomi, walked partway down the long road leading to the rural community Naomi called home, the agricultural hilly hamlet known as Bethlehem.

Ruth's future seemed bleak but obvious—it was expected that both Moabite sisters would return to their family and rebuild their lives as the princesses that they were. As Ruth and her sister kissed Naomi good-bye and wiped away their tears, something invisible, something intangible, something uncontrollable arose in Ruth's heart with an unavoidable imperative—"I'm going with you, Naomi."

Orpah kissed Naomi and abruptly turned to go back to her Moabite memories. When it was Ruth's turn, she had no interest in her natural home. She would "go back" to Naomi's home. She was unprepared and unpacked, but she went nonetheless, not knowing what the next sunrise would bring.

What made her take such an impossible gamble with her life? She knew that she must find her way to a place that filled the empty ache within her heart. An ache that a new husband, a new boyfriend, or the familiar landscape of Moab could never fill! She felt guided to the decision that "home" lay before her, not behind her.

What Takes Us from "Famine of Land" to "Famine of Soul"?

What had caused Naomi to leave a place that years later looked appealing enough to return to? There was no food. The opening quote for this chapter tells us succinctly that there was a famine. A tricky path can lead us from "famine of land" to "famine of soul." Pursuing our material needs can take us to places that leave our souls hungry. Naomi awakened to the fact that a full belly does not equate with a full soul! How do we lose touch with what is innately valuable?

What would make one pull up roots, abandon all that was once valuable and leave home? Is it the wearing ravages of poverty or the tiring search for prosperity? Could it be the stress of the endless reach for a higher-paying job? The cost in relationships for these actions can be staggering. Such pursuits can unseat the beliefs and deep convictions that grounded us and—at one time at least—made us decent, loving, and connected.

Home

There are three types of homes mentioned in the wisdom of the Bible. There is the literal home in which you dwell on earth with your family. Secondly, there is Jerusalem, called by the Bible the "mother of us all" (which is a perfect picture of the religious or spiritual "home").[3]

King Solomon described the third home with this metaphor for eternity: "Man goes to his *long home*."[4]

If there is a *long home* there must be a short one. If eternity is your *long home*, then your *literal home* and your *religious home* must be *short homes*!

How you value and conduct yourself in the first two homes may help indicate where your "long home" will be.[5] Eternity, the "ever after," only has two address options in two neighborhoods: one good and one bad—heaven or hell. Your value choices on earth determine which neighborhood you will be enjoying or enduring for eternity. That's why you need an "EPS" more than a GPS! Where one leads you is temporary, where the other leads you is eternal. Which is more important: where you take a short trip to, or where you will live permanently?

You can know the price of everything but the value of nothing.

I've met people with a gutter mentality while living at a penthouse level. You can know the price of everything but the value of nothing.

If life were one big game show such as *The Price Is Right*, they would win! They know the dollar cost of every brand-name designer item on earth. But they don't know the value of a quiet cup of coffee with an old friend or family member. This is the driven, unsatisfied life of the "homeless" and unhappy.

Have you ever wondered why matchmaking companies like eHarmony.com or Match.com have become such Internet juggernauts? People want to be connected! They innately value long-term connections and old friends, as well as new challenges.

Obviously, money, influence, and unlimited indulgence in personal pleasures do not meet this deep inner longing we have to return to "something." If we only knew *what* or, more importantly, *where* it might be!

Everybody longs to belong!

You long to *belong* somewhere, but it certainly isn't just here. You sense a clock is ticking somewhere—you're getting *impatient*. It isn't enough just to exist and feel good for a moment...something in you wants to shout out loud, "I am important to someone, to something somewhere! I *matter!* If I only knew where or to who."

For most of us, it takes a while for this sense of something missing to register. Perhaps it is the flood of temptations and their ready availability that causes the college freshman, freshly out of the protected comfort zone of home and seeking a college education, to lose touch with and throw away familiar values—only to try to reconnect with the values they casually discarded when a crisis, marriage, or children enter their life.

We are often influenced by the "Columbus factor," that nagging feeling that the cost of exploring new worlds may well be the loss of the old world. But even Columbus knew there was a time to go back.

What is lost haunts us. It's time to find the way to who you really are. To no longer believe the lie that happiness is always found by abandoning tradition, this is to begin the journey back.

To use "*the road home*" as a collective catchphrase and definition may not interest you if it triggers memories of childhood abuse, an absentee parent, or a place where your comfort and security was not valued. "Home" is not necessarily a good term to everybody.

If the home you remember and know has always been a place of painful memories, then why would you want to go home? What if the thing you long for is something you've never actually had before?

You may be the product of a troubled, anger-filled home, or of a home where the things you innately needed were never supplied. If the only home you've ever known was marked by those painful memories, then "home" is not a good term to you. That's *not* where you want to go. Yet, even *saying* that seems to jab that hurting place deep inside.

As a Western society we've done a fairly good job of culturally deconstructing the family. Even in TV Land, one must observe the *stereotypical* cultural shift. *Leave It to Beaver* is not even in reruns anymore. Its replacement, the blended *Brady Bunch* family, became the next cultural icon, only to be followed by a parade of single-parent families, odd couples, and *Friends*! Unfortunately, having demolished the valued home of yesterday, where do we go today?

If marriage is an outmoded idea from yesteryear, what takes its place when the "twenty-something" years are replaced by the third and fourth decade of life? If lifelong commitment has no place in human relationships, then why is it so difficult to be happy, fulfilled, and content with only one-night stands? In short, who do you want to grow old and wrinkled with? Someone who values only the external or someone who values you for who you are on the inside?

Searching For a Place Where You Are Valued

Perhaps you only know where you *don't* want to go.

But I think I know where you *do want* to go.

You really want to find your way to a place where you are valued, where you are loved, where you are comforted and supported. And where your destiny is important too. We may be thankful for the support of psychologists, psychoanalysts, and psychiatrists, but can they replace what God really intended—a secure, comfortable environment in which to grow? We all need the support of a loving extended family, whether it is "biological" or "by choice."

Where is this Shangri-La, this sanctuary of the soul, this place of unconditional love?

Is there really a place where someone believes in your security, and values your destiny and your happiness? Where someone is actually committed to you achieving that destiny and accomplishing that success?

Now *that's the home we're talking about.*

The road home may not always be the expected road, or the familiar path that pulls into your familiar driveway, or cruises through the familiar neighborhood of your memory.

You know deep inside that somehow you just "don't fit in," not where you find yourself now. You feel homesick sitting in the middle of the place others think *is* your home.

You feel like the title character from the vintage Steven Spielberg science-fiction movie *E.T. the Extra-Terrestrial*—no matter how many Reeses Pieces you eat in your adopted home, they just don't satisfy. Something inside says, "E.T., go home." This road home just may be the road never traveled that takes you to the very place you've always longed to be.

Have you ever driven through a neighborhood where the houses were beyond your financial reach? How many times have you longingly looked at such a place once, twice, and even a third time before thinking or saying out loud to yourself, "It would be nice to live there"?

Expensive houses do not always represent loving homes.

That's the Place I'm Talking About...

I'm not talking about a house of brick and mortar, but of a place where things that bring comfort, security, and fulfilled destiny and purpose are valued.

That's the home I'm talking about.

In fact, if your *home* is bad, if you *feel* fatherless, if you feel issues of abandonment and isolation, then I do have a promise for you. It is a promise from One who has never broken a promise—*that He would be a Father to the fatherless.*[6] In other words He would provide a *home* for you!

Now *that's* the home I'm talking about.

Something—perhaps the beginning of hope—is rising up inside you: your desire to return to what really matters. To perhaps where you've never been. To what is really important. There is always something spiritual about the search for the intangible.

Perhaps your unconscious pursuit of the "home" you've dreamed of has led you to a place of temporary and counterfeit comfort. The fleeting sanctuary offered by a pillbox, a bottle, the career ladder, or the arms of an illicit lover.

Instead of providing that place of security, comfort, and valuing your destiny, all those dead-end paths and wrong choices only made you more uncomfortable and less happy. Perhaps you've even believed the pop culture lie "That's as good as it gets."

Maybe you just changed lovers, spouses, jobs, or your drugs of choice, justifying it all with the phrase "Everybody deserves to be happy." Have those choices brought inner contentment?

How Did I End Up So Far from Home?

You *know* it's time for a real change. You're just wondering how you ended up so far from that place called home. An awakening has taken place, one that made you realize temporary pleasure can never replace the joy of permanent covenant.

Sometimes life's greatest losses come so slowly that *the journey from "have" to "have not" becomes indistinguishable from daily routine.*

For decades some live life as they should, with strength and good health. Then, on an ordinary day just like ten thousand others, an odd weakness seems to come from nowhere to take over their bodies and drain away their strength. The diagnosis—whether it is cancer, neurological impairment, Alzheimer's, or the simple but inevitable effect of natural aging—is shocking. Or could it be the sudden awareness of the slow, corrosive effects of a series of bad decisions that robbed them of all companionship, leaving them broken and alone, feeling as if there is no one left who really cares?

Famine of the soul often comes softly.

It is the *undetected stealth of it all* that produces the greatest shock and surprise. Famine of the soul often comes softly while escaping suspicion under cover of "the usual."

This form of famine is rooted in the loss of what is valuable. Whether it is health or relationship, it comes with a directive to kill the well-worn youthful notion "It will never happen to *me*."

For a few, the unpleasant surprises in life may be traced to a single decision made on a certain day. For most, however—even those with relatively "traceable" tragedies—loss may involve entire sequences of seemingly unimportant choices made day by day.

How does it happen? This invading accumulation of wrong decisions or minor missteps seems to escape attention by flying *under the radar* of the conscious mind. They come disguised or cloaked as unimportant, inconsequential details hidden in plain view among the usual, the ordinary, and the routine.

Painting a Life Meltdown in the Making

Very few of the isolated decisions we make each day would qualify as the proverbial "smoking gun" behind the damage done. But link one bad decision to another, allow the bad decisions to accumulate and outnumber the good ones, and they may paint a painful portrait of a scandalous secret debacle and a life meltdown in the making. Or perhaps just an awareness that "I'm heading in the wrong direction."

Few of us want to invest a lot of time in the "whys" behind a crisis, but when unpleasant reality arrives, it inevitably becomes an unwelcome disruption to our dreams.

This cunning thief of what is really important and what is valuable to our inner peace is seemingly empowered to steal everything we consider "normal" out of our lives. If we aren't careful, we may discover we've lost our personal value system somewhere during the mindless glide into the oblivion of mere existence. This journey to "the usual" has often gone very badly.

In the story that inspired my observations, two women from totally opposing worlds—Naomi, a Jewish mother, and Ruth, a princess of Moab—met during Naomi's flight from famine. This is carefully recorded in Ruth's book. We watch these women endure publicly what are normally private sorrows. They then share their public triumph, all placed on eternal display by biblical narrative. But it all began with Naomi leaving home.

Thanks to the benefit of hindsight, we understand that Naomi's everyday life as a normal Jewish wife and mother was caught up and intertwined with the machinations of something far bigger than herself.

She didn't cause the famine. It wasn't her fault. Where you are may not even be your fault. You could probably say, legitimately, "If I had only known..." But you didn't! Naomi didn't have the advantage of hindsight either.

This woman made her decisions the same way you do—armed only with her mind, her heart, her convictions, and her sometimes feeble faith. The very process of "blind navigation" and survival sometimes makes God seem distant and unconcerned about your present plight!

Have you ever heard the sound of tires screeching, horns honking, metal colliding, windshields shattering? Life as you knew it changed forever. Perhaps it was not that dramatic or drastic, but have you ever felt as if it was the end of normal for you?

CHAPTER 3

How Do I Get Back on the Road?

The End of Naomi's "Normal"

Growing up, I knew that bad things sometimes happened in life. I covered my teenage fears by driving my red Ford Mustang and loudly playing and singing hit songs from the radio. Singing about them seemed to bolster my courage—whether it was after the death of John Kennedy, John Lennon, Martin Luther King Jr., or my cousin, a soldier who went to Vietnam. The arrival of tragedy signaled the end of an era. Nothing would ever be as it was.

Today's generation deals with public tragedies so ubiquitous that they've been nicknamed—"9-11" for instance. They also deal with tragedies so private that they don't even know how to tell their parents. How do you tell your parents you've had an abortion, and that life will never be completely "normal" again? How do you explain to your children that you and your spouse are getting a divorce, and that "normal" family life is over? They will move on, but numbly at first.

Maybe you remember the day when "normal" ceased for you. You awoke to a day after which nothing would ever be the same. So you made a decision—you would quit the job or leave the marriage; or you would just pick up and move.

Naomi was a woman who reacted as we do to shocking news of tragedy—an empty refrigerator, the proverbial "pink slip," or a regional famine. Naomi's life story is a tale of two journeys and two destinations. Between them we find episodes of unspeakable sorrow and immeasurable joy. Her story begins in the first verse of the only Old Testament Bible book named after a non-Jew, and it marks the end of Naomi's "normal."

> *Once upon a time—it was back in the days when judges led Israel—there was a famine in the land. A man from Bethlehem in Judah left home to live in the country of Moab, he and his wife and his two sons.*[1]

Naomi and her husband lived in tiny Bethlehem, an ancient cluster of dwellings clinging to a hill in the rugged rural region of Judah. Bethlehem was not famous then. Not a tourist destination and not connected to Christmas or a virgin birth. This place was just the backwater suburban shadow of an important city.

This family of four lived only about five miles south of the site that we now know as Jerusalem, perhaps history's most important and hotly contested city.

We don't know very much about Naomi's life in Bethlehem-Judah *before* the famine, but we do know that some things never change in human life.

It can be deceptively easy to make a bad decision while thinking it was a good decision or a "God" decision. We can all fall victim to the seduction of "the monotony of the usual" and lose our way by napping when we should have been looking for road signs. It can happen in any era, in any culture, and in every life.

Sometimes the decision that feels right is fundamentally flawed.

You cannot always be led by what feels right. The deceptive nature of our own emotions mixed with our natural human tendency to avoid pain can lead to a disastrous decision. The heart can be deceitful, therefore "feelings" can lie.[2]

It is easier to go straight than turn, but turns are essential to destinations. Change is never easy and it always takes more courage than imagined. Courage to stay the course during trying times is perhaps the most formidable type of courage in existence.

We know that famine forced a *change* in the home of Elimelech and Naomi. Everyone who lived in the region of Bethlehem was confronted by famine and lack, but it seems that most people elected to stay and wait it out (or perhaps I should say "endure" it out).

At least one family decided to leave their dwindling hopes and their dwelling home of Bethlehem and strike out for places unknown at the risk of losing everything.

Their noble goal was to build a better life in a place that seemed to offer more potential—more opportunity for them and their children to achieve success than in their hometown. The goal wasn't the problem—the fatal flaw is found in the choices that landed them in a place called Moab.

> The man's name was Elimelech; his wife's name was Naomi;
> his sons were named Mahlon and Chilion—all Ephrathites of
> Bethlehem in Judah. They all went to the country of Moab
> and settled there.[3]

Names carry great weight in the Old Testament, and the weight of bad times coming seemed to overshadow this family of prominence. Elimelech's name means "My God is King,"[4, 5] and Naomi's name means "Pleasant."[6] The parents were named well, but the sons must have looked to the future with dread.

One source translates their names respectively as "Weak" and "Sickly," while others translate them into even more shocking terms: "*Sickness*" and "*Destruction*"![7] Mahlon and Chilion are always paired together and for good reason—their names sound as if they were given leading roles in a movie detailing every frightening judgment of the Apocalypse.

I think that within every parent is a hope that our children embrace the good things in our life and a bright future, or else there would be more daughters named Jezebel and sons named Judas. Perhaps history re-renamed these boys after the fact. Let's hope so.

(How will your history name you?)

Elimelech was a man of means, a respected and wealthy landowner, a man of great stature and prominence in his community. No one can be sure of his reasons for leaving all this behind, but perhaps he feared the famine would continue long enough to wipe out any remaining wealth he had accumulated in Bethlehem.

Decisions made in fear often lead to disaster.

Perhaps the fearful nagging of Naomi, legitimately concerned about her children's future, pushed their family panic button. Decisions made in fear often lead to disaster. Running from a famine of the land led them into a famine of the soul.

It is possible that the Midianites—ancient enemies and distant cousins of the Jews[8]—seriously compromised the productivity of the land of Judah and the region around Bethlehem during a seven-year military occupation.[9] We can all get "occupied" dealing with a crisis, and make hasty incorrect decisions.

This crisis may well have set up the devastating famine that drove Elimelech—a landowner and farmer—to consider an emergency immigration as a refugee to Moab.[10] His peers probably did *not* approve or welcome his flight from his hometown to the cursed land of strangers. It's not just "that" he moved, it's "where" he moved. One writer comments:

> His defection to Moab is therefore shocking; his name's promise was not accomplished. The Jewish tradition imagines that Elimelech left Bethlehem with bag and baggage to (perhaps) avoid dividing his wealth with the remaining population who were victims of the famine.[11]

If this suspicion of Jewish tradition is true, then Elimelech embarrassed his extended family members who were left behind in Bethlehem. They had all been taught from childhood, *"Share your food with the hungry* and to *welcome poor wanderers* into your homes. *Give clothes* to those who need them, and *do not hide from relatives who need your help!"*[12]

He Would Not Survive His Fateful Decision

Elimelech's decision to uproot his family from Bethlehem and move to Moab was a life-changing choice with significant consequences. The urgency of their crisis must have completely overwhelmed them. We know this: Elimelech, and his sons, would not survive his fateful decision.

Despite his impressive name, Naomi's husband made some unwise decisions that earned him criticism over the centuries. Looking back at his actions thousands of years later, it seems that most of the people who remained in Bethlehem made it through the famine just fine.

Elimelech *could have* stood his ground in faith. Perhaps he *should have* thrown his lot in with the community and ensured his place in the future of the country of Israel. Instead, he decided to take things (specially his wealth) in hand and cross the forbidden fence to a place where the grass looked greener.

I can't help but think of Esau, the elder brother of Jacob in the Bible. Esau was a walking stomach who foolishly sold his lifelong rights as a firstborn son and chief heir in an ancient Hebrew family for *a single bowl of red beans*.[13] It appears he had a case of the same modern disease that cripples many of us today, the infamous "instant gratification syndrome"!

How many memories of unwise choices and foolish decisions have we attempted to stow away in the locked cavities of our minds? Have you ever allowed yesterday's regrets to strangle the life out of today's possibilities? Have you ever been overcome by the stench of a decision "gone bad" that you made two weeks earlier? Are you *still* paying for a mistake made ten or twenty years ago?

The empty pursuit of the proverbial "brass ring"—the rich opportunity of wealth and success, the prize everyone reaches for—can put you out of touch with the important things in life.

When merry-go-round carousels were first created, they had a brass ring that one could reach for as the ride spun around. The prize was an additional free ride. The practice was dropped when too many fell while reaching for the brass ring.

"Reaching for the brass ring" became a cliché meaning to reach for the prize or to live life to it's fullest. It also implied the danger of falling.[14]

Sometimes, the bankruptcy of values slips up on you unawares as you lean out beyond what wisdom tells you, extending yourself as far as your appetites and physical body can take you, with your eyes focused only on grabbing the ring. Suddenly you lose your balance...and fall, all the while "reaching for the brass ring."

The world may even applaud the aggressive push within you—after all, the materialistic urges of society tell you, "You only go around once! The blind pursuit of desire, power, and sensory satisfaction is the key to all happiness! It is right there in that brass ring!" Notice it's called a *brass* ring, not a *gold* ring. It shines like gold, but tarnishes when touched.

Unfortunately, we often fail to see the reaching arms and hopeful eyes of our spouses, our children, those we love. They are *not* reaching for the ring—they are reaching for us! They crave our attention, our love, and our company! While we blindly chase our empty pursuits.

We may find ourselves callously stepping on or pushing away the very people we love and care about the most! It usually happens when something (or some*one*) obstructs our focus or slows our progress. We justify insensitive methods and even brutal tactics saying, "They blocked my vision. They got in my way. I'm determined. I've already made up my mind. I am going to grab the 'brass ring'! *That thing is* my prize! I must have it at *any* price." We justify our intensity by saying, "It will make things better for all of us."

We like to think that "everybody deserves to be happy." That may be true, but it can easily become the first step into a very insidious web of wrong thinking. This "happiness principle" simply cannot justify or drive every action or decision in life. We must peel our bleary eyes away from the tarnished brass ring and use our peripheral vision to see the truth.

Sometimes you must give up what you want to do
for what you need to do.

The urge to run when a crisis occurs is natural. The decision to stay, endure, and possibly help is heroic. Have you ever noticed that

sometimes people who often are overwhelmingly happy live suppos-
edly "deprived" lives devoid of many of the luxuries and vast array of
entertainments, opportunities, and pursuits common to modern life?
Whether it's the Amish in Ephrata, Pennsylvania; or Haitians in a poor
seaside village in the Caribbean, *their dependency on one another
brings it's own peculiar brand of happiness!*

In certain regions of the United States of "Plenty," there is a group
of people who live intentionally "deprived" lifestyles. They are the
Amish, a legalistic religious order that shuns all modern conveniences,
including electricity and modern vehicles, they live as if in the 1800s.
In turn, they have become a tourist attraction.

Why are the Amish a tourist attraction? It is because everyone
appreciates or enjoys observing what the Amish value, and the way
they live out those values. You may not want to pay the price of driving a horse and buggy instead of a car. However, I think you would
like the camaraderie and support they enjoy among one another, along
with the community focus on what *matters* more than on what *flat-
ters*. When looking back, children often remember experiences shared
together above things you give them.

When the Clutter of Life Seems to Hitch a Ride

Many parents take their kids on family vacations, but the clutter of life
seems to hitch a ride even on these special trips. Imagine a family driving through Pennsylvania Amish country when the mom says, "Hey,
I want you guys to see something." So the family pulls into the parking lot in an overloaded high-tech SUV. The kids pull headphones off
their ears, turn off their Game Boys, and walk into an Amish museum.
They then sit down to a family-style home-cooked meal.

The mother enjoys the conversation, but the kids look at the exhib-
its and representative souvenirs and say, "I can't believe people live like
this. There's no electricity, they can't drive cars...!"

Their focus is on things made of steel, plastic, resin, and glass (which
includes the SUV, an item that will probably end up in a junkyard before
the kids finish college, and Game Boys, soon to be replaced by expensive
"new" models and ultimately new technology before they finish high
school—or even before they pull back into their driveway).

The reason the Amish shun electricity and live a simple, separated lifestyle is their heartfelt desire to live untainted or unspoiled by the distractions of the world. They don't hate outsiders; they just want to honor their God and their traditions, and live lives that remain focused on the values they feel matter more than all others.

Principle must take priority over comfort.

In other words, they value other intangible things more than modern conveniences. I'm not an advocate for embracing the Amish lifestyle, but I *am* an advocate for embracing good values.

It is one thing to be poor or to live a separated, simple life, and it's another thing to be unhappy. I learned a great lesson from my grandparents' experiences coming through times of the economic Great Depression. The stories of their poverty were many, but the stories of their happiness during their poverty always outnumbered their stories of the poverty.

Yes, I remember my grandparents telling me stories about what they *had* to do to get by. More than that, I remember them telling me stories of what they *did* to get by. How they did it *together*. How family stuck together, how friends stuck together. How relationships were formed, bonded, and lasted a lifetime.

Sometimes, I wonder if our great mistake is that we are so afraid of the "famine of the land" that, before we know it, we have isolated ourselves into the "famine of the soul" syndrome.

Perhaps it is because when all else is stripped away, we have nothing left to value except what truly is valuable. Often that is *one another*. Sometimes, in the pressure to flee poverty, we also leave behind those things that we should take with us—our values and priorities.

It can even happen in your own home! Think of the businessman workaholic who works around the clock remaining totally separate from his family—in his own mind he is fleeing famine, but in reality he is a victim of famine of the soul.

Perhaps if Elimelech and Naomi had known the future pain that

---

In the pressure to flee poverty, don't leave behind true prosperity.

Moab would deal them, or if they had known about the future blessing that would come to Bethlehem, they would have made a different decision. But they didn't know, and neither do you. They made mistakes and so will you. Mistakes can be corrected.

I can't help but think that Elimelech, a man who uprooted his family and headed for the high plains of Moab, must have thought Moab would be a better life. It probably seemed easier than sitting out a famine. The problem was that Moab wasn't exactly on the Top 10 list for "The Most Desirable Places to Live." Especially for children!

The people of Moab (and their cousins, the Ammonites) were ancient relatives of the Jews descended through the two daughters of Lot. He was Abraham's nephew, the lone surviving male with his two daughters of the Sodom and Gomorrah catastrophe, where fire and brimstone from heaven destroyed twin cities because of their sexual depravity.

Lot had two sons, Moab and Benammi (better known as Ammon), birthed through incestuous conception[15] *with his daughters*. The nations that came from these two sons were so antagonistic against their "cousins" (the children of Israel) that when Moses brought them from Egypt God Himself cursed them.

No Ammonite or Moabite is to enter into the congregation of GOD, even to the tenth generation, nor any of his children, ever.

Those nations didn't treat you with hospitality on your travels out of Egypt, and on top of that they also hired Balaam, son of Beor from Pethor in Mesopotamia to curse you.[16]

It seems the king of Moab was afraid because there were so many Israelites following Moses from Egypt. That is why he hired a religious "hit man" named Balaam to curse Moses and the Israelites (the equivalent of hiring a witch doctor in Africa or the Caribbean).

Later on, another Moabite king named Eglon oppressed the Israelites for eighteen years from a captured stronghold in Jericho during Elimelech's lifetime. That probably didn't earn Moab any points with Naomi's hometown either.[17] Little did she know her life would become intertwined with Eglon's.

One of the few positive things supporting Elimelech's decision was the fact that Moab was considered "the more civilized half" of Lot's descendants, known for it's "plentiful fields, hay, summer fruits, vineyards, presses, [and] songs of the grape treaders."[18] In modern vernacular, the economy was good and there was a good job market.

It Is Mixture That Gets Us

It was also well positioned for security and defense from outside raiders (something that was likely to be on Elimelech's mind as a man of means).[19] We would like to label the land of Moab as totally evil, but as it is with so many things and situations in this life, it was a place of *blessings* as well as curses. This makes a dangerous environment for nurturing deeply held values. It is easy to throw aside things that are clearly evil or dangerous. It is the mixture of good with evil that often confuses us.

It was in the plains of Moab that the children of Israel made their last encampment before entering the land of Canaan, and it was in Moab that Moses climbed to the top of Mount Nebo and died after gazing across the valley into the Promised Land.[20] For these reasons, Moab had some good memories attached. Yet, the sexual deviancy only grew worse after its shocking beginning with Lot and his daughters. The Moabites worshiped bloodthirsty demon gods such as Molech that required child sacrifice! What a mixture! The blessing of plenty mingled with the curse on families.

Things were about to get confusing for Naomi. She faithfully left everything behind to follow her husband to Moab with their sons. She had no idea that a part of Moab would come to live in *her* house and share her future—with all of it's *sorrows* and *blessings*.

Elimelech died and Naomi was left, she and her two sons. The sons took Moabite wives; the name of the first was Orpah, the second Ruth. They lived there in Moab for the next ten years.[21]

No one knows how long Elimelech lived after he moved his family to Moab, but his stint as a resident of Moab must have been very brief. Circumstantial evidence implies that he was received with honor upon arrival. We don't know if it was partly due to his apparent wealth or his way of presenting himself among Moab's leaders.

You Want to Marry Who?

One reason we think Naomi's family was received with honor is because it seems her sons married sisters who were also *Moabite princesses*. According to Jewish rabbinic tradition, Ruth and Orpah were the daughters of King Eglon of Moab—the king who oppressed the Israelites for eighteen years until his assassination by Ehud, an Israelite leader.[22]

The Jewish Talmud teaches that King Eglon gave his daughter Ruth in marriage to Mahlon.[23] We don't know how Naomi felt about her new Moabite daughters-in-law in the beginning, but it must have been a shock. In the words of one writer:

> She is a Moabite. She belongs to an enemy people, callous, pitiless, a people who deal in lethal curses....
> It is hard...to swallow a Moabite bride.[24]

It was really *worse* than that. Any mother of worth is concerned about the home life and background of any potential future daughter-in-law. It is hard to think of any worse scenario for Naomi than Ruth and Orpah's personal pedigree. Their father had been (or would be) assassinated by a Jewish agent for oppressing the Jewish people.

Ruth and Orpah's father was so obese that when the left-handed assassin, Ehud, shoved a knife that measured almost two feet long into his stomach, it literally sank so deeply out of sight in the rolls of fat on King Eglon's body that the handle disappeared and the knife couldn't be retrieved![25]

Coming from a place of famine to a place of so much food, Naomi and Elimelech must have been shocked to learn the nation of Moab was led by such a dramatically obese person. (Eglon appears to be the most obese person mentioned in the Bible.)

While Bethlehem had *none,* Moab had *plenty*; and it's leader apparently flaunted it by "fatness." Perhaps Elimelech and Naomi's boys were impressed by the obese opulence and the extravagant abundance of the home from which Ruth and Orpah came. (Perhaps the boys' parents, in their maturity, may *not* have been as impressed.) Maturity can often filter out the "bling-bling"[26] that camouflages the absence of good priorities and values.

Immaturity is often blinded by the "bling-bling" of "thing-things"!

They as parents now had a different battle to contend with. No longer were they struggling to keep their kids alive physically as in Bethlehem; now the battle was to keep their values alive in Moab. Have you noticed that a simple move won't eliminate your struggle? It just changes the battlefield!

In a modern society that is "obese with opulence," our children are at risk—not from famine of body, but from famine of the soul. If your family life is dysfunctional in Newark, New Jersey, or Riverside, California, it will still be dysfunctional in Des Moines, Iowa. There may be fewer "outside" dangers pressing in, but that which is *missing* on the inside will still work its way out to affect your day-to-day life until the void is filled with something of value.

You Can Choose Your Friends, but Not Your In-Laws

It is very logical and even likely that fat King Eglon, the father of Ruth and Orpah, was unclean in every imaginable way. His was no mere weight problem or metabolism imbalance—his spiritual heritage as the head Moabite was a contaminated pool.

Remember, the nation of Moab was conceived through incest, but each generation added it's own layers of ritual sexual perversion and extreme demon worship through child sacrifice! They would wrap babies and roll them into the gaping mouth of an idol named Molech where a hotly burning fire would consume them.

This sordid history forced Naomi to contend with the Israelite mind-set and stereotype that female Moabites were "no better than prostitutes."[27] For all she knew, her daughters-in-law may have been the original "Twisted Sisters"!

Picture one of those sisters added to your family tree! Now embrace *two* daughters-in-law from this same man's household. God Himself had leveled a curse on this deviant Moabite clan that ranks as the strongest curse ever leveled on any enemy of the Jewish people! *Both* of Naomi's boys married into that contaminated clan (and both died prematurely)! You can choose your friends, you can choose your spouse, but you can't choose your in-laws.

It seems the two new family "additions" came *after* Naomi's sudden loss of Elimelech, her husband, sole provider, and primary protector in a foreign land. The comfort and security of home and extended family must have seemed far away during her painful season as a struggling single mom.

Naomi's crisis points to the *lower priority of values* in her choices. A series of painful choices and debilitating consequences brought her to the brink of bankruptcy in body and spirit.

Most of the choices weren't even *hers,* yet Naomi is reduced within three brief sentences in Ruth's book from a place of honor and fullness (back home in Bethlehem) to the precarious position of a desperate widow in a foreign place. And she was expected to support her two sickly sons and two foreign daughters-in-law from a cursed people.

Important vs. Urgent

Loss often initiates at the place where *urgent things* begin to crowd out *important things*. The truth is that you can only hold on to just so many things with your hands.

Have you ever been so busy that urgent matters seemed to take priority over truly important ones? I have only to be reminded, "Dad, you promised," to think of the times I let the current crises of the day drop to tend to what really mattered—my daughters.

I remember one day I was spending a few moments with my youngest daughter in our swimming pool when the housekeeper called out from the back porch the name of an internationally renowned minister. She said, "Tommy, he wants to talk to you."

We are friends, but it was unusual for him to call. And it was even more unusual for him to call me at my house. My housekeeper assumed I would jump out of the pool, but when I looked at the face of my then eleven-year-old daughter, I said to her, "Tell him I'll call him back. I'm in a meeting." The look of astonishment on my housekeeper's face gave her away, but she turned to go in the house to dutifully do as I had asked.

My daughter turned to me and said, "Daddy, you're not in a meeting. You are just playing in the pool with me." I told her, "No, I *am* in a meeting—*with you*. And it's more important than talking to him. I can talk with him at any time, but you are going to be eleven only once."

I often make wrong decisions, but on that day I made the right decision. I did not let an urgent phone call take priority over an important moment with my daughter. Later I learned how much my decision affected her. A few days after that I passed her bedroom door and overheard her bragging to her friends, calling out the name of the famous minister. "My dad wouldn't talk to him because he was playing in the pool with me."

Yes, I heard the words of her mouth, but I also felt the imprint on her heart and knew that I had made an indelible impression about what really mattered.

Never let urgent things take priority over important things!

You can lose what you want to keep by misplaced priorities. Set your values and stick with them. (It's easier said than done.)

Naomi *knew* her boys weren't exactly perfect, but she never stopped loving them or their wives (even though they were Moabites). Naomi's unconditional love must have been the endearing factor, the "God showing through" that captured the heart of Ruth the Moabite.

There was a special something about Naomi, perhaps an inward ability or virtue that gave her the ability to produce extreme loyalty. The seed of a fruit is always in the fruit. Somehow, Ruth the Moabitess saw something in Naomi that assured her there was something very special inside herself, something even *she* longed for.

She who never lacked for anything as a princess of plenty suddenly felt a hunger for something she never knew existed. And in the process, it seems that Naomi would become "the unlikely evangelist to the non-Jewish[28] "un-churched" pagan princess, Ruth. She didn't do it by preaching or by perfection, nor by some knack of always making the right choices. She did it by love and acceptance, along with a large dose of transparent honesty.

Naomi's eventual return to Bethlehem and the conversion of Ruth is an example of how to keep your passion alive in the midst of your pain. In her worst crisis, Naomi remembered what was *most important* to her—she had kept alive a flickering passion for Bethlehem and what it stood for. Don't let the pain of your present circumstance kill the passion for what is really valuable to you.

> She comes forth out of Moab, an idolatrous people full of wantonness and sin, and is herself so tender and pure....
>
>   Ruth's confession of God and His people originated in the home of her married life. It sprang from the love with which she was permitted to embrace Israelites.... *[through] the conduct of one Israelitish woman [Naomi] in a foreign land.*[29]

Naomi's love both for God and people had a striking effect on her daughters-in-law, even though she was passing through her most painful circumstances in life. Naomi was forcefully *disconnected* from her husband by death. And distance had disconnected her from her extended family. Yet, Naomi forged new connections with her small family in Moab, forming the nucleus of a new covenant community with her sons and daughters-in-law under the very shadow of the land of the curse.

We Long to Feel Connected

Your journey away from values may be unintentional, but you will gradually begin to feel the effects of lost "*connectedness.*" It is the great common complaint about the "exciting urban life"—even in the world's greatest cities: "*We long to feel connected.* We have cell phones, instant messaging, text messaging, emails, and satellite videophones; but we *still feel disconnected.*"

People may be all around you as you attend church, shop for groceries, or go to school. But somehow in your journey, you just don't feel connected with people.

It has been said, "The typical *modern individual* does not have any history, *only episodes,* like the soap operas on television."[30]

We often lose what we have not valued.

It's one thing to lose a cheap giveaway plastic pen. You just shrug your shoulders and dig around in the clutter for the next one. But if that pen was a "golden" gift from someone valuable to you, the search suddenly turns frantic. Why, it could easily be replaced...right? The pen could be replaced, but *not* the memory and the relationship that *gives it value!* I'll never forget the day I lost a "gold" pen that my aunt gave me for graduation. I now have some pens far more costly than that simple gold Cross pen. But occasionally when I am digging through some old stuff I harbor hope that it will show up. Cost and value are not always the same.

Once, when I was a boy, my grandfather taught me a lesson about losing things.

I couldn't find my comb! He reached into the drawer and pulled out a reddish-colored old-fashioned tapered comb. Holding it in his hands, he said, "How you take care of small things sets a pattern of how you will care for big things."

He then told me that he bought this comb before he went to be a missionary in Alaska at the time my parents were first married. That was at least fifteen years prior to this moment. Then my grandfather handed the comb to me and said, "Don't lose it!"

His lesson to me was, "This comb has been to Alaska and back to Louisiana with me, and I didn't lose it. I don't want you to lose it. At any point," my grandfather told me, "I might ask you where that comb is."

My grandfather has been long gone, but I still have that comb. I know right where it is. Fifty-five years, two owners, and three generations of memories later, I still have that comb. It's now locked away. It is too valuable to lose. It's not the value of the comb; it's what it represents.

We often lose what we do not value.

"How you take care of small things sets a pattern of how you will care for big things."

It's time to *re-value* true "connectedness," to establish and nurture covenant relationship instead of throwaway trysts and mutually beneficial "hookups."

Naomi was mourning her tragic loss of the people she valued and her lonely separation from the things she valued, yet she still managed to introduce her daughters-in-law to quality relationship and "life with a purpose" that they had never before seen or experienced.

Naomi may have questioned why her husband had died so suddenly and why she found herself so far away from home. "How did I get here?" Yet, she still had a sense of passion and purpose in her life. Naomi still had her sons and her daughters-in-law, and she knew that sometimes God does, or allows, things—often the most important things—*on* purpose *for* a purpose.

The Accumulated Fruit of "More Good Decisions than Bad Ones"

If Naomi felt as though she was trapped in the lottery of accidents, she still knew there are no accidents, only incidents, where God is concerned. Some may call it "good luck," but perhaps it is more a result of the accumulated fruit of "more good decisions than bad ones." In any case, it can *never* be called the "Lord's Lottery."

The steps of a good man are ordered by the LORD.[31] The Bible says the steps—and I might add, *the stops*—of a good man are directed by the Lord. In other words, *you are not a throwaway relationship to Him.* The hand that holds you sometimes holds you up, sometimes delays you, and stops you. God may "*step you*," and "*stop you*," but He will never "abandon you."

Naomi was about to experience another crippling fall, yet in her stumbling struggle alongside a young foreign stranger she discovered that *shared hardship often births sincere friendship,* and *your strength is often found in how you handle another's weakness.*

Shared hardship often births sincere friendship.

CHAPTER 4

Past Loss Magnifies Present Pain

It's Going to Feel Worse Before It Feels Better...

I remember hearing the words, "It's going to feel worse before it feels better." My memory of those words goes back pre-kindergarten when my mom took me to the dentist for the first time. So vivid is it in my memory that I can still picture the long-defunct Rexall drugstore over which the dentist's office was located.

That day, the dentist hurt me—all the while telling me it *wasn't* going to hurt. I'm fifty-plus years old at this writing, and I still fight a lifelong semi-phobia of dentists. As a Christian, I have to love them. As a human, I sometimes wonder if they are going to heaven.

The problem persisted into my adulthood. On one occasion when I had to have some major dental work done, I went to a dentist who proceeded to put me in much pain—all the while claiming, "It has to feel worse before it feels better."

Even after that indignity, the dentist told me he couldn't finish the work that day, and I would have to come back for another torture session. I was determined to not be lied to again with the claim, "It's not really going to hurt," so I concocted a plan.

The next day, I walked into the office, sat down in the torture chair, dutifully opened my mouth, and placed a hammer in my lap. When the dentist who was appointed to conduct the "painless" torture came in, he noticed the hammer and said, "What's *that* for?"

I calmly replied, "You told me you weren't going to hurt *me,* so I tell you I won't hurt *you*." With a chuckle, he smiled and said, "I get the point." Then he turned to the nurse and said, "Knock this guy out." That is when I discovered the heaven of sedation dentistry. Now, every time I visit the dentist, it is a known fact—they just knock me out. And when I wake up, they are finished and everybody's happy.

What causes a fifty-plus-year-old, semi-intelligent man who is the author of numerous books to have to be treated like a small child at a dentist's office? It is because *past pain can magnify your present circumstances*.

For those going through a loss like Naomi's, a day with the dentist may seem trivial (although it wasn't for me at the time). Naomi's pain was the pain of *loss*. Not the loss of a tooth or of a job, but *real* loss. She had suffered the loss of her husband and of her two sons.

> *And Elimelech, Naomi's husband died;* and she was left....
> *And Mahlon and Chilion died also both of them;* and the
> woman was left.[1]

It is one thing to get *lost*, and quite another to be *left*. Memories and their attached emotions persist for decades. Virtually every one of us can recall a childhood experience of stark terror birthed in the sudden realization: *My parents aren't here. Where are they? I've been left behind!*

It happens nearly every Christmas season, when the shopper population in crowded malls reaches alarming danger levels. From time to time you will hear the piercing scream of a child facing for the first time that same terror that has become familiar to us.

I call it "terror" because the feeling of being left behind far surpasses mere fear. It is a terror that I'm convinced never quite leaves the human psyche. Perhaps it is bound up in the fundamental human fear of death and eternal separation.

Naomi knew about death. She was still feeling the painful twinges of loss over Elimelech's sudden death less than a decade ago. And she still had fresh memories of her struggles as a single mother trying to raise two sons in a place where they were still seen as little more than strangers. *And death suddenly came to her door again*, this time with double vengeance.

Things seemed to be going well after her sons grew older and displayed their father's skills in leadership and business. Naomi's sons rose to hold positions of authority in the region, and their needs were met. The family brought skills and abilities in leadership with them that must have attracted the personal attention of the king of Moab, and he immediately put the sons of the Hebrew to work and gave them positions of great influence in return.[2, 3, 4] It seems he even gave them his daughters in marriage—even though their father, Elimelech, had already died.

For centuries, Torah and Bible scholars have compared Naomi with Job, the number one human sufferer in all of history. She is also compared with another close contender, Abraham, who left home, family, and tribal lands for a promised land he never found.

Yet, Naomi had *less* than either of these great leaders of the Bible, and she had even *less* to look forward to (or so it seemed).

Unlike Abraham, Naomi had no divine promise to anchor her through her torment. Unlike Job, this wife, mother, and homemaker didn't set her own course—she followed her husband where he led, and then she remained with her sons who preferred to marry and settle in the foreign land of Moab rather than return to their ancestral home in Bethlehem.[5]

Naomi Experienced the "Ultimate Identity Theft"

Past loss *magnifies* present pain. First, this wife and mother lost the financial security she enjoyed in Bethlehem. The famine didn't destroy them financially, but it greatly reduced or hindered their ability to add to or maintain what they had, and it forced Elimelech into an emergency mode.

Naomi experienced the "ultimate identity theft" at the hands of drought and natural disaster, combined with human decision making. She was no longer a woman of prestige and prominence, well known in her environment. Now she was a nobody, with comparatively nothing, going nowhere.

Far greater and more painful than the loss of money was the loss of friends and family. Naomi was a product of the ancient covenant society of the Jews, and specifically of the area around Bethlehem. It was common for multiple generations of one family to live, work, and eat together from birth to the grave. Every significant personal event became a significant community event and vice versa.

With one simple decision, Elimelech had cut off all access to his family's cultural roots (along with all personal obligations to help his community survive the challenges of drought) and set out for forbidden lands.

Clinical psychologist Mona DeKoven Fishbane said something about "cutoff" that strikes at the very heart of the "journey away from values" that afflicts so many people, whether they find themselves separated "on purpose" or by accident. She described something that we literally see displayed "in living color" in the lives and sorrows of Elimelech's family members.

> "Cutoff," in the language of family therapy, refers to *the action of people who remove themselves totally from their family of origin*, rejecting contact with them. Clinical data suggests that *such cutoffs create havoc* in the family system, especially for the person who cuts off, and *may negatively affect subsequent generations* if not resolved.[6]

No longer would Naomi greet the morning sun with warm salutations to sisters, brothers, aunts and uncles, or lifelong friends. She wondered if she would ever again observe the great feasts and the countless other excuses for community worship and celebration.

It's One Thing to Leave a House. It's Another to Leave "Home."

Ten years is a *long time* in the life of a close-knit extended family. When Naomi moved her things out of the house that had perhaps been her home since her marriage to Elimelech, she left behind much more than a roof, four walls, and a smoky cooking hearth.

Naomi almost certainly knew she was leaving family members behind who would probably die before she ever made it back home again—*if* she ever made it back.

Many of her dear friends were probably in their peak childbearing years when Naomi left Bethlehem. How many of them would give birth to children and share the landmarks of motherhood with all of the same friends Naomi loved so dearly—*but not Naomi.* She was moving to Moab!

I can hear her perhaps taut-lipped reply to Elimelech's decision:

"I don't want to move to Moab!"

"But, honey, we have to! There is no future here. No jobs, no money, nothing!"

"But Elimelech, Moab is a bad place, a dirty place!"

Her imaginary comment has a good precedent. Psalm 60:8 says that Moab is God's wash pot. Who wants to live where God washes dirty laundry?

Parents, uncles, and aunts were left behind—some of them forever. Her dreams of seeing her sons marry the prettiest girls in Bethlehem with the whole village attending the gala wedding feasts? They were dashed the day the last building faded from view and she took a final glance at the last field bordering her home village.

Much of what makes for a joyful marriage—dreams of cuddling and spoiling grandchildren, and of watching a husband work with his sons to prepare his grandsons for the passing of the family heritage to the future—those dreams and hopes were dashed and seemingly forever buried.

And speaking of grandchildren, will she even be able to communicate with them? They may not even speak the same language.[7]

When Memories Make You Miserable

We can only imagine the feelings of pain and loss Naomi experienced on the long journey from Bethlehem-Judah to Moab as face after tearful face flooded her memory of those she left behind in the only world she had ever known. That pain, combined with a normal and natural fear of the future, is a recipe for misery.

Many people today still battle emotions of loss, anger, or disappointment over the memory of being pulled out of school, the neighborhood playground, or a treasured close relationship for sudden moves across country or to another nation. Those without your memories cannot understand your pain.

I grew up in a preacher's home, and my sister and I knew what it was like to be separated from Dad at times when he couldn't take the family along on ministry trips. We also knew how to live out of suitcases and prepare for Sunday meetings using only the rearview mirror in the well-worn family car and a service station bathroom sink. (I think I've perfected the art of mobile grooming since then!) A few are born to the traveling life. Most are not. The "glitter-ous glamour" of travel is not glued on well; it tends to fall off rather quickly.

Those without your memories cannot understand your pain.

With her departure, Naomi lost even more than money, memories, and moments with her friends and relatives. She was forced to leave behind many of the shared values that were most important to her and the community she loved. I can only take a well-educated biblical guess as to what the values were that she left behind in Bethlehem.

The Things That Really Matter—Values

But I can make a well-observed count on the central values disappearing from *our* societal landscapes now. I feel we may be losing ground on:

Family
Friends
Character
God

You may have your own list of what is valuable. It may be longer, but it most probably would include some form of these four.

Family

How connected are you to your family—your parents, siblings, and adopted or extended family? Friends are important (as they show up on the values wish list also), but friends cannot take the place of family. It *seems* as if we have created the disposable throwaway family—block it out and start over. When you do that, you lose a part of yourself every time. It's like cutting off your fingers one at a time. Sure, you can live without them—but it hurts, it is very inconvenient, and you can't grow them back.

Don't cut off your family. Again, it may not be your biological family that I'm referring to. It could be your "by choice" family. Father figures are essential, and a mother's nurture is irreplaceable. The loyalty of a sibling (always peppered with a little competitiveness) is invaluable. The sense of history and heritage that comes with being connected to grandparents is life changing.

Friends

Friends are not just acquaintances. There is a difference. Friends are crucial. They *help* one another. This is so fundamental that "even a caveman knows this." Humanity has been living in groups since history began.

When I'm down, you are up. When you are sick, I'm well. Cities are made up of groups of friends, and not just short-term friends. Of course, there will be some of those, but you need some "twenty-year friends." If you can be friends with somebody for twenty years, it says much about your character. It generally means you've learned how to forgive and to be forgiven. You've learned how both to eat "humble pie" and to fix humble pie in such a palatable way that others can eat it. You can't be friends with someone that long and not be offended and offensive. The fact that your friendship has survived speaks loudly of your ability to walk together.

Character

And as far as the value we call character, it is the integrity with which you live your life. It might best be described as "what you would do if you knew no one would ever find out." *That* is your character. If there are people you really trust, it is because those people have trustworthy character. There is little pretense about them. They are exactly what is in their character.

I could make references to the fact that the Judeo-Christian foundation of the Ten Commandments from Exodus 20 is the benchmark of good character:

1. You shall have no other gods before Me.
2. You shall not make for yourself an idol, or any likeness of what is in heaven above or on the earth beneath or in the water under the earth.
3. You shall not take the name of the LORD your God in vain.
4. Remember the Sabbath day, to keep it holy.
5. Honor your father and your mother, that your days may be prolonged in the land which the LORD your God gives you.
6. You shall not murder.
7. You shall not commit adultery.
8. You shall not steal.
9. You shall not bear false witness against your neighbor.
10. You shall not covet.*

These ten commandments are the essential manual on how to build character and to maintain healthy relationships with friends and family.

God

Interestingly enough, these ten commandments (not the ten *suggestions*!) are tied directly into the last and most important of the "big four values"—God. They are simply God's value statements. He will *never* break these—they represent who GOD is, and why you can feel safe with God.

Think this through: One commandment says, "You shall not covet." God does not want anything you have; therefore, your "stuff" is safe with Him. Are you on speaking terms with Him? I know that sounds like a simplified way to put things, but it works for me. I've been married (happily) for over thirty years. But when I'm not on speaking terms

---

*Adapted from the New American Standard Bible.

with my wife, I have offended her value system. (It *has* happened. Try cutting down the wrong rosebush!)

Do you value what God values? If so, you value God—and don't want to offend Him. This is not simply because He is "the big Policeman in the sky," but because you value Him.

It is like this: If you love and value God, then you will value what He does—whether it is human life or family relationships. You will be a trustworthy character, develop friends who are faithful, and cherish family. In turn, you will be loved and cherished by those who embrace the same values. And perhaps you will not be particularly liked by those who don't.

That Naomi moved away from Bethlehem infers that she was changing values. Just as the currency changes when you go from one nation to another, Bethlehem's "coinage" of family, friends, character, and God was not the same value system she found in Moab. After her painful losses, her journey back was a re-embracement of Bethlehem values—family, friends, character, and God.

It's not always true that when you "move" you always lose, but it's often true! And I'm not just speaking of geographical moves. I am also referring to "moving on" in relationships, and "moving out" or even "moving in"! The problem is not the "move"; it is the changing of values when you move!

To Moab and Maybe Back

The dangers of a family foray into Moab, the land of twisted values, cannot be overstated. You might venture there, but will you come back?

Elimelech and Naomi no doubt thought they were making the best decision possible. In fact, they were attempting to save their children.

Meanwhile, they also knew that exposing them to the valueless excess of Moab would be dangerous. But they probably reassured themselves and their questioning family members, saying, "We will only stay there a little while, just until things get better here in Bethlehem."

There is no vaccination against the virus of lost values.

Moab truly *was* a place of "plenty"—plenty of food, plenty of money, but also plenty of idolatry, and plenty of child sacrifice.

I can hear Naomi's response: "I'll *never* let that happen to my family."

The sad fact is that it did.

She lost a husband and her two sons. The twisted corruption of Moab claimed three more victims.

If Naomi were to advise us today, I think it would be on this wise saying:

"You cannot take a vacation from values."

Eternal vigilance is the price one generation must pay to secure the safety of the next. Moab was not *that* far away. Moses died in Moab on Mt. Nebo, looking into the Promised Land. So Moab is not far from the promises of God, just outside the door.

But why leave the safety of the promise? You may take your family to Moab, but you have no guarantee you will bring them back!

By most outward appearances, Elimelech's gamble had paid off. What began as a "sojourn" or temporary visit to Moab seemed to be working out. *He had been received well in the region, and the family felt prosperous again*. Now, if they could ever get past losing Elimelech before his time.

In reality, all was not well.

The "sojourn" had transformed into permanent settlement through marriage. But after as many as ten years of marriage, neither of Naomi's sons and daughters-in-law had been able to have children. A dark blanket of somber dread had settled over the entire family. The lack of an heir was deeply troubling, but it evidently remained mostly unspoken concern.

In accordance with ancient Near East tradition, Orpah and Ruth (rather than their husbands) were probably blamed for the infertility at the time. But in Naomi's mind, her Moabite daughters-in-law had been very good to her sons, and she genuinely loved them.

Many people in modern Western societies fail to understand the depth of this concern for having an heir to carry on the family name and traditions. Modern ideas aren't necessarily "better."

To Be "Cut Off" from Kin Was Worse than Mere Death

The term "shall be cut off from among his kin" appears repeatedly in the Old Testament as a severe punishment for serious crimes punishable by death.[8] This was *worse* than mere death itself!

> The continuity of the generations is at the heart of the survival of a family, and ultimately of a people. The notion of the end of a family line, or of a person cut off from his or her family or people, is anathema in the biblical and later Jewish world.... Such a cutoff represents the worst punishment a person could endure. A medieval tradition has it that the souls of the dead find rest in their heir, whereas a person who dies with no children can find no rest.[9]

We know today that this concept of "the souls of the dead" finding rest in their heirs is contrary to the Scriptures, but this information helps us understand the fears felt by people in biblical and medieval times.

Our modern culture has inflicted countless wounds on the family through it's blind pursuit and worship of *individual* rights, self-absorption, and selfish living over the selfless life taught and modeled by Christ Jesus. In our race along the road—or perhaps we should say "the super speedway"—*away from values*, we have virtually decimated the stability, joy, and strength of our families (especially our extended families).

We've Simply Lost Our Way

No family unit can operate in an environment of selfishness and lawlessness, which should go a long way toward explaining why some of today's families are such a mess! Our thin outward veneer may look good, but even the slightest examination probing below the surface reveals fractures, wounds, and magnified pain. We've simply lost our way.

Inner pain and fear of the unknown may have haunted everyone in that fractured family of five. It centered around a disturbing question, no matter how mathematically unlikely it might seem: "What if all of the males in the family died? How would the three widows survive?

How would they preserve the family name, work the family fields, and keep the family inheritance—even their very lives?"

Then the unspeakable happened. Word came one day that Mahlon *and* Chilion had died *simultaneously*. How could such a thing be?

We don't know any verified details behind their deaths, but we have lots of opinions. Rashi,[10] a prominent rabbinic scholar from the medieval era, believed that the Hebrew phrasing of Ruth 1:5, translated "also the two of them," means that first the two brothers were punished by losing their money. Then their camels died, followed by the rest of the herd. Finally, they themselves died.

In her modern commentary, Rabbi Ruth H. Sohn said Mahlon and Chilion "died together on the same day. And how did they die? They died as a result of a fall, when the roof they were building for their new house collapsed."[11] We know that however it happened, once the brothers died, all hopes died with them for the three widows left behind.

In explaining why the two young husbands died, the *Targum*, an ancient translation of the Hebrew Bible, said, "*Because of their transgressions, their days are cut short,* and they die in an unclean land." One scholar explains that "for the *Targum*, any place outside of Israel, particularly Moab, is considered unclean, that is, not fit for the raising of a Jewish family."[12]

Naomi Suffered the Longest, Lost the Most, and Was Left with the Least

This hit Naomi the hardest. She had suffered the longest, lost the most, and was left with the least. On top of everything, she was also the farthest away from her extended family, friends, and home.

Remembering is one of the most important components of mourning, despite what you may have heard from various ill-informed sources.

Naomi had to endure three funerals—she tearfully worked her way through three "scrapbooks" of memories, touching the faces of her husband and two children in tearful remembrance with her daughters-in-law at her side.

If Naomi was the least bit "Jewish" (and she was), then she had taken in her new daughters-in-law from the very beginning and had begun to teach them what it meant to be Jewish and how to be wives to their husbands. In ancient oral tradition, she would have been inclined to share with them the Ten Commandments and the Law handed down through Moses, and instruct them in the complete Jewish history of Abraham, Isaac, and Jacob.

After spending up to ten years together as mother and daughters linked through marriage, at her sons' deaths Naomi, perhaps, once again took up the tools of the mentor to teach her two Moabite daughters-in-law how to "mourn and remember" as Jewish wives and women facing *loss*. And remembrance was *vital*.

The tragedy of the situation was that the deaths of these three men left little social status, personal worth, or potential future available to Naomi, Ruth, and Orpah. Ancient rabbis studying these passages are openly horrified over Elimelech's immigration to Moab and the subsequent marriage of his two sons to women from the accused nation.

R. Hanina comments, "She became like a remnant of remnants."[13] According to the prescribed law, the priest would take from the mincha [flour offering] a handful which included oil, flour, and an expensive, imported fragrance and burn them upon the altar. The remainder was eaten by the priests. The Midrash describes both tragedies according to this paradigm. First, Elimelech, the head of the family, died. He was like the chosen handful. Next, the sons, the remnant, were consumed. Their widows remained, *the ghostly remnants of the remnants*.[14]

Shakespeare calls this "sorrow's crown of sorrows." It is when pain and sorrow bear children and multiply.

Elimelech and His Sons Had Left Ephrata— the Land of "Fruitfulness"

Something seemed to be obviously wrong with the family's future, because a possible ten-year span was enough time for any normal marriage to produce children.

Perhaps the problem was because Elimelech and his sons had left Ephrata, the land of "fruitfulness,"[15] to make Moab their home. Then Moab became for them the land of barrenness and death. Neither son produced an heir, and neither daughter-in-law had become a mother or had given Naomi a grandchild.

The irony of the situation was that Ruth the Moabite would soon step away from her house of mourning, leave all behind, and follow her mother-in-law Naomi into the Divine Scheme of God.

She would one day be called "Ruth, the mother of kingdoms"[16] and she "join the Matriarchs as one of the Mothers of the Jewish People."[17]

Experiences of loss either bond people together or divide them. The test was about to come. There was nothing left for Naomi in Moab except for the two young women she had come to love. I remember my grandfather, a pastor, after he'd passed his ninetieth year, telling me in the last years of his earthly life, "There's no one left alive who witnessed my childhood."

Shared loss often bonds you to your partner in pain.

My grandfather's words remain in my mind as one of the saddest statements about old age in the human experience. They are especially sad when no provision has been made to pass on those memories, beliefs, accomplishments, or loves to the generations that follow.

If you step into the carefully maintained homes of healthy families with relationships that are intact, you will usually find walls covered with framed photographs. Some will obviously be new because they sparkle with brilliant colors and backgrounds that reflect the modern era. You will also find faded or yellowed black-and-white photographs, and the nearest family member will eagerly tell you the *story behind the smile* (if you display even the slightest interest or appreciation for what you see there).

My grandfather was correct in the sense that he could think of no one living who had witnessed his childhood. But there were—and *are*—multiple homes filled with people who will joyfully tell you *stories* about my wonderful grandfather's childhood, personality, tall tales, and anointed ministry!

Naomi looked around at her now empty home in Moab, filled with stark reminders of her deep loss. Every room housed emotional barbs just waiting to pierce her heart anew with painful memories and very little else.

It was time to go home.

Even if nothing awaited her there, for sure nothing awaited her here. At the least she had heard the rumor that there was bread in Bethlehem. And...it was *home*.

> *Then she arose with her daughters in law, that she might return from the country of Moab: for she had heard in the country of Moab how that the LORD had visited his people in giving them bread.*
>
> *Wherefore she went forth out of the place where she was, and her two daughters in law with her; and they went on the way to return unto the land of Judah.*
>
> *And Naomi said unto her two daughters in law, Go, return each to her mother's house: the LORD deal kindly with you, as ye have dealt with the dead, and with me.*
>
> *The LORD grant you that ye may find rest, each of you in the house of her husband. Then she kissed them; and they lifted up their voice, and wept.*[18]

CHAPTER 5

Stumbling onto the Right Road

Your Personal Crisis May Trigger
Another Person's Epiphany

The last lingering moments before leaving the place you've called home for years are the worst. Some of us will go to almost any length to avoid the tearful embraces and hold back the wellspring of emotions they trigger.

It is not the same when you leave for a two-week trip, or a two-month journey to a far place, or even to a college for four years. You will be coming back. Somehow, someway, the place left behind remains at home in the heart.

Not this time. Not for Naomi. Not when leaving Moab. She thought for a moment how different she felt when leaving Bethlehem ten years ago. Everything that mattered in this place had died, everything, that is, except for the two young women who had spent most of those painful years with her and her now deceased sons. She was ready to leave without a moment's hesitation.

She had come to the realization that good people can be trapped in bad places. But now she was free to go back.

Good people can be trapped in bad places.

What she had not yet realized is that good people can *come* from bad places.

Naomi knew what she had to do. She knew where she had to go, but she was certain her two daughters-in-law could not and would not go with her. It was a different world, a different place, a different destiny.

Rumors that rumbled at the trading tents of the caravan merchants had made their way to her ears from Moabite acquaintances, and from sources inside the royal palace where her daughters-in-law were from.

It was being said along the trade route that the invisible God of the Israelites in faraway Judah had visited His people once again. The famine in that land had been removed. It seems there was bread once again in *Beit Lechem*—Bethlehem—literally named the "house of bread."[1]

Hope is the "bread" of the soul. Without it, life seems to wither and ultimately risk death by soul starvation. We all want to live in a house with plenty of food available. In the same way, we all need a sufficient supply of hope available for our souls.

Naomi's desire for home was preceded by a "good" appetite. (Note that I mean an appetite "for that which is good," not just an intense hunger for anything consumable.) This is the same process as with the prodigal son.[2] Physical hunger ignited a spiritual hunger for "home."

Types of bread are found sprinkled throughout the Bible. All of them have a prophetic meaning. "Shewbread" was a prophetic bread; manna was a prophetic bread.[3] Naomi was pursuing prophetic bread spawned by a prophetic appetite! Let your appetite for what is "good" lead you to a place where your destiny can be fulfilled!

She would return to a place where a manger would become a bakery for the bread of life! And she would play a part, but she didn't yet know it!

Your hope supply may rise and fall in the normal course of life's ups and downs, but a drought season—that dark night of the soul—can be frightening. These dry and dark places can easily breed desperation and hopelessness in us over time. But you have no idea what your destiny can be! Keep hope alive!

Naomi had suffered as much as twenty years of pain and diminishing hope. On this day, seemingly poised at the far end of hope, she made a decision and committed her entire future to it.

I can almost hear her whispering to herself the night after she'd made her decision, "If I can just make my way back home, then at least I won't starve." She could hope for little else it seemed. As the old Hebrew saying goes, "*M'shaneh makom, m'shaneh mazal—With a change of place comes a change of luck.*"[4]

> *And they [Orpah and Ruth] said to her,* "No, but we will surely return with you to your people."
>
> *But Naomi said,* "Return, my daughters. *Why should you go with me? Have I yet sons in my womb, that they may be your husbands?*
>
> "Return, my daughters! *Go, for I am too old to have a husband. If I said I have hope, if I should even have a husband tonight and also bear sons, would you therefore wait until they were grown? Would you therefore refrain from marrying? No, my daughters; for it is harder for me than for you, for the hand of the LORD has gone forth against me.*"
>
> *And they lifted up their voices and wept again; and Orpah kissed her mother-in-law, but Ruth clung to her.*[5]

Did you note that last line? "Orpah kissed" but "Ruth clung." We are about to discover the difference between the "kiss" and the "cling." They are as fundamentally different as dating and marriage. Both imply passion, but one implies commitment, while the other implies convenience. Ruth and Orpah were at a point of decision! Should they stay or go back? Should they join or separate?

The Place of Separation Reveals the Truth about a Relationship

It is precisely at the place of potiential separation that the true depth and foundation of a relationship shows up. It can't be hidden anymore—this is the final hand, the last opportunity to cast the deciding vote. The ability to leave is what confirms the power in a decison to stay.

Action must follow words at this tipping point between the pain of the past and the possibilities of the future—whatever those words may be.

Naomi's crisis had changed everything. Whatever the three women had come to accept as "normal" was normal no more. Things would change, and *they* would change from that moment of decision onward with lifelong, history-altering effects.

None of the three grieving women realized on that day just how much change they were about to experience. Nor would they ever have imagined that entire nations would be transformed and come to define part of their identity in the decisions they made that day on that road![6] Many decisons made "on the way" have intractable consequences for the future.

The Chorus of Spoken Commitment Came Quickly

Both of Naomi's Moabite daughters-by-marriage quickly committed to their mother-in-law. It reminds me of another time and place many generations later when the chorus of spoken commitment in crisis came quickly. Sadly, the spirit was willing, but the flesh was proven to be too weak.

> *"Tonight all of you will desert me," Jesus told them. "For the Scriptures say, 'God will strike the Shepherd, and the sheep of the flock will be scattered.'*
>
> *But after I have been raised from the dead, I will go ahead of you to Galilee and meet you there."*
>
> Peter declared, "Even if everyone else deserts you, I never will."
>
> *"Peter," Jesus replied, "the truth is, this very night, before the rooster crows, you will deny me three times."*
>
> "No!" Peter insisted. "Not even if I have to die *with you! I will never deny you!"* And all the other disciples vowed the same.[7]

We see it again and again. Abraham and Lot. Jesus and Judas. Jesus and Peter. David and Jonathan. Esther and Mordecai.

Now it is Naomi, Orpah, and Ruth. Affectionate kisses and terms of endearment are revealed for what they really are—expressions of commitment or signals of separation. But never make the mistake of thinking that a kiss means commitment!

Mafioso kiss their intended victim to seal their fate. Judas kissed the door of heaven but wound up in hell. This is the point where actions truly do speak louder than words.

If the words are followed by actions that demonstrate lasting commitment, they were genuine expressions of covenant. If separation follows, then the words spoken are reduced simply to public expressions and advance signals of polite *separation* (or even worse, of bitter betrayal).

The Scriptures picture this bittersweet point of decision in this distraught family with a single, simple line:

Orpah kissed *her mother in law;*
but Ruth clung *to her.*[8]

Shared hardship reveals sincere friendship. When you share hard times with other people, those difficult experiences and the pressures they create have a way of separating fair-weather acquaintances from true friends. Are you a "kissing cousin" or a "clinging friend"?

In our artificially friendly society, "air kisses"—even if on both cheeks—are essentially meaningless.

After you wipe the lipstick off your cheek, check your back for a knife. Backstabbers often precede their attack with a kiss. Ask Jesus.

The glaring light of crisis has a way of placing family ties and the bonds of friendship under a penetrating light that reveals true heart motives and inner values. It should be no wonder to us that crisis seems to quickly separate our "handout" relatives from our "count me in" kin.[9]

If the death of a single loved one is enough to put us into shock, can you imagine what these three women endured? Funerals often bring out the best in people, and the worst. Grief overwhelms our sensibilities, and sometimes irrational statements are made.

The tenuous threads of in-law relationships often break after the death of a mutually loved person. In fact, we often only "endure" those who are kin to the one we really love. I am not sure how that played out with Orpah. All I know is that she had some attention from Naomi, "enough to kiss, but not to cling."

Even though Naomi suffered alone the loss of three, while Ruth and

Orpah lost only one, she seems more stable, lucid, and able to process the loss. She is speaking reality to Ruth and Orpah.

Expanding the Grim Situation for a Reality Check

Parents and *real* friends sometimes resort to shock therapy to help us face a difficult situation with greater clarity. Less-intimate friends may often be less-truthful friends as well. It takes real love to tell the truth even when it hurts. Naomi truly loved her daughters-in-law. She loved them enough to share the stark truth about their shared crisis.

Three times Naomi expanded the grim situation facing the two young Moabite widows. To invoke the reality check needed for the crisis, she said in essence: "If you're waiting for more sons of Naomi to marry, understand that I have no babies now. I'll have no babies later. And if you wait too long counting on my womb, then there won't be any babies for *you* then either!"

First, there were no babies in Naomi's womb to be born over the next nine months who might possibly mature in time for them to marry and bear children by them.

Even worse (and more unlikely), even if Naomi were to marry again and quickly become pregnant by some miracle, the timing would be even more difficult.

And finally, Naomi asked them if they really wanted to put their lives—and their ticking biological clocks for potential childbearing—*on hold* for decades in the face of such certain disappointment.

Naomi's bitter last statement was said for the benefit of her daughters-in-law, but it also revealed Naomi's personal condition at that moment:

> No, *my daughters; for it grieves me very much* for your sakes
> *that* the hand of the LORD has gone out against me!"[10]

Would Naomi's Calamity Leave Her Daughters-in-Law Childless Too?

Naomi was expressing her bitter surrender to what she felt was the will of God for her life. And she feared her calamity would leave her daughters-in-law childless and destitute as well.

If the *content* of her words wasn't enough, then the *emotional bankruptcy* of Naomi's soul became the final catalyst or spark igniting the process of decision leading to concrete action. This was the "telling blow" that finally revealed which direction each person would go.

For whither thou goest, I will go; and where thou lodgest, I will lodge: thy people shall be my people, and thy God my God. Ruth 1:16

After another round of crying and tears, Orpah kissed her mother-in-law good-bye while Ruth "clung" to her tightly in covenant commitment. Sadly, this "great divide" seems to affect virtually every type and kind of commitment in the human experience. When trouble or adversity comes, most people call it quits—including many who say they follow Christ.[11]

Orpah returned to Moab—to its gods, its culture, and its destiny. In fact, according to rabbinic literature, Orpah married and bore four sons—all of them *giants* who were slain in David's reign![12]

This young widow really *did* love her mother-in-law, but as one recent writer puts it:

> What Orpah loses is the last three thousand years of being present in history. Israel continues; Moab has not....
>
> Does it matter to Orpah that her great-great-great-grandchildren have tumbled out of history, and that there is no book of Orpah, and that she slips from the book of Ruth in only its fourteenth verse?
>
> Normality is not visionary. Normality's appetite stops at satisfaction.[13]

Ruth Saw God Through Naomi's Life in the Midst of Adversity

So what about Ruth? How did this young widow respond to Naomi's attempts to talk her out of a desperate venture to an uncertain future in a foreign place so far away?

Her passionate reply to Naomi paints a portrait of epiphany. Do you know what an epiphany is? It's when you have a "Eureka!"

moment, a flash of revelation, a sudden realization or comprehension of something.

In the Bible, these epiphanies seem to always happen on or near roadways. Jesus' disciples realized it was Him only after walking with Him on the Emmaus road.[14] Paul had an epiphany on the Damascus road.[15] Even the proverbial "three kings" with their long journey are connected to an "epiphany."[16]

Ruth had a sudden realization, an awareness of what was really valuable to her. Thrust by evil circumstance and personal loss to the edge of ruin, Ruth saw God through Naomi's life in the midst of adversity. And she chose her path. She *saw* God through Naomi at her most painful crisis. And ironically, she *met* God at the most painful time in her own life.

One more time Naomi intreated Ruth to turn back:

> *And she said, "Look, your sister-in-law has gone back to her*
> *people and to her gods; return after your sister-in-law."*[17]

Ruth then began to vocalize perhaps the most anointed covenant contract ever recorded in human history. The words of this brokenhearted Moabite widow to her discouraged Jewish mother-in-law *set the historic "gold standard" for devotion in human relationship and spiritual identification*:

> *But Ruth said: "Entreat me not to leave you, or to turn back*
> *from following after you; for wherever you go, I will go; and*
> *wherever you lodge, I will lodge; your people shall be my people,*
> *and your God, my God.*
> *Where you die, I will die, and there will I be buried. The LORD*
> *do so to me, and more also, if anything but death parts you and me."*
> *When [Naomi] saw that [Ruth] was determined to go with her,*
> *she stopped speaking to her.*[18]

Some people find faith in the same circumstances
where others lose it.

Apparently Ruth had seen too much—too much love, too much compassion, perhaps too much wisdom, and too much faith. The moment Naomi experienced her greatest crisis of faith on the road to Bethlehem coincided with one of Ruth's highest moments of revelatory faith! It is at this point that we become aware that Ruth *realizes* Naomi has a God. And this God was very different from those of her Moabite background.

It is ironic that some people find faith in the same circumstances where others lose it. One person may get mad at God and another may find great faith—even as they negotiate the same crisis point.

The Seven Values of Ruth's Commitment

There are seven powerful values to Ruth's "covenant of identification":

1. I will not leave or abandon you.
2. I will not stop following you.
3. Where you go, I go.
4. Wherever you live, I will live.
5. Your people shall be my people, your family is my family, your friends are my friends.
6. Your God shall be my God.
7. Where you die and are buried, that is where I will die and be buried. We're in this together to the death.

Is it any wonder so many wedding services include the words of this ancient commitment made by a daughter-in-law to her mother-in-law? The marriage covenant made between husband and wife is the strongest and most solemn human agreement on earth. Ruth's covenant commitment to Naomi and her God is just that strong! Both contained the total commitment of "leave and cleave" (although in different ways).[19]

God has a promise connected to this level of commitment. We often try to "keep" our commitments but fail and fall short. That is why we need His promise "to keep that which we have *committed*."[20] The only thing God ever promised to "keep" was that which was "committed" unto Him. We would be wise to also value *commitment* if God does.

Ruth's Commitment Fueled and Strengthened the Bond of Love

Some believe Naomi's relationship with Ruth didn't really begin to bloom in depth and intensity until after Naomi's sons died.[21] It is here, at the pinnacle of Naomi's crisis, that Ruth's covenant commitment began to fuel and strengthen the bond of love between her and Naomi.

Ruth had decided to become what is still called "a Jew by choice." Her decision—and the depth of her commitment—was so important to the future of the Jewish people that her name has been permanently linked to Shavuot, the ancient sabbath feast that marks the giving of the Torah to the Jewish people "and their *acceptance* of it."[22]

Whatever it was Ruth saw in Naomi's life, it so captivated her that she wanted it badly enough to abandon all of her previous life and embrace the unknown. Naomi's crisis cracked open the door of Ruth's epiphany.

To observe another person gracefully and heroically deal with life's problems often inspires one to find the source of that person's strength.

Ruth was seeking to *belong, to have a relationship with the God she saw in Naomi's life*. The only route she knew was to align her life with Naomi's. She was seeking to embrace values she had never known before—until she met Naomi.

Ruth's example teaches us three things:

1. If you love somebody, never let it be unsaid.
2. If you want to connect with someone, never miss the opportunity.
3. Pursue relationships.

Normally, parents who want to add a child to their family by adoption will choose the baby. Whether it is the brown eyes, the cute dimple, the head full of hair, or simple availability, *the parents choose*. This is the natural world's way.

In the realm of the spirit, many things are reversed. The way up is down, the path to leadership is servanthood, and the list goes on. Why not the law of adoption?

I believe that in the spirit realm, one chooses whom to adopt as a spiritual father or mother. Ruth makes this choice.

The only time a son or daughter can choose a father and mother is through the spiritual law of adoption. Ruth had no say in the matter when Eglon the ruthless Moabite king became her physical father. But she had *everything* to do with choosing Naomi as her adopted spiritual mother. (She could have gone the path of other young wives and rejected a relationship with her mother-in-law.)

This is the heart of the spiritual and natural principle of mentoring. Wise people of every era and culture have understood the value of connecting with people who improve their destiny. When you reach out for help, it is best to reach up to wisdom. It elevates your destiny.

Princess of Darkness or Follower of Naomi's God?

Ruth followed that path all along. She started out as a Moabite princess, the daughter of Eglon of Moab. If we look at her through the stern looking glass of the Law, then Ruth was a princess of darkness, the daughter of an obese, abusive, anti-God king, the chief opponent of God's people for a time. Yet, she had embraced the God of Naomi in lifelong commitment.

Obviously, God wasn't using that legal looking glass. He didn't need it, for He sees things differently from us—He peers directly into the heart through heaven's lens of grace.

Some people brag about friends in low places, but Ruth was learning the lesson of adopting friends and mentors whose understanding was higher than hers. Her first wise choice was the adoption of Naomi as her spiritual and adopted mother.

The most effective mentoring relationships are based on love. Naomi and Ruth drew so close that their destinies became hopelessly (or joyously) intertwined.

One writer tried to describe this relationship through a fictional account: "Ruth is wedded to Naomi's friendship and her wisdom. Orpah has often had the sense that *a single soul inhabits the bodies of both Ruth and Naomi.*"[23]

Naomi was totally capable of bad decisions, because even good people—*all* good people—are capable of bad decisions. However, the mistakes *should* get smaller as we move forward toward God's good plan for our lives. One of the odd things about God is that He delights in using flawed, ordinary people to reveal His extraordinary love and perfection.

"I Like You, But I *Really* Like What You Represent"

Despite Naomi's losing battle with bitterness, the virtues of her loving God were showing through! It happens in us too. We still get upset or make others upset, we fumble our way through life leaning on divine wisdom every day and are shocked to hear someone say, "I like you, but I *really* like what you represent. I don't know how to put it, but it is even higher than what *you* represent individually...I guess I'm saying I like what you symbolize and what you stand for, even when you mess up! It means there's hope for me."

Covenant is commitment carried to the highest level.

When Ruth began to express her heart on the road to Bethlehem, Naomi was, in essence, "out of the picture." What had begun as a personal commitment from one woman to another had become an eternal covenant in the making between Ruth the Moabite and the God of Abraham—even if Naomi was a beneficiary!

Sometimes the young can help the older ones renew the chase for their dreams. The good decision of Ruth to go with Naomi was so powerful that it offset the weight of five or six bad decisions! It effectively shut the painful door of the past and opened a new door to the future—for *both* Ruth and Naomi. *Commitment can be the bridge from good to great.*

Yet, the very fact that this parting of ways took place *on the journey* somewhere between the place they'd left in Moab and the place they were headed in Bethlehem proves that "part-way home is *not* home." One correct turn does not equate with arrival at the destination.

But what of Orpah? She came partway; should she be "partly" honored? She did have some affection for Naomi. Her life had obviously been impacted. But the pull of the past was too great.

I am reminded of the "Columbus factor" again. There came a time when his men wanted to go back. Columbus himself pondered turning back from the great unknown oceans. No one would have blamed him. Had he done so, no one would have remembered him.

Orpah went back. Her fear was greater than her faith. Nobody blamed her, but nobody remembers her.

The only thing that would take them the rest of the way "home" to Bethlehem was to continue to walk out physically what they had decided mentally. The initial impulse was a rumor of God's goodness that they decided to pursue.

Naomi's mature desire to return to her ancestral home was borne out of a hunger and heart-desire to return to the values of her father and mother, to the people chosen and set apart by the God of Abraham, Isaac, and Jacob.

Loyalty precedes royalty!

And Ruth? Her loyalty preceded her royalty. Because she was loyal she later found herself in the royal lineage—a pagan princess promoted to the bloodline of King David of Israel.

> Ruth's confession of God and His people originated in the home of her married life. It sprang from the love with which she was permitted to embrace Israelites.... *The conduct of one Israelitish woman [Naomi] in a foreign land was able to call forth a love and a confession of God like that of Ruth.... Ruth loves a woman, and is thereby led to the God Whom that woman confesses.*[24]

Like the woman with the issue of blood who touched the hem of Jesus' garment, Ruth touched something (or *someone*) that was touching God and was healed.[25]

She didn't even touch Jesus, just something that was touching Him. And she returned home healed. We could use a few more Naomis. The necessity of a Naomi cannot be overestimated. Many "Ruths" only connection to God is when they brush up against our lives. Then they have their "epiphany"—they see God through us, even when we are in pain and crisis.

Ruth touched someone who had touched the holy, who had come from the Holy Land. She would never be the same. Neither would history.

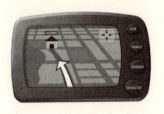

CHAPTER 6

The Journey Back

Muddling Through the Mess

Even with a GPS, the journey back home is a process of "muddling through the mess" with frequent backtracks and help needed from the direction-givers in life.

My grandfather loved to watch *Laurel and Hardy* films. If you are from a younger generation, you may not even know who Laurel and Hardy were. In the early days of filmmaking, they were the equivalent of the Blues Brothers or perhaps the comedy duo of Jim Carrey and Jeff Daniels who starred in the 1994 movie *Dumb and Dumber*. (No, I'm not endorsing the movie, just providing a "memory handle.")

One of Laurel and Hardy's trademark phrases inevitably turned up when the duo found themselves in some kind of a mess. At that point, the heavier-set Oliver Hardy would strike a pose and say to his soft-spoken partner, Stan Laurel: "Well, this is *another fine mess* you've gotten us into." (And usually, it was Hardy's mess.)

Have you ever felt as if all fingers were pointed at you, perhaps from your family or your boss? Can you still hear the phrase "Well, this is another fine mess you've gotten us into" ringing in your ear?

I know I've felt that way. I have a very patient wife. Our long-lived, thirty-something-year marriage is not a testimony to my great wisdom, extreme kindness, or dashing good looks. The strength of our marriage has really been the patience of my wife. No matter what "mess" I happened to get us into through the immaturity of my decisions, she seemed to have some inherent assurance that I would somehow muddle through my mess.

We had our ups and downs. There were times when, financially, we were so "down" that we wondered, literally, how we would survive. The physical challenges were just as difficult. I remember one time when Jeannie had three surgeries within eighteen months and I had just taken temporary charge of a church going through a very troubled time.

I'm not sure I made the right decision in going there. I'm not sure I made the right decisions *while* I was there. But I am grateful that while I muddled my way through, my wife found the patience and strength to walk through it with me.

I haven't always written best-selling books, or been involved in making motion pictures, or had life "all together." Sometimes, we felt frazzled around the edges. But we *just kept going.* Life is not scripted or controlled. It is *unpredictable.* (That is precisely what makes it so exciting—and so frightening at times!)

Anyone who has ever stepped onto a theatrical stage, or played even a small role in a play or musical, knows how hard it is to "get everything right" for the first performance (let alone *keep* it right for a long string of performances).

If it is that difficult for those playing a scripted and controlled role to polish their performance for a brief three- or four-act play, then why are we so shocked that *life* is so difficult to "get right"? Oh, and there are *no* rehearsals to life!

What makes life so unpredictable? For one thing, we must deal with the variables of life—the things that can *change* everything else that follows. That would be things and events such as a serious illness, a market crash, the unexpected betrayal by your best friend, or the oncoming car that suddenly crosses the center median to head straight toward you.

Then we must deal with the fixed uncontrollables—the family we were born into, the DNA we received at conception, the fact that we were born blind or allergic to peanuts. Perhaps the most difficult variable of all is simply *the unknown.*

If these variables and the unpredictability of life aren't enough to make life "messy," then all we have to do is factor in the *flaws* we *do* know about—our disdain for authority or organization, our fear of heights, or our compulsion to lie, to overeat, to view pornography, or to gamble away our last dollar over almost *anything*. If the list seems endless, then so will the frustration of it all. From our fear-driven phobias to our dislike for veggies, it all has an impact.

We should understand that perfection isn't the goal, nor is it demanded on the road home. The successful journey requires, first, that you be headed in the right direction. So the first step out of our mess turns out to be a simple decision: muddle through it to something better.

> When [Naomi] saw that [Ruth] was determined to go with her, she stopped speaking to her.
> Now the two of them went until they came to Bethlehem.[1]

The journey home to values is a process of "muddling through the mess" with frequent backtracks to the maps and direction-givers of life. It's improbable that any of us can go through our muddling journeys without fighting, squabbling, getting hurt, or feeling guilty over our failures. Muddling through life's mess is—excuse me—messy!

It was only a decade or two earlier that Naomi had everything she thought she wanted: a good husband who was well respected and successful in the community and two sons to carry on the family name and business. And all of that was based in the same town where she'd grown up with lifelong friends and a large extended family.

Muddling through is always messy!

Then came the mess. First, the famine hit. Then her husband, Elimelech, decided to move the family to Moab to wait out the drought while establishing new business in another country. That is when Naomi's life began its agonizingly slow slide into the pit of personal loss and despair. First it was Elimelech's death, followed by the dual deaths of her two sons, and well...it's a mess. It's a mess financially. It's a mess emotionally. It's a mess!

Things started to look up just a little when the news of bread in Bethlehem sparked a long-forgotten hope and longing in Naomi's dreary thoughts. She quickly made up her mind to go back home. Naomi must have thought to herself, *Well, I used to have a farm. Maybe I should go back and see...maybe I can get out of this mess in Moab.*

Every mountain is a servant of your faith. It must obey faith.

The return home must have seemed mountainous. But every mountain is a servant of your faith.[2] It must obey faith. But then she had to "muddle through the mess" of breaking the news to her two faithful Moabite daughters-in-law.

Ruth Veered "Off Script" and Messed Up Naomi's Escape Plan

Naomi felt she would be accepted, welcomed, and cared for among her old friends and family in Bethlehem. She also knew that no Moabite would be welcome in Judah—not with God's curse over their heads and after the Moabite oppression several years ago.

When an actor or actress begins to speak their own words or rewrite their part, it is called "veering off script." Ruth veered "off script" and messed up Naomi's escape plan with her unexpected commitment to follow Naomi home to Bethlehem and stick with her for life—no matter what. This is what I call "*risky* faith in a *certain* God."

This was a complication—perhaps a comforting one, but a complication nonetheless. It was time to muddle through yet another mess again.

After Ruth's declaration and determined embrace, what could Naomi do? She was glad for her companionship and loyalty, but she was worried on her behalf, and uncertain about the future. And what could she say after Ruth's impassioned speech?

Naomi was genuinely concerned about Ruth's uncertain future in Bethlehem. There was no love lost for Moabites in her hometown, and Ruth was a beautiful young widow with no children or authoritative male to protect her. As an unattached female foreigner, she might almost be considered "fair game" by the less-scrupled males of that society.

Yet, even the prodigal had his last day in the pigpen. Naomi intended to extend her stay in the pigpen of bitter attitudes toward Jehovah's indifference. She was convinced that she had become a target for His vindictive "punishment" toward her for her husband's decisions.

Naomi fully embraced bitterness. Even while her feet were pointed toward the Promised Land, her mind was mired in Moab. But she had the "prodigal's advantage": when all else is lost, *they at least know their way home.*

It seemed obvious to her that the God of Israel had marked her off of His "blessed and most highly favored" list. What a mistake she made! (In other words, be careful when you judge people because you never know when *this day* will be their *last day* in the pigpen—or *in Moab.*)

Thankfully, one of the benefits of the "muddling through the mess" process is that *you see immediate improvement* or positive progress when the muddling begins to take on *direction.*

As soon as she leaves Moab, it ceases to be her home. Moab is now only the place she has left behind. The hold of Moab falls from her as a garment draped loosely over one's shoulders might drop suddenly to the ground. And now, the place that is named is **the land of Judah**, the land to which she is returning. Now Naomi can turn even more fully to the future, with the image of Judah burning brighter before her eyes.

From Naomi we learn that *teshuva*, "repentance" or "return," is a process that seizes upon the glimmer of hope present in the report that God has remembered her people and is providing them with bread.[3]

Perhaps Naomi felt her fate was subject to "the lottery of happenstance." She felt she was outside of God's favor, at the total mercy of "whatever happens."

Sometimes betrayal is the best friend your destiny ever had.

Learn to befriend any circumstance in life and it will serve God's purpose. Even befriend the betrayals and the betrayers—Jesus called Judas "friend"! Judas's betrayal, as painful as it was, served a higher purpose.[4] Sometimes betrayal is the best friend your destiny ever had.

> *And it happened, when they had come to Bethlehem, that all the city was excited because of them; and the women said, "Is this Naomi?"*[5]

An Unfriendly Incursion into a Vulnerable Place of the Soul

Have you ever walked into a party and realized you were seriously underdressed? Have you walked into someone's party as they were celebrating a great life—when all you could think about was the pain and sorrow of a great loss in your life? Bitterness and sorrow may easily creep in as an unfriendly incursion into a vulnerable place of the soul.

Perhaps you have noticed that it's actually easier to mourn with those who mourn than to rejoice with those who rejoice. Naomi had just left a land of mourning filled with pain, loss, and unwelcome displacement. Once she made her decision, she must have felt a growing sense of freedom rise up in her heart. She never performed a postmortem autopsy on her past. Once the decision was made, it was straight ahead.

Naomi must have replayed those moving images again and again, with imagined scenes of laughter, warm hugs, and open delight over her dramatic return home. These were the expectations fueling her excitement over seeing her friends after years of separation, but Naomi's haunting thoughts of loss burst through her facade and exploded in the middle of her reunion. Once again she stepped into a mess.

Naomi's Haunting Thoughts of Loss Burst Through Her Facade

As she took her last few steps up the hill toward her hometown of Beth-lehem, we can almost see her pick up the pace. When she stepped into the sight of her friends, she carried with her all of the accumulated thoughts of hope and excitement over her reunion with her lifelong companions of the heart.

> *And it came to pass, when they were come to Bethlehem, that* all the city was moved *about them, and they said,* Is this Naomi?
> *And she said unto them,* Call me not Naomi, call me Mara: for the Almighty hath dealt very bitterly with me.
> I went out full, *and the LORD hath* brought me home again empty: *why then call ye me Naomi, seeing the LORD hath testified against me, and the Almighty hath afflicted me?*[6]

We see the disintegration of a dream and the death of hope all in just three short sentences. With one three-word sentence, Naomi's fragile dream of hoped-for positive images was crushed with the onslaught of a flood of painful memories from more than a decade of back-to-back disappointments.

Keep the lesson but throw away the experience!

With the painful memories came a wave of bitterness that shattered Naomi's fragile heart. They found instant expression in her words of personal pain. "Don't call me Pleasant! Call me Bitter, for the Almighty has dealt bitterly with me." Rabbi Ruth H. Sohn captures the emotions of the moment with these words:

Where Naomi had hoped to find comfort, her searing sense of loss tears at her all the more strongly in the face of her memories.... "Naomi, is it really you?" her friends cry when they see her. They hug her fiercely amid laughter and tears, touching the lines on her face with tenderness.

She says, "I went out full but came back empty."

'I am not the same woman as when I left....'[7]

I wish I could have said to Naomi, "The road back is the road to better! Keep the lesson but throw away the experience!" I can't scream back through history to Naomi, but I can tell you—*keep the lesson and throw away the experience.*

Naomi Was Not Alone—God Had Sent Along His Own "Care Package"

Ironically, as Rabbi Sohn also points out, Naomi didn't even remember or think to introduce Ruth.[8] The wonderful truth is hidden right under Naomi's nose—she was *not* alone. In fact, God sent His own "care package" along with her for the journey back home.

In all the time of Naomi's negative thinking and bitter talking, God had already prepared a place for Ruth in the genealogy of Jesus. At her lowest moment Ruth was already carrying the highest seed. This is a beacon for all of us on the road home to restored values. Our lowest moment carries within it our highest destiny!

(Future generations would testify that there was enough provision in this underrated gift to preserve her family line and set the stage for King David and the Messiah to enter the world through her ancestors!)

Our lowest moment carries within it our highest destiny!

Life doesn't come to us neatly in prepackaged single-serving units. We rarely have the luxury of focusing on one problem or opportunity at a time. The twins may come the same week Dad loses his job. You may get two lucrative job offers in your field the same week you make the decision to try *something else* in a different field. The choices and decisions are rarely clear-cut or easy.

> *So Naomi returned from Moab accompanied by Ruth the Moabitess, her daughter-in-law, arriving in Bethlehem as the barley harvest was beginning.*
> *Now Naomi had a relative on her husband's side, from the clan of Elimelech, a man of standing, whose name was Boaz.*
> And Ruth the Moabitess said to Naomi, "Let me go to the fields and pick up the leftover grain behind anyone in whose eyes I find favor." *Naomi said to her, "Go ahead, my daughter."*[9]

The purpose of life is to find your master, not your freedom.

Notice how Naomi speaks and Ruth questions. It is as a master teacher to a student. How wise Ruth was. She knew that the purpose of life is to find your master, not your freedom.

The family and friends who gathered around the two new arrivals were in the middle of full-strength celebration over the second straight harvest in one year. This followed nearly a decade or two of stark drought when there were no harvest celebrations.

They Were Still *Outside* of the Community

It was difficult for the two widowed women to get into step with the community because they were still *outside* of the community. *Community sustains you through loss* and Naomi had direct links to the life of the town. But in her outburst of bitter grief, she may have managed to put off most of her friends—at least for a time.

We don't know this for sure, but Naomi and Ruth seemed to have an immediate need for food and income. No one seemed to be helping them, which seems unusual for a close-knit agricultural communal town like Bethlehem.

Life just isn't some kind of fast-food restaurant where everything you want is dished up fast and hot. Nor is it a cosmic smorgasbord, a "choose-what-you-want, as-much-as-you-want" diner some folks would have us believe it to be.

It is more like, well, the physical world we live in.

Good and bad things alike seem to flow in and out of our lives like streams flowing through an arid area. At times, favor appears to rain down on us like unexpected summer showers. People love us, we get raises and promotions on the job, and we have money in the bank.

Then we go through tough seasons that resemble hot dry spells in summer. Everything just seems to get dryer, browner, and crispier with each relentless day in the oven of life. Tempers wear thin at home and at work.

Every uninsured driver in your area seems to be targeting *your* car. If not the automobile drivers, then the grocery store parking lot "buggy drivers" dinging your doors! Nothing you do seems to work, and your timing always seems to be off. You miss a step and break an ankle; you get your proposal in five minutes later than the sales representative from the *other* firm. The doctor *didn't* make a mistake—it is cancer and you have to go through chemotherapy *now*.

This Is Life in "The Muddle Zone"

Even the "good days" can nearly do you in from time to time. The start-up company you risked everything to launch six months ago nearly folds through lack of capital—until the orders start coming in and just keep *flooding* in! When the inevitable backlog drives away your brand-new customers permanently, your good news is reduced to the sad, last gasping breath of a titillating but false grasp on new life.

This is life in "the muddle zone." You can't quite grasp anything with concrete certainty. You somehow sense that good may be coming your way, but it gets mixed in with bad news or old disappointments come to revisit your life. This process is so common that the rabbis have a term for it—*teshuva*.

The path of *teshuva* [return] **is not always a clear ascent; there are dips and valleys.** Naomi's hope gives way to despair before finding fulfillment in the birth of a grandson. And so it is with us: the process of *teshuva* is often one of overcoming obstacles and feelings of hopelessness as we move slowly toward the hope of renewed life and redemption.[10]

This is what it means to muddle through the mess of life. The redeeming virtue to the "muddling" phase of life is that at least there is some forward progress. It may not be fast, it may not be in the exact direction you'd planned, but at least it is moving *away* from loss and stagnation.

To put things in perspective, if you finally straggle back home after losing everything like Naomi did, then your reference point for "normal" life includes large helpings of ruin, hopelessness, and *the rock-bottom* human experience everyone tries to avoid!

When you're coming from that vantage point in life, *even muddling through a mess looks good!* At least there are signs of *life* and the possibility of hope in that mess!

Ezekiel warned us that there would be times when things are looking good with green pastures and clear water, and then someone (or something) muddies up the water. Have you ever had another sheep muddy up your drinking place?[11]

Patience, my friend! Just wait awhile and it will clear up. That's how you "muddle" through life. Patience, my friend! It will clear up!

Real life tends to come to us in totally unmanageable swells and overwhelming waves, framed by seasons of drought when life barely survives. For a *survivor*, that simply means it is time to adjust.

God Seems to Send along Surprises from Unexpected Sources

Since you can't control what comes your way, you must control the number and the quality of voices you listen to while trying to navigate the road and manage the mess. *What voices are you listening to?*

Life generally refuses to follow our personal script ideas or plans for how we would like to see things play out, but God seems to send along surprises from unexpected sources for those who trust Him as they journey on the road home.

All it takes to loosen a log-jam in a river is a sudden shift of water, intervention from other logs entering the stream at the right time and place, or an explosion of power carefully positioned at the front where the blockage is.

If I can find a way back—there will be a way in.

Naomi launched the expedition on the road home with her determination to walk out physically what they had decided mentally. It was as if she said to herself, *If I can find a way back—there will be a way in.*

Once Naomi made it back home, she was ambushed again with overwhelming disappointment. The Bible says we tend to speak from our mouth what is brewing on the inside.[12] Desire finds a way; lack of desire finds an excuse.

Naomi's pain was plain for everyone to see, and it almost paralyzed her. She was in dire need of some intervention to break up the log-jam of bad news and pain in her life.

God had already supplied her need years ago in the form of her humble Moabite daughter-in-law. Ruth seemed to have an ability to look past all of the objections, obstacles, and procedures of protocol in Jewish society.

Ruth's first moments in Naomi's hometown were spent in the shadows, but it didn't take her long to perceive the most important need of the moment and come up with a way to meet that need through *direct action.* They needed food! And quickly! Apparently, while Naomi was still licking the wounds from the past, Ruth was providing for the present. What a gift! Everyone needs a Ruth!

But God Was in the Details...

When she asked Naomi for permission to do something that was really very risky for a single, foreign woman in a hostile culture, Naomi mumbled an answer through the fog of distraction—but God was in the details.

> *Now Naomi had a relative on her husband's side, from the clan of Elimelech, a man of standing, whose name was Boaz.*

And Ruth the Moabitess said to Naomi, "Let me go to the fields and pick up the leftover grain behind anyone in whose eyes I find favor." *Naomi said to her,* "Go ahead, my daughter."[13]

There is no traffic jam on the second mile.

This is the first time in the passage Naomi calls Ruth her "daughter." Before this it had been "daughter-in-law." Ruth's willingness to go seemed to put her in lineage. There is no traffic jam on the second mile. It changed her relationship...commitment leads to relationship.

One of the most important values in Naomi's covenant culture was expressed in the command, "Remove not the ancient landmarks."[14] For this reason, when she returned to her hometown after a ten- to twenty-year absence, she already *knew* the boundaries of her land and property were still intact.

It is possible Elimelech sold the fields or leased them before they left, or that they were taken over to pay debts. Even if the lands were free until Naomi sold them to pay for expenses for some reason, the harvest was on. It was too late to get any seed in the ground for a harvest (assuming they could even afford seed or get it planted without workers).

In any case, it seems Naomi and Ruth at least had a place of their own to call home after they arrived in Bethlehem, but no crop in the field. And judging by Ruth's request, their first order of business—their most urgent need—was to gather grain for food and income.

The scriptural account clues us in to the fact that a wealthy, close relative lived in Bethlehem at the time. We know that, but Ruth *didn't* have a clue. Evidently, Naomi forgot to tell her. Ruth doesn't have a clue that Boaz exists, that he owns land, or that she will mysteriously choose his land instead of anyone else's in that town.

All she knows is that she has cast her lot. She's made her commitment to trust in the God of Naomi and in the values of the village Bethlehem. It was time to go rummaging for food. Tomorrow would take care of itself.

Often when reading a fiction book, you are introduced to a new character. If the writer is good, it will be a character who is essential to the story—one who is so crucial that without him or her, the story could not be told.

On occasion, when writing a non-fiction book, you must be introduced to a "word." This isn't just any word, but a "word" that is essential to the story. You are about to meet such a word. It is a Hebrew word, so it may be a little odd to you. The word is *hesed*.

The loss and lack of Naomi and Ruth were about to meet *hesed*, and the log-jam of lack was about to be hijacked by *hesed*—the ancient Hebrew virtue of *kindness*. And the first kindness shown was the kindness of a foreign princess who refused to leave the side of the Jewish mother-in-law she loved.

Hello *hesed*. Hello kindness.

Aren't you just a little bit glad that on the road home you begin to meet kindness?

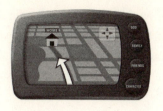

CHAPTER 7

Coming Home to a Place You've Never Been

"Déjà Vu the First Time"

Have you ever walked into a place and felt as if you had already been there? I went house-shopping with my wife one time and at one particular stop on our tour, she walked into a house she had never seen before and announced to me, "This feels like home. I could live here." Now we do!

I don't know how she discerned that, and I'm not sure any man could put it into words. But I'm sure a wise woman could. But I do know that Naomi returned, and then we are told that Ruth "returned" with her:

> *So Naomi* returned, *and Ruth the Moabitess, her daughter in law, with her, which* returned *out of the country of Moab....*[1]

How do you return to where you have never been?

I'm convinced that everyone has a longing for something "more" than what they see, hear, or experience here. We may not be able to put words to it, but the longing is there. While I totally reject the old Freudian idea of some "primal memory" in the human psyche, I suspect we *all* have a "paradisal memory" implanted by the Creator and passed down from generation to generation.

A greater mind than mine described this as "a God-sized hole" in the human soul that can only be filled by God. And another said, "Our hearts are made for Thee and will not rest until they rest in Thee."[2]

It's the faint memory that defies words, the fragrance that can't be expressed. You get a fleeting sense of it in the shiver that runs over you in the brief instant you walk to the edge of the Royal Gorge or the Grand Canyon and sense an even more majestic and vast Presence that dwarfs our world and everything in it.

Implanted deep in each of us is a vague memory and longing for the "paradise lost" that our first forebears once called home. We spend most of our lives trying to regain that place of peace, searching for the road home, longing to "return" to a place we've never been.

Whether you consider yourself part of the "Gen-X" generation, the Boomers, or "the Late Bloomers"—we all seem to be engaged in a relentless search for "a place we've never been."

The post-modern generation is desperately seeking that "unknown something" they feel was lost during the so-called modern era, when everything could be had through science, logic, or mindless hard work, or simply created through plastic resin technology. They want to reclaim the missing values of previous generations, but without the cultural contamination of their rigid traditions.

The Most Important Word for Any Genuine Searcher

The word *return* literally might best fit Naomi. She had once lived in Bethlehem and was now coming back. *Return* is also one of the most important words in Ruth's life story, and it may be the most important word for *anyone* who is genuinely searching for the road home. The word *return* first appears in the sixth verse of the first chapter of the book of Ruth, but not for the last time.

Have you ever been away from home for a long time? I'm talking about a separation from home that is long enough to wear you down and weigh you down with heartsickness. Thoughts of *return* can begin to dominate your every waking moment (and invade your sleeping hours as well)!

They Leave Home Behind and Part of the Heart as Well

It happens to dads and moms who are called into active military service far from home for six months to a year. It happens to sailors who are out to sea for extended tours of duty. It happens when businesses expand to overseas markets and send their top people on-site to set up operations. In every case, they leave home behind and part of the heart as well.

These expatriate parents and family members count the weeks and months eagerly, looking forward to the moment of their *return* home. In one brief moment, everything is all right and life seems good again.

Prodigals and runaways seem to go the farthest and the longest before they finally crash into the brick wall of their own hearts. Perhaps it is because their journey *away* from home often begins with explosive emotions, deep hurts, and a supercharged hunger to go *anywhere* but home.

Adults who grew up without a mom or dad to draw them close in parental love and intimacy often spend their lives looking for "a place to lay their head." Many of these spiritual orphans spend their lives in a desperate search for the significance that usually springs organically from healthy parent-child relationships.

A few may one day find a father figure or a mother-by-choice who will take their hands, look into their eyes, and say, "I'm proud of you, son. I'm proud of you, daughter. You did well. Now go with my blessings and succeed!"

Seeking Directions to the Road Home

One Man spent thirty-three years away from home on a mission that could not be cut short, put off, or avoided. He lived among people of all kinds—some loved Him, some hated Him. Some were broken and were quick to admit it while seeking directions to the road home.

Others were so proud of their self-help accomplishments that they could not or would not admit their need. They felt they were already home, but were actually lost.

As for the Stranger on a mission, He couldn't take the road home until His mission was complete. He understood homesickness as no one else could. He didn't leave home in anger or boredom; He left for love, sent on a mission to help *the rest of us* find the road home.

He knew the people around Him were homesick for a place they had never seen—because *He had been to that place.* In fact, it was His home! He cried out in the busiest shopping area of the capital city at the peak of His nation's greatest and most holy holiday season: "Hey, everyone who is thirsty! Come to Me, all you who are worn out and overloaded. I will give you rest. Follow Me."[3]

Jesus came to show us it *is* possible. The Way *is* known, but we've often got it all wrong. It isn't the *Tao*, or *Zen* (the road home to inner peace according to many oriental religions). Their way, they say, is found in personal enlightenment and self-discipline. No, *the Way* is a Person.[4]

We Secretly Long to Touch God Because It Is "Hardwired" into Our Makeup

We instinctively hope heaven is real—even as we assure everyone around us we don't believe in God. I'm convinced that we secretly long to touch God because it is "hardwired" into our makeup.

This "image" or "likeness" of something you can't quite put your finger on can be traced all the way back to our beginnings when the first created beings enjoyed garden walks with the Creator in the cool of the day.[5]

Something deep inside us cannot agree with any hypothesis which reduces us to less than what our Creator says we are. I have no interest in debating the relative values of arguments about our origins, whether they terminate in images of monkeys, amoebas, cosmic accidents, or mere incidental conglomerations of water, proteins, and minerals.

It isn't about the science (which is incapable of *disproving* the existence of God and of *filling* that "God-sized hole" within us); it's about the burning desire we carry from birth that cries out to know our lives "count for something" more than mere existence.

With eternity bound up in our souls and infinity burned into our thinking, we seem to be poor candidates for death without hope beyond the grave. And so our desperate and often secret search for paradise lost continues. We feel like modern cell phone citizens with a dropped call, continually crying out: "Are you there?"

Many would-be "road maps to Paradise" have surfaced over the centuries bearing marks and endorsements claiming some degree of accuracy. There is a Way, but it cost the Guide everything to pave the road and offer us the ability to "return" to the Garden of Eden—one of the symbols of that place we've never been before.

Ruth was willing to risk everything if it meant that she might rediscover the "home" and connections she'd never known before. She was a daughter of King Eglon, whose physical appearance, and perhaps whose immoral and hedonistic behavior, was renowned for its repulsive and self-seeking nature. She longed for something—anything—beyond what she had witnessed or experienced in the royal dwellings of Moab.

Could it be that Ruth's initial introduction to *hesed* (that Hebrew word meaning loving-kindness[6]) through her relationships with her late husband his other family members triggered this longing?

Heaven Can Even Show Through a Hellish Life on Earth

Perhaps through Naomi, Ruth could catch the faint scent of eternity from time to time. Divine loving-kindness is so attractive that it would have the capacity to captivate Ruth's heart *despite* the distractions and sorrow Naomi experienced through the disappointments, bitterness, and pain of her personal life. In other words, bits of heaven can even peep through a hellish experience on earth.

Naomi's husband and sons were still Jews, regardless of whether or not the men were in sin through Elimelech's choice to "leave the Holy Land" or his sons' decision to marry Moabite brides. And Jews, for the most part, have maintained the ancient tradition of *hesed* or showing loving-kindness toward "outsiders" ever since their own sojourn as foreigners and slaves in Egypt.[7]

One Jewish scholar says, "Anyone who does not have family to provide and care for them—the widow, the orphan—is to be the focus of our special concern. In the book of Ruth, however, it is the stranger-widow-orphan Ruth, who has left her family and come to a new land, who is the exemplar of kindness."[8]

Sometimes, we need a road map to return to things that really matter. Most of us don't plan to get lost. Park rangers in large parks and nature reserves spend a sizeable portion of their time and resources rescuing people who get lost or stranded far from their original starting point. Few of us intentionally lose our way, but we often arrive in that desperate place through casual navigation.

Like a new visitor to Yosemite National Park, you launch out on an adventure armed only with a day pack, a small snack, and a particular mountain peak that captured your eye. You put your head down and follow the path, but fail to check your compass or consult a map. (This may *not* be your style, but walk this out with me.)

If You Only Knew the Way...

As the sun goes down, it dawns on you that every step you've taken *away from home* must now be replaced with a step back toward home. Your adventure has now become a nightmare with miles of wilderness dividing you from food, water, a warm bed, and safety. Perhaps you could make it back safely *if only you knew the way.*

We also get into trouble by trying to hold on to too many things at once. Logically, you can hold on to just so many things with your hands. We relentlessly pursue the "stuff" and the perks of what we call "the good life," stacking one thing on top of another without reevaluating and restructuring to preserve what matters most.

With each added focus in life—a full-time job, a career, ministry, children, etc.—comes more complications, conflicts of interest, time-management challenges, and on it goes. And every step taken away from what matters the most requires a step back toward home if we want to return.

Then the company decides to "downsize" just before Christmas, and *your position* is part of the corporate diet plan.

Do you drive home from work each day with an empty heart? Get a fresh perspective on your full house, full bank account, new cars, new furniture, and broken marriage. There's nothing wrong with having material things, but have you taken care of what matters most in your life?

Perhaps it's time to simplify and preserve what is most important in life. Perhaps your homelife would improve if you sacrifice that third car, work fewer hours, and reinvest that time and energy in that wonderful person you once pursued so relentlessly.

What if the place to which you "returned" actually considered you a foreigner?

What if there was no familiar home and hearth and no neighbors known by name? What if the place to which you "returned" actually considered you a foreigner?

> For Naomi, the journey to the land of Judah, once her home, is clearly a *return*. But in what way is this a return for Ruth? For Ruth, isn't this journey a venture into unknown territory? From here we learn that any time a person turns toward the Holy One it is experienced as *a return*, as *coming home*.⁹

Naomi left behind the fields of Moab and the mistake of living only for the present associated with Moab's plenty. She made a conscious decision to *return* to the values of her youth. Ruth abandoned the only life she had ever known—she left life as she knew it altogether! She literally died to her Moabite roots to join her heart and future to Naomi, her Jewish mother-in-law! Ruth the Moabite didn't realize it, but she had just taken a major step toward becoming a *Jewish* heroine.

> *And Naomi had a kinsman of her husband's, a mighty man of wealth, of the family of Elimelech; and his name was Boaz.*
> *And* Ruth the Moabitess *said unto Naomi,* Let me now go to the field, and glean ears of corn after him in whose sight I shall find grace. *And she said unto her, Go, my daughter.*
> *And she went, and came, and* gleaned in the field after the reapers: *and her hap was to light on a part of the field belonging unto Boaz, who was of the kindred of Elimelech.*¹⁰

What possessed this young, beautiful Moabite princess to lower herself to the social level of a slave or homeless, aged widow who had nowhere else to go but harvest the leftovers reserved for the poor? (The modern equivalent would be someone "Dumpster-diving" outside a posh resturant, digging through others' leftovers to have enough to eat.) And Ruth was a princess!

To understand the shocking humility of Ruth's request, it may help to put it in a modern context. Imagine the daughter of the king of Norway or the queen of England's daughter coming to the United States with her American mother-in-law.

Once they land in New York, she volunteers to her mother-in-law, "If you will allow it, I would like to go down to the Public Welfare Office and submit forms for food stamps and financial assistance. And on the way, I'll stop by Goodwill to see if they have a nice dress and shoes for us, and I'll bring you some food from the Salvation Army soup kitchen."

Please understand that there is *nothing* wrong with folks who must rely on food stamps or financial assistance to get by—that is exactly what they are there for. My wife and I have known times early in our marriage when I took her to a hamburger place and acted as if I wasn't hungry because we only had enough money to buy one hamburger.

My point here is that Ruth gave up her royal title and privileges to associate herself with a widow from a foreign nation—a nation that traditionally hated and looked down on "people like her." For her to walk onto a dusty grain field during harvest was as shocking as seeing a movie starlet or a glamorous and world-renowned princess sit down at the job center to apply for a minimum-wage job—*because she had to.*

Ruth Volunteered and Naomi Agreed—Because They Needed Food!

What isn't obvious until later in the narrative is that Ruth was venturing onto dangerous territory. Ruth *volunteered* to do this, and Naomi agreed to let her go *because they needed food!*

> *While she was there, Boaz arrived from Bethlehem and greeted the harvesters. "The LORD be with you!" he said.*
>
> *"The LORD bless you!" the harvesters replied.*
>
> *Then Boaz asked his foreman, "Who is that girl over there?"*
>
> *And the foreman replied,* "She is the young woman from Moab who came back with Naomi.
>
> *"She asked me this morning if she could gather grain behind the harvesters. She has been hard at work ever since, except for a few minutes' rest over there in the shelter."*[11]

According to one rabbinic tradition, the newly widowed Boaz was returning home after burying his wife.[12] Any way you look at it, the number of "coincidences" stretch the likelihood of "accident" in this meeting. We must believe either that Ruth carefully planned out and orchestrated each detail of her meeting with Boaz, or that God was orchestrating things according to His perfect will. Given the historical events that followed this "chance" meeting, I know which way I'm going!

Somehow Ruth managed to pick the right field (belonging to a relative she didn't even know about yet), she won the favor of a field foreman, even though she was obviously a foreigner, and she successfully gleaned behind the workers all day, finishing and showing up just as Boaz returned from Bethlehem. Accidents may happen, but *this was no accident scene—this was the scene of a miracle.*

The very same God who orchestrated things in Ruth's life still works "accidental miracles" for those who seek Him and trust Him in difficult circumstances. *He still works from the heart outward!* God will disregard every mountain of rules, regulations, and excuses that presumes to exclude honest seekers from His love and grace.

The Princess and the Promise

As for Boaz, he stood out from the crowd from the moment he opened his mouth. Even the way he greeted his workers marked him as a powerful leader.[13] He literally exchanged priestly benedictions with his workers, which tells us a lot about the man's character and management style.[14]

The next question Boaz asked was blunt and direct. Someone had caught his eye, someone who did not blend in. In fact, it was someone who could not blend in.

Boaz assumed at first that Ruth was a servant girl. After all, "field gleaners" were usually servants, older widows, and aliens. What property owner in his right mind would expect a beautiful young widow, let alone a foreign princess, to be "Dumpster-diving" on his property?

The answer he gets tells him why: "*'Who is that girl over there?'* And the foreman replied, *'She is the young woman from Moab who came back with Naomi.'*"[15] Twice the servant mentioned Moab in his answer to Boaz, along with the all-important details concerning the woman's relationship to Naomi.

It becomes obvious that Ruth *first* won the heart of the field foreman before she conquered the heart of the field's owner.[16] He knew Ruth was from the cursed land of Moab, so she wasn't necessarily protected by the laws established for poor Israelites or aliens. He decided to take the risk of granting her request, gambling that Boaz would approve:

> *She asked me this morning if she could gather grain behind the harvesters. She has been hard at work ever since, except for a few minutes' rest over there in the shelter.*[17]

This Woman Didn't Fit the Usual Stereotype

The servant foreman couldn't help but offer extra information about Ruth that he wouldn't have normally mentioned. It seems he had taken a liking to Ruth, and he felt a strong need to let his master know that this woman didn't fit the usual stereotype of a loose, amoral Moabite woman.

He stressed her relationship to Naomi, and then he volunteered even more information about Ruth's unusual work ethic. (Luck is when preparation meets opportunity. "The *harder I work*, the luckier I get!"[18]) She stayed at her task all day long, and she rarely sat in the shelter used by the workers for rest and shade from the sun.[19]

Luck is when preparation meets opportunity.
"The harder I work, the luckier I get!"

It sounds to me as if God provided an advocate and "inside friend" to Ruth on her very first day gleaning in the fields! Have you ever met somebody that you just knew you wouldn't like, but you couldn't help yourself? Whatever it was—Ruth's stunning beauty;[20] her chaste manners; the fact that despite her former social standing as a princess, she was willing to learn the new rules and abide by the new lifestyle; or the information shared by the foreman—Boaz had dramatically altered his speech by the time he spoke personally to Ruth. Her humility only made her all the more a princess... from the inside out.

> *Boaz went over and said to Ruth, "Listen, my daughter. Stay right here with us when you gather grain; don't go to any other fields. Stay right behind the women working in my field.*
> *"See which part of the field they are harvesting, and then follow them. I have warned the young men not to bother you. And when you are thirsty, help yourself to the water they have drawn from the well."[21]*

Boaz no longer had any illusions that Ruth was a servant girl, because he now addressed her as "my daughter." He clearly took on a voluntary responsibility as her protector and provider. It was extraordinary, and it took great courage. Ruth was still a Moabite, and Boaz was a prominent leader who probably served as a senior judge and elder at the city gate.

Boaz Dredged Up and Reversed the Root Cause of the Curse

In the course of a single sentence, Boaz dredged up and reversed the root cause of one of the most deadly curses in biblical record. This incident was discussed over hundreds or thousands of campfires from generation to generation of Jews and Moabites alike.

The Moabites were distant cousins of the Jews, but they refused to sell bread and water to the Jewish refugees trying to reach the Promised Land. They finally gave in and reluctantly helped the Jews, but jealousy and fear got the best of the king of the Moabites. He hired a rogue prophet—similar to a witch doctor—to put a curse on Moses and the Jews. When that didn't work, they had their prettiest women use sex appeal to draw the Jewish men into idol worship. That is when God brought a curse of His own down on the Moabites.[22]

Add to that King Eglon's ruthless oppression and you have full-fledged ethnic hatred toward the Moabites. (And Eglon was *Ruth's father*!)

Within minutes after meeting Ruth the Moabite princess, Boaz told her to glean nowhere but in his field, and then told her to drink from the water the men have drawn when she is thirsty. This is a reversal of Moab's original sin against Moses and the Isaelites. Boaz was basically saying, "Regardless of the fact that your ancestors denied water to mine, I will quench your thirst." What a picture of forgiveness!

It also seems that the language Boaz used in his conversation sent some very clear signals to his workers in the field: "This woman is under my personal protection . . . and she isn't available, so don't even think about it."[23]

Somehow, Ruth experienced a deep sense of belonging, coming home to a place she had never been before. She was beginning to feel a very real connection with her unexpected new benefactor. That is not just my opinion. Here is what another scholar says:

> Ruth hears these words (of Boaz) as "comfort," as words spoken directly "on her heart" (2:13), not merely as social acceptance or the assurance that she will get a meal. Rather, she experiences a deep sense of belonging, of coming home.[24]

It's amazing, isn't it? How can you "come home" to a place you've never been? It's like *déjà vu* for the first time! Coming home is not just to a place, but to people. It is just a house until relationship turns it into a home. The prodigal did not say, "I am returning to my father's *house*." He did say, "I will go to my *father*." Ruth felt at home when she felt relationship. Boaz called her daughter too!

The Formula Is No Formula at All; It Is a Supreme Act of Love

Wouldn't you like to know the formula for reversing every curse, mistake, failure, or family fault in your long (and probably twisted) family tree? The good news is that the formula is no formula at all; it is a supreme act of love by your Creator.[25]

You, too, can "come home" to a place you've never been. You can be embraced by comfort and security, but you must embrace something yourself: the values of your "new neighborhood." In order to be blessed by Bethlehem, Ruth had to embrace its culture (even if it seemed strange at first).

It is at this point, so early in Ruth's miraculous story, that she is established as "a returner." This Moabite widow who left everything behind in the name of covenant relationship and adopted her mother-in-law's people, homeland, and God dared to come home to a place she'd never been before. The tide was turning. In the words of Tamar Frankiel:

> Even though she is a Moabite by birth, she is now treated as a "returner," one who belongs to the land and is under the stricture of not leaving....
>
> Ruth the returner is accepting the bounty that the land has to give her: not only physical sustenance, but spiritual refreshment and homecoming.[26]

This is a nice story up to this point, but stories don't accomplish much unless they somehow relate to *our* situation. Are you still searching for something or some place that is "larger" or greater than you are? Are you still struggling and searching for a road that will take you "home" to a place you've never been?

Experiencing *déjà vu* the **first time** is only possible if such a place or state really exists. It does!

The closer you come to the home you've longed for, perhaps the place you've never been, the more you will rediscover "true values." They are the home you've been looking for.

CHAPTER 8

Finding Your Way to Things That Really Matter

What's It Really Worth?

I love wristwatches. I guess if I have a weakness in the area of material possessions, it's my fondness for really nice wristwatches. Not quartz wristwatches, mind you, but "mechanical, automatic, made-in-Switzerland, day-and-date, precious metal" wristwatches.

I don't know when it started, but it was at least thirty years ago. Some men tinker with cars, others favor, perhaps, guns or fishing rods. With me, it's watches. I have owned and traded scores of watches over the years. I even have framed mechanical drawings from the 1800s on my walls revealing the inner workings of watches.

To put it bluntly, I am just fascinated by them. I have been given many nice watches as gifts, including a gold watch my wife gave me on our twenty-fifth wedding anniversary. Yet, there is one brand of watch that I have always wanted but felt I could not afford. It is a Patek Philippe.

This brand of watch is obscure and expensive. The price of the most expensive ones is literally astronomical. Even the simple models are ridiculously priced for one reason: a Patek Philippe is considered *the ultimate expression* of the watchmaker's art.

Every time I am in an area exclusive enough to host a jewelry store carrying the Patek Philippe line, I bore my family by ogling what I cannot justify buying. I think of how many mission trips could be sponsored, how many students in our Bible school could be given scholarships, and on and on, ad infinitum. But, I always say to myself, "Someone could always give you one!"

Guess what! One day it happened! My wife and I were dawdling through an art show to while away a rare afternoon off in a major city. We were doing our best to be incognito, when someone recognized me. I was slightly bothered by all the semi-celebrity attention, handshaking, photos, and autographs. I wanted to get back to just spending time with my wife—without the distractions of being recognized.

While making small talk with those who had recognized me, I noticed a Patek Philippe watch on one man's wrist and commented, "Nice watch!" To my amazement he immediately took if off and, with tears in his eyes, said, "It's yours!" I protested, because I knew how much a watch like that could be worth. Yet, he insisted, telling me over and over how much my books had touched his life.

What could I do? So I accepted. Wow! Double wow! I could hardly believe it. I kept checking the time. It was so cool! I rejoiced. I thanked God. I hugged my wife. It was a good day!

While eating lunch in a restaurant, I took off the watch again contemplating the question, "I wonder what it's worth?" My wife suggested that I have a jeweler look at it so we could have it insured. Striding excitedly into the most exclusive jewelry store in the city, I walked to the case where the Pateks were kept. When the sales lady asked if she could help me, I proudly inquired if she had any models like this, as I pushed up my sleeve to reveal the Patek Philippe of my dreams. "I'd like to know what it's really worth. It was a gift," I told her.

She asked me to take it off, and I complied. She gently turned it over a time or two and said with a smile, "Sir, this watch is a fake..."

My face flushed, and I stammered around a minute while she added, "We see counterfeits all the time. Would you like to see a real one?" By then my excitement had dissipated, my joy evaporated, and in its place was just embarrassment. "No," I politely replied, as I slunk out of the store with my proverbial tail between my legs.

Later that night my wife and I had a good laugh at my expense over how I could be so excited over something so fake!

I still have that watch, and amazingly, it actually keeps good time.

Nevertheless, I can't bring myself to wear it. Why? Because *I know its true value*—it's only worth about fifty bucks. Maybe.

Sometimes we can go a long time in life treasuring something only to find out it really wasn't worth what we thought. Others can even be fooled by false values. I believe the man who gave the watch to me thought it was valuable. (At least I'm giving him the benefit of the doubt!)

If there was a fire at my house and I had to scramble to save a few things, that watch would not be one of them. But right next to it is a Timex that is so old it barely works. And next to that is an old Hamilton that definitely does *not* work.

Those old watches belonged to both of my grandfathers. Being the family watch "fanatic," the watches were given to me. They are the watches that are *really* valuable to me, and maybe *only* to me. What makes them valuable? It's their heritage and history, not their gold and mechanics.

Too often in life we know the price of everything but the value of nothing. I think it's time we rediscovered true value.

Why do we value "home"? Who could put a price on loyalty? Why do we have to be so old before we really understand the value of community, or family, or legacy? We are too often discount shoppers where price is more important than value.

How do you discover the difference between price and value? How do you find your way to what really matters? How does Naomi find her way back?

Rediscovering True Value

What made Naomi want to go back to Bethlehem? Was property cheaper there? How did Ruth end up in the field of Boaz receiving such words of praise? What did she want from him?

A series of crises in Naomi's life forced a realignment of values. Isn't that the way it often is? She knew her life was off track. She set out to rediscover the true values of her life, even if it meant turning loose of everything that had been her life for the previous ten or twenty years.

Naomi also set out to reconnect with her *valued relationships* and the *community lifestyle* they used to share.

As she quickly discovered in her first reunion with her old friends, Naomi didn't really need "the old days," and it wasn't necessarily even the old *ways* she was after. What she really longed for were the *old values*—the ones anchored in truth. These are the core values that remain valid from generation to generation, from era to era, and from culture to culture.

"It's true that I can't bring back my husband and sons, but then again, there are *some things* I *can* retrieve."

Perhaps she didn't see God at work in her difficult circumstances, but Naomi was about to discover an important principle in God's kingdom: *Your re-connection[1] may create a new connection for someone else.*

In the old days when Bethlehem struggled under the weight of Moabite domination, a woman from Moab like Ruth may not have been entirely safe on Bethlehem's streets.

According to the old *ways*, strangers in the land had some protections and rights under the Law of Moses, but Ruth the *Moabite* would definitely be labeled as an outsider and denied even the most basic of privileges for the rest of her life. "Nothing personal, Ruth, but you are a Moabite. That's just the way it is."

Your re-connection may create a new connection for someone else.

Through the wisdom of Ruth's book, God seemed to reveal a higher set of values where He created a way to let others into the secret of community covenant and shared values. How else could a Moabite become connected to the messianic lineage! But for that to happen, not only did God have to adopt Ruth, but Ruth had to adopt God *with all the subsequent value changes.*

When you cross a border into a different country, very often you must change currencies because the previous currency has no value in the neighboring nation. Ruth faced some major changes. Some things that were highly valued in Moab would get you stoned in Bethlehem. For instance, try offering your baby as a child sacrifice on the town square of Bethlehem! You might be applauded in Moab, but you would be abhorred in Bethlehem!

Life itself becomes more valuable, family opinions matter, no others gloating over what you lost, only help in trying to restore it. The poor are cared for by the powerful! Are you ready to move?

Look what Ruth got for "moving," not just geographically but literally with her allegiance. History holds her in high regard as the great-grandmother of David. Christ was born of her lineage, and her words of wisdom to Naomi at the point of her decision are used as a litmus test for conversion and covenant to this day.

What if I could promise you a better future and a chance at making history *if* you just moved and changed your citizenship? But it's more than that. Her impact came not just because she moved from New York to Florida, or Ohio to Arizona.

Her influence came because something moved inside her! She no longer felt loyal to her natural family—including her father, King Eglon. She honestly saw the flaws and made an inward change of heart before her feet ever touched the soil of Bethlehem.

It is proved by her statement, "Your God will be my God!"[2]

In other words: "I forsake the edicts, commands, and values of what I previously held! I reject Moab and all it stood for. I value your God and His request more than mine."

There was an inward shift that indicated an appetite change.

I am not sure when it happens, but in most children somewhere around adolescence they begin to be willing to diversify their eating habits. They will try a bit of this, a veggie here, or a salad there. Maturity changes the value of what they choose to eat.

For many of us, that time has come. Nightclubs no longer do it for us. Partying only leaves us more empty in the morning (despite our denials otherwise). Call it the "biological clock" or the "theological clock," the incessant ticking within is driving our dissatisfaction. We long for a place of stability, trusted friends, complete confidence, loving family, and no fear.

How long has it been since you "took your guard down"? When was the last time you felt like you were in a place or with people safe enough to know your secrets and love you anyway? How long has it been since you were "home"?

In order to go to that place you must embrace that place, *and* its values! Can you be trusted? Can you keep a confidence? Are you loyal? Do others have anything to fear from you?

Until you swear allegiance to the values of Bethlehem, you can never become a citizen. It's not a geographical trip of the body that will take you home; it's a spiritual trip of the heart!

Listen as Ruth begins the journey:

> *But Ruth said, "Do not urge me to leave you or turn back from following you; for where you go, I will go, and where you lodge, I will lodge. Your people shall be my people, and your God, my God.*
>
> *"Where you die, I will die, and there I will be buried. Thus may the LORD do to me, and worse, if anything but death parts you and me."*[3]

Ruth plugged into what Naomi really was.
Ruth connected in a way that she never had before.
Ruth changed values.

What we all really long for in our souls is a return to true values.

All around the globe, trendy Starbucks coffeehouses have become the "town squares" of the twenty-first century, where people from all walks of life meet and mingle. Although many may gather in the same place longing to connect, some never speak though they often sit only one table away.

They often *text-message* or "IM" (instant-message) *others in distant cities* (individuals who may, themselves, be enthralled by words on their laptops, PDAs, or "smartphones" in yet another coffee-house).

An even larger "community" has emerged on the Internet in the form of blogger networks and virtual communication forums, but with questionable results. Yet even this strange anonymous "anti-community" based on the Internet still loudly proclaims one of the deepest longings of the human soul—the desire to connect with others. The problem is that "connection" *without values* can be very lonely and even deadly.

For example, you and I live in what the Amish[4] call "the Devil's Playground," or "the outside English world." Amish teenagers are allowed to "connect" with our forbidden world of temptation at the age of sixteen for a "wilding." The Amish call it by its Pennsylvania Dutch name, *rumschpringe*, or literally "running around."

The thinking behind this loosening of rules is that these teens must make a lifelong decision to enter the strict communal life of the Amish. The feeling is that before they make that decision, they should have the opportunity to explore what life is like *outside* of their insulated community.

Should You Take a Vacation from Values?

A new set of problems is plaguing the Amish now. This "vacation from values" is becoming more risky. The average Amish teen enters our twenty-first-century world with the cultural trappings of the eighteenth century, and the collision of cultures and values (or the lack thereof) has turned even more deadly than usual. Perhaps it is because the temptations—including alcohol, sexual promiscuity, and exposure to newer and more volatile drugs such as "crack" or "crystal meth"— are getting more addictive and excessive as well.

The serene settings of the tourist-friendly Amish community in Lancaster, Pennsylvania, were turned upside down in 1998 when two young Amish men faced charges that could have earned them up to forty years in prison. These twenty-somethings were caught dealing cocaine to Amish youth for "hoe-downs," teens on "wilding" sprees in informal gatherings held in barns or the new living places of older "wilding" youth. (This is a "vacation from values" gone very, very wrong.)

Both men cooperated with federal officials, repented, and returned to their Amish roots. At their sentencing, one of the men said, "We lived a terrible life for a while. We want to try to be better."[5]

A reporter for the *New York Times* noted in his article on the case, "In many ways, they [the Amish] have been poster people for all that

America cherishes: strong family values, accountability, responsibility, a deep faith in God."[6]

We *do* cherish these qualities in the Amish and Mennonite communities—possibly because we've lost track of those values in our own lives. So much so that to find these values preserved created a tourist attraction. More than five million tourists per year travel to Lancaster County, Pennsylvania, to look through the window of tourism and observe values in action in such Amish communities as Lancaster, and strangely named townships such as Bird-In-Hand and Paradise.[7]

What happens if you have a flat in "Amishland"? Your neighbors will probably help you, even if they don't have an automobile, *or* tires to go on the car they do not own.

What if you truly need food? Your neighbors will share what they have with you.

Lodging? Your neighbors may put you up for a night or so.

Comfort? Your neighbors will weep with you or stay up through the night at your side.

What happens when your *barn burns*? Your neighbors will show up early one morning with all of the supplies and people necessary to raise a new barn for you in one day.

Do you have an innate sense that you would be helped? What is the source of these values?

Millions of stressed-out Americans with disintegrating families look longingly at the simplicity of the separated life of the Amish and Old-Order Mennonite communities. At the same time, they consider it virtually unthinkable that they could ever give up the modern conveniences and freedoms of high-tech life in "the Devil's Playground."

Time to Choose

This struggle to choose ultimately comes to a head among Amish youth who taste the temptations of modern society and lessened values, and then contemplate a lifelong commitment to the community values honored by their parents.

A film documentary entitled *The Devil's Playground* focused on this struggle with temptation and the need to choose. Its producers focused on Faron Yoder, an Amish teen who said he felt called to minister like his father—ironically, even as he battled with a crippling addiction to "crank," or crystal amphetamine.

Another Amish teenager described to the film crew how she felt divided between the temptations of the world and the values of her parents:

> God talks to me in one ear, Satan in the other. Part of me wants to be like my parents, but the other part wants the jeans, the haircut, to do what I want to do.[8]

Between 85 and 90 percent of these Amish teens ultimately return to their families and tight-knit communities within two to four years of going on their *rumschpringe*. Those who return choose to embrace community life rather than life *outside* the values and separated lifestyle the Amish have nurtured since 1693.

The only limits to our realization of a bright tomorrow are our doubts of today!

It isn't my purpose to promote the Amish lifestyle or the virtues of a life lived in extreme separation from the outside world, although I deeply respect their commitment to a holy life lived in community. It's just that the backdrop of their extreme embrace of traditional values along with traditional trappings paints a vivid picture for a close and easier observation.

I believe in a bright tomorrow led by a generation that values life, God, and each other. The only limits to our realization of a bright tomorrow are our doubts of today!

How Do Some Choose to Preserve the Values?

My personal conviction is that the *values* we cherish and honor are larger and greater than any temporary outward trappings they may produce. Those outward indications might include things such as clothing preferences, lifestyle guidelines, or limited associations with others who do not share them. Often, as with the Amish, the urge to preserve values creates its own problem. Legalism!

While many would embrace the values of life, kindness, hospitality, ad infinitum, that the Amish possess, they don't want to abandon modern transportation nor adapt to a life without electricity (much less the style of dress). To think you must have the trappings of tradition in order to imprison value is legalism. I love the values; I despise the legalistic definition we tend to give them.

The key question for anyone evaluating the values of history might be, "How can I learn lessons from the old values without living in the old legalism?"

Perhaps it helps if to understand that the *legalism* seen in many faith-centered or value-based societies (such as in the biblical Israelite society in Moses' day) is merely the "safe" used to preserve the treasured values within.

Why do we venerate "the safe" holding the treasure, when we *know* we should seek the treasure it contains and look forward to revealing its inward beauty to the outside world? We become worshipers of the "safe" rather than its contents. We genuflect to the container, while we disrespect its contents.

I think it's probably good that no one has ever found the ark of the covenant like Indiana Jones did. Millions would be worshiping the box rather than the testimony of who made it and the miracle of its contents. I don't care if it is the baby blue of Tiffany & Co. paper wrapped around the box you've just been given as a gift. The value of the container is insignificant compared to the contents inside. Bethlehem is great, church is good. But what church contains is where the real value is . . . Him and the community of human covenant!

Our deep longing to connect to something or someone greater than we are is, perhaps, one of the inner forces driving our deep interest in the Amish and the Old-Order Mennonite communities.

One of the enduring symbols of their strong community values is the tradition of community barn-raising, where families in the community show up with lumber, tools, and enough food for everyone. This often occurs after a tragic fire destroys someone's barn. By the time everyone goes home, a new barn has been erected and community ties have been strengthened.

The value **is not in the barn,** *it's in the time spent together.*

Something in us longs for simpler times with fewer distractions and complications. Unfortunately, life can be complicated no matter who you are. It is in times of crisis—in those moments of urgent need or crushing loss—that *"values"* matters the most. Always remember that *the value* **is not in the barn,** *it's in the time spent together.*

What do I mean by "values"? One definition from *Merriam-Webster's Collegiate Dictionary* says a value is "Something (as a principle or quality) intrinsically valuable or desirable."[9]

It seems that Ruth learned a great deal from her mother-in-law, but she must have brought some of her own personal values to the table as well. For instance, credibility is the human equivalent to a credit check.

> *Boaz replied, "I've been told all about what you have done for*
> *your mother-in-law since the death of your husband—how*
> you left your father and mother *and* your homeland *and came*
> *to live* with a people you did not know *before."*[10]

Ruth's loving treatment of her mother-in-law and the memory of her deceased husband became the initial deposit in her "favor account" with Boaz, and with the entire Jewish community of Bethlehem as well.

Her loving-kindness, the *hesed*, created the bridge that would span the gap between the black-and-white rules of the Judaic Law and the heart of God toward those who seek Him out and who share and demonstrate His eternal values. Could the unthinkable happen? Would she be accepted by the community of Bethlehem? Only if some upstanding citizen would vouch for her.

Credibility is the human equivalent to a credit check.

It doesn't matter what we *think* we are longing for—we may think our heartache is all about home or belonging, but at its core it is about our longing to return to the intimate relationship with God that once existed.

Modern Jewish rabbis clearly understand the virtue in Ruth's covenant commitment toward her mother-in-law, and later toward Boaz. At the root of it all was a deep longing to connect with the Creator who made her. And the only path available to her was to find Him through Naomi, and later through the community of Bethlehem and the Jewish Torah. One rabbi based in Jerusalem points out Ruth's obvious sacrifice and focuses on her desire for "attachment":

> Ruth was a Moabite princess according to tradition. She was used to the best things in life. She was also a beautiful young woman in the prime of life. The step she was taking would introduce her to a life of poverty; her mother-in-law had lost everything she had through her misfortunes and was returning home entirely destitute. So, in going with Naomi, Ruth was leaving a life of high status to become a lowly convert of questionable status. It was not even clear if a Jew would even be permitted to marry her....
>
> Ruth was torn. But what she wanted was closeness to God, she wanted attachment....She decided to go with Naomi to join the Jewish people no matter what....Naomi understood Ruth and saw that she was after an attachment to God. She had absorbed the true message of Judaism.[11]

"Tell Me What He Looks Like...I've Almost Forgotten"

One of my best friends, a pastor named Jentzen Franklin, tells the story of a mother and dad who were about to have another baby. While they tried to explain the upcoming new arrival to their little girl of about four in an age-appropriate way, she blurted out in true childlike fashion, "Where do babies come from?"

Caught off guard and desperate for an answer, they said, "Well, babies are from God in heaven."

Shortly after their baby boy was born, the couple's older daughter experienced the usual adjustment time accommodating the new family member. As is often the case, there was a bit of sibling jealousy.

Finally, their daughter said, "Mom and Dad, I've gotta talk to him [her brother] when no one is around." At first they were hesitant to allow the "private meeting," but finally they decided to allow it with some discreet eavesdropping.

They left the door slightly ajar and quietly listened to discover what would happen next. Their daughter walked over to her baby brother's crib and said, *"I know you come from God in heaven, but will you remind me what He looks like? I've almost forgotten."*

What a picture of "returning to a place you've never been before"! Several writers and thinkers attempting to describe the intangible and the impossible came up with sentences and ideas that came to be simply framed with the phrase, "There is a God-shaped hole in all of us."[12] A piece of the puzzle of life is missing that only He can fill. When a "piece" is missing the picture is incomplete.

That deep desire to connect, to return, to be reunited with our eternal Creator, is inherent in all of us. All of these values we're talking about point us back to God. They are signposts confirming the existence and continuing influence of the One we all seek, pointing us back to Him who is Himself the timeless Answer.

Separating the Urgent from the Important

Sometimes the only way to leave the "State of Chaos" and go "home" is to rewind portions of your own life, learning along the retraced steps of the journey what was urgent and what was really important.

As a child I often went to a resort at the Lake of the Ozarks in Missouri with other family members and friends. I remember it as one of the best seasons of my life. I can close my eyes and still see my family and other relatives as we gathered to enjoy each other's company. Kids were running every which direction and laughter filled the air as memories were created.

Those images, sounds, smells, and emotions are literally etched into my memory. When my wife and I married, I told her about "the most wonderful vacation spot in the whole world" that I had visited every summer as a child.

Finally, I convinced her that we, too, would have the time of our lives there. To make this long story short, we went back to that "wonderful spot" for our honeymoon only to find it was a huge disappointment to us both!

When we arrived, all we found awaiting us there was a run-down motel. There were few attractions and nothing else to do...*for miles.*

What went wrong? I learned that the *location* had virtually nothing to do with what made that place special. The "special" quality was in my cherished relationships, in the fellowship and the people. The "people" weren't there! There was no sense of community!

The Treasure Isn't in the Geography—
It's in the Connections

My beautiful childhood memory lost its appeal when I tried to go back and re-create it. The joy and the treasure weren't in the geography—they were in the connections.

It was the relationships that I missed and sought after. Even though I retraced my steps to the location of my memories, I still felt disconnected because the *people* weren't there.

The city of Bethlehem in the book of Ruth is not merely a geographic location. Bethlehem also represents a connecting point, a crossroads, a birthing place, a gateway or spiritual matrix between human life and God's eternal plan for man.

Perhaps this is why Micah the prophet pointed out lowly Bethlehem as the birthplace for the Messiah, and why the Magi or wise men from the east believed his predictions and followed a star to Bethlehem more than seven hundred years later looking for the King of the Jews who would be born there.[13]

Perhaps this is why Herod is always trying to kill the babies in Bethlehem.[14]

Even Mary and Joseph had to take the road home to Bethlehem once Herod and his son had died.[15]

Even David longed to drink water from the well of Bethlehem.[16]

* * *

What is so special about Bethlehem? What attracted Naomi back to Bethlehem fueled only by a rumor that things were better? It all funnels down to God. And what He values! Every household has its own peculiar set of rules. In some houses, everyone takes their shoes off at the door; in others, it's another particular custom. These customs preserve values, even if it's just the carpet!

In the household of faith where Jehovah God is Father, there are rules. We call them the Ten Commandments. They are actually statements about what our Father values. Honesty, respect, forgiveness, purity, clean hands (thou shalt not murder). They are our house rules. They make community and create the atmosphere where we can live with and tolerate one another.

We long for this place where unconditional love makes us feel valued and unique. We ache for a permanent sense of belonging in an impermanent world. We hunger for significance, for something worthwhile to burn for. It is actually a preview of eternity, because that is our true home and destiny. We long for "Bethlehem" and its values.

Sometimes our children or grandchildren must re-dig the ancient wells of our values by consciously searching them out, by digging deep into our memories to find out why they matter. In this way, they "rediscover the memories through us."

We see it happening in the lives of Naomi and Ruth. Through Naomi we find Ruth "rediscovering" values she instinctively knew were there, but had never known personally. And Naomi began to rediscover her core values through Ruth as she watched her daughter-in-law awaken under the influence of God's kingdom principles, and through her own godly influence. For Naomi it is a trip back; but for Ruth, daughter of King Eglon of Moab, it is a journey to a place of value.

The Reality of Mortality Is Forcing Many to Make Hard Decisions

Millions of people are stumbling into their middle-age years despite their best efforts to avoid, delay, or deny them. (You can only "botox" away so many years!)

The reality of mortality is forcing many to think deeper and make hard decisions about "what they want to be when they grow up" because the chronological aging of the body has already happened. Now it's time for the soul to catch up before it's too late. You can only discover what you really are by "growing in." It's dangerous to "grow up" before you "grow in."

It's dangerous to "grow up" before you "grow in."

As if our own confusion and longing for a return to values wasn't enough, even our kids seem to be going back to where we or our parents came from. They want to understand why we believe and live as we do—and why we didn't do *better.*

In fact, we're seeing *more* than just returning to values. We are *redefining* our values.

Values Reversed and Tainted with the Pain of Circumstances

By Naomi's own words, she returned home with her values reversed and tainted with the pain of her circumstances. She cried out to her closest friends in anguish and bitterness:

> *"Don't call me Naomi," she told them. "Instead, call me Mara, for the Almighty has made life very bitter for me.*
> *I went away full, but the LORD has brought me home empty. Why should you call me Naomi when the LORD has caused me to suffer and the Almighty has sent such tragedy?"*[17]

Naomi was correct when she said she was *full* when she left Bethlehem but *empty* when she left Moab. This was obviously not a reference to the fullness of the belly. She left Bethlehem hungry with an empty belly—she was leaving Moab with a belly full of food but saying she was empty! She decided that *full means family.* But Naomi was mistaken when she said God had testified against her and afflicted her.

It was God's *mercy* that placed her on the road home with a covenant daughter at her side, and it was His *grace* that restored Naomi to her true values once again. Her emotions had lied to her; grief can lie to you.

In one instance a father named Jacob was handed a torn, bloody coat that belonged to his beloved son Joseph. The antagonistic brothers did not say, "Joseph was dead"; it was Jacob's grief that lied to him and told him so.[18]

God was not the author of Naomi's losses or disappointments in Moab—those came about through human choices based on man-centered values. But God *was* the author of the divine plan to elevate Naomi and Ruth the Moabite to the level of matriarchs of Israel.

It is entirely possible to have a *full bank account* and yet live a totally *empty life*. It is also very possible to have an *empty bank account* and yet live a *full life* marked by joy, happiness, and divine purpose.

It is entirely possible to have a **full bank account** *and yet live a totally* **empty life.**

True wealth has very little to do with financial riches; but true poverty of spirit *often* includes entanglements and misperceptions about the acquisition of *love* of money. We all know the reality of the statement, "I've lived with money and I've lived without money—it's a whole lot nicer living with money than not." But if we have learned anything in this life, it's that the lack of spiritual nutrition for the soul cancels out any earthly riches we may have obtained.

If I lose everything but keep my relationship with God, I am not broke. If I keep everything and lose my relationship with God, I am broke! "For what shall it profit a man, if he shall gain the whole world, and lose his own soul?"[19]

Contentment in the Absence of Things

If you have ever visited an Amish farm or talked with an Old Order Mennonite, your first impression might be that they live lives of contentment in the face of the obvious absence of things we might consider "minimum standards of living" for happiness. How could we live without computers, cell phones, instant hot water, microwave ovens, or automobiles for every family member of driving age?

We tend to mistake "things" for "values" and material possessions for genuine personal happiness. If you are privileged to travel and minister in other nations—especially nations that don't have living standards common to Western industrialized nations, you may notice the richness of family relationships and community identity they possess.

While it is true that genuine poverty (which is very rare or unheard of among the Amish) in impoverished nations brings its own kind of sadness, you also notice that their dependency on one another brings its own *peculiar* brand of happiness.

The odd truth is that when all else is stripped away, poverty often leaves us with nothing left to value except what *truly* is valuable. And part of that value is found in *one another*.[20] Sometimes, when we feel overwhelmed by the pressure to flee poverty, we may accidentally leave behind those things that we should not.

Poverty that leaves us with nothing of value *except* what is really valuable is not truly poverty. It is simply the "absence of things." If you still have good relationships with family, good health, enough to eat, and faithful friends, are you poor?

Poverty that leaves us with nothing of value except *what is really valuable is not truly poverty.*

What causes this slow erosion of values? What destructive catalyst would cause an otherwise happy and fulfilled young person to marry a stranger and divorce her close-knit family and her values?

It doesn't matter whether you are fleeing famine (like Elimelech) or fleeing your hometown for "a better job" in Chicago...the price of abandoning your core values is a price too high to pay. Before you leave "home" make sure it is God transferring you, and not just IBM.

There are predatory con men who frequent the bus stations in New York and Hollywood, waiting for the steady stream of young people with fresh dreams who step off of those buses from Des Moines, Iowa;

Topeka, Kansas; Bristol, West Virginia; and a thousand other places people call home. These predators wait to prey on their false hopes so they can entrap them with drugs or a "free loan," and force them into addiction, prostitution, or worse.

It happens to "older" people too. Sometimes we have to move to find work or improve life for our families, but just make sure you are not seduced by bright lights and false promises parading as a "better life." Don't get mad at the circumstances if your choices put you in an even worse place.

Millions Flee "Famine of Land" Only to Create "Famine of Soul"

It is a terrible thing to lose touch with family and never reconnect again. Sadly, there are people who manage to do the same exact thing while living in the same house! One ancient prophet named Amos spoke of a famine "hearing the words of the LORD."[21] Not a famine of the Word, but of "hearing" God's words. You can be in the presence of the Word and not "hear" the Word. To have wisdom available and not be tuned into it is tragic!

I suspect there are millions of workaholic fathers who, in their own minds, are "fleeing famine of land" and the poverty of their youth— only to "create famine of soul" through their blind pursuit of money at the cost of their family relationships, broken marriages, and spiritual bankruptcy.

If you are living in a famine of the soul, then I encourage you to drop everything and pay attention to the rumor—there's *bread* in Bethlehem again. There's hope for you if you will take the first step on the road home to true value in life! But you must make the first step! You may feel as if you can't do it alone, but God will send you help along the way...

CHAPTER 9

Family Is Not a Do-It-Yourself Project

But Does It Take a Village?

One modern writer said, "It takes a village to raise a child." I think she was correct. But don't let the voice of the village speak louder than the voice of the family! I have quite a large extended family despite the fact that I have only one sibling.

In fact, I have people whom I call my uncles who are not my uncles; and we taught our children to call them that when really they aren't. My extended family, for the most part, is put together and made up of people who aren't even biological relatives—but they sure feel that way.

I will never forget the young couple that babysat me. I still call them Uncle and Aunt, even though they are not related to me. I've never called them anything else, and I'll never forget them.

I wonder if the loss of family is the root cause behind a lot of unsought-for solitude in our modern society. You see, when you embrace the values of an extended family, you embrace the places, the things, and the history and heritage of that family.

That is why every time I pass a little hamburger stand in Lake Charles, Louisiana, I *remember* my babysitters, Uncle Murrell and Aunt Joan. That is why I connect certain places with certain people. Those voices have often spoken loudly in our lives.

I'm trying to do the same thing with my children. I surround them not only with a large biological family but also with a large extended family of people I trust. I refuse to let CNN, MTV, or FOX TV speak louder into their lives than their extended family.

This is what Bethlehem was for Naomi, and this is what it became for Ruth. Community! I still live in a relatively small community where I know the mayor and the policemen. There are advantages to living in a small town. One time my wife did not realize she was speeding. She was totally unaware of the flashing lights behind her until she pulled into our driveway. When the officer pulled in behind her, she was totally shocked. A ticket was issued with much apology. Because she was *known* and *respected*, because of relationship, mercy was extended to her by the folks at city hall (along with a warning about being more mindful of her speed on city roadways).

While you may not live in a small town like ours, situations like this can help you appreciate the benefits of community. Whether it is within the context of a church or some other form of association, a support group of some kind must be created to reap the benefits of extended family life.

I have a room at my house that I call "The Coffee Room." The furniture and décor is varied, but it is unique in that it has no television or computer within its walls. That is because its primary purpose is the promotion of conversation. And since I live in Louisiana, when I think of conversation I think simultaneously of coffee. So our coffee room contains a coffeemaker, plenty of cups, and a layout specifically designed to encourage and accommodate discussion.

On the back wall of the coffee room there is a shortened version of a church pew. It came from the church where my grandfather served as pastor, and the church where I grew up. I learned that the church was being remodeled and the pews would be pulled out, and while I was appreciative of the progress being made, I arranged to rescue one of those memory-laden pews.

Once the pew was shortened to accommodate use in our home, we had a commemorative plaque attached in honor of my grandfather. It still sits in a commanding spot in the Tenney coffee room. Why did I go to all of that trouble? So I could always *remember* the blonde oak pews in the church where I came from and the people who helped impart to me the *values* that made it so special. I'm not advocating that you put pews in your house, but I *am* advocating that you place values in your life. Values like loyalty and good work ethic help create community. Ruth obviously had these values in her life.

> *"So much!" Naomi exclaimed. "Where did you gather all this grain today? Where did you work? May the LORD bless the one who helped you!"*
>
> *So Ruth told her mother-in-law about the man in whose field she had worked. And she said, "The man I worked with today is named Boaz."*
>
> *"May the LORD bless him!" Naomi told her daughter-in-law. "He is showing his kindness to us as well as to your dead husband.*
>
> *That man is one of our closest relatives, one of our family redeemers."*[1]

Naomi most likely began to coach Ruth, her Moabite daughter-in-law, in the ins and outs of the Jewish world from the very beginning of her marriage to her son Mahlon. (This training role of the mother-in-law was part of the ancient structure of Jewish homes and society then, and is still the case in many Jewish families today.)[2]

Yet, once these two women made a covenant and took the road home together, the training process had to speed up and became even more vital. Their lives and destinies could literally depend on Ruth's ability to learn the ancient paths of Abraham's descendants and embrace his invisible God. She had to learn to fit in with the culture of Bethlehem while en route.

Naomi also faced another immediate challenge: it is much more difficult to plan, support, and administrate the needs of two people than it is for one.

It seems Naomi fully expected to make the lonely trip home alone. She probably knew she could count on the generosity of close relatives and friends for the few needs she might have as a single widow. She also knew that generosity would probably be "off the table" once "the young Moabite woman" entered the picture.

So Naomi had to forge a new plan. She would have to blend the ancient elements of Jewish religious tradition and social protocol with the new elements of Ruth's fresh choices. As a new convert to the culture of Judaism, mistakes would be made.

Naomi may have been walking on a familiar road to a familiar town, but she and Ruth were treading *new ground with uncertain outcomes* when they left Moab for Bethlehem. She couldn't do this alone—Ruth had to do her part.

No Turning Back for Half-Hearted Travelers

When Ruth and Orpah first made their commitments to stay by Naomi's side, the brokenhearted mother-in-law functioned as a discourager. Her job was relatively easy simply because the picture ahead *was* dark and hopeless. Her path of return was a permanent one—there could be no turning back for halfhearted travelers, and there would be no nursemaid service for the easily discouraged.

In our modern era, thousands of Jewish people living in lands distant from Israel face similar decisions each year. These are called by some the *diaspora* (Greek for "a scattering or sowing of seeds"), and today the term refers to any Jewish person living outside of Israel.

Will they "*aliyah*" or make "*the return*" to their ancestral homeland and all of the Judaic values and spiritual heritage it represents? Or, will they remain embedded among the adopted nations they've called home for generations?

The very question of whether or not to return to "the promised land" involves a *return to the promise* and perhaps to "the Promiser."

One thing any of these pilgrims can tell you is that *taking the road home* demands a definitive decision. As the Wisest of all has said regarding a similar journey home:

> No one, having put his hand to the plow, and looking back, is
> fit for the kingdom.[3]

There is no room for looking back. The cost is too great; the separation from the old life is too permanent to permit indecisiveness.

The journey to an inner kingdom implies that there is a king. If there is a king, there must be protocols and regulations. Some would want the protection of life in the kingdom without embracing the values of the king. Once you "swear allegiance" to the king, you embrace his values.

And the kingdom embraces you. You are protected by its power and policies. The king has made certain promises to the citizens of the kingdom.

He promised to not put more on you than you can bear. In other words, you will *not* be overtaxed.

He will become a father to the fatherless; orphans and widows will receive special care.

He desires that "above all you would prosper."[4] He demands that injustice be banished.

How would you like for a kingdom like this to be your home?

Naomi did her best to discourage the daughters-in-law whom she had grown to love so dearly. She knew she really *was* too old to provide another son as a potential husband for them. Besides that, the ancient curse on the descendants of Moab was very real.

It was written in the scrolls of the Law and was burned into the memories of the Jewish people:

> *No Ammonites or Moabites, or any of their descendants for ten generations, may be included in the assembly of the LORD.*[5]

And the scrolls even explained **why** *they were cursed:*

> *These nations did not welcome you with food and water when you came out of Egypt. Instead, they tried to hire Balaam . . . to curse you. (But . . . God would not listen to Balaam. He turned the intended curse into a blessing because . . . God loves you.) You must never, as long as you live, try to help the Ammonites or the Moabites in any way.*[6]

Others who were not Jews were not to be "abhorred" like the Moabites!

> *Do not detest the Edomites or the Egyptians, because the Edomites are your relatives, and you lived as foreigners among*

the Egyptians. The third generation of Egyptians who came with you from Egypt may enter the assembly of the LORD.[7]

Much time and distance later, Naomi and Ruth entered the city of Bethlehem, and it almost seems for a moment as if Naomi forgot that Ruth was there. This is understandable to a point. Naomi's homecoming brought up uncontrollable waves of grief and despair over what she had lost and left behind in Moab. Grief can be all-consuming when memories bring emotions to the surface.

Ruth appeared to be essentially lost in the shadows, *or was she?*

My family and I still live happily in a relatively small town, and I've had many experiences in *really* small towns. With little to do except keep up on the gossip about family, work, and friends, I have *no doubt* that those astute ladies in Bethlehem had evaluated, calculated, classified, and formed fixed opinions about every aspect of Ruth's appearance.

Any one of them could give a complete and detailed rundown on this Moabite widow's skin color, her hairstyle, her approximate age, whether she had borne children, and the approximate danger she represented to their own *personal* marital bliss (as a measure of her potential ability to attract their husbands' attention). *Who is this over made-up "hussy" who came to town with Naomi? Her skirt is too short! Her hair is too wild! And she is a Moabite. You know what they are like!*

Naomi and Ruth Made an Uproar and Agitated the City Greatly

The historical biblical account says that when Naomi and Ruth came to Bethlehem, "all the city was *moved* about them."[8] Many modern translations say the city was "stirred" by their arrival. The original Hebrew root of the word literally means "to make an uproar, or agitate greatly."[9] So it is more than possible that the uproar may have been caused—at least in part—by Ruth's Moabite style of dress or some physical attributes of her ethnic background.[10] For whatever reason it may have been, we know that Naomi and Ruth *made an uproar and agitated the city greatly!*

Perhaps Ruth's clothing and appearance shouldn't even have entered the picture, but it probably did. Just as it does for us many times. That is why most of the time any questions about what we wear, eat, drink, or say in the presence of others really shouldn't include discussions of our "rights." It usually has more to do with *who* we represent and *how* that person or entity wants to be represented at the time.

The president of the United States and the prime minister of Great Britain certainly have the same freedoms as you and I—they have the "right" to dress like slobs on Saturday mornings or to wander outside of their official residences with their hair all awry and a four-day growth of beard or their makeup smeared and smudged (depending on their gender, of course); but that doesn't make it the right thing to do. They happen to represent their nations, and on a 24/7 basis as well.

Since we've referenced the Amish often, let's view this scenario through their eyes. Remember that their women don't wear slacks, their hair is long (and is often totally covered and in a bonnet or kerchief), they wear no makeup, and, in general, their dress is very modest and plain. Some sects even deny the use of buttons and bright colors.

Naomi returns to her "Amish" roots. She no doubt had forsaken many of the "old order" ways, but probably had not completely embraced the Moabite style of dress. It takes a while for them to recognize her—"That's Naomi!" (But at *least* she seems a bit repentant about the situation.)

"But who is that with her? Dressing like a Moabite! Hair short, dress short, cleavage showing. Over made-up!" Can you hear the tongues wagging? *"Too little dress trying to cover up too much woman!"*

It is possible that a similar scenario occurred the day Naomi and Ruth entered the city of Bethlehem, fresh from the fields of Moab.

I wonder if Naomi had been gone so long that she didn't even know the stir they were causing.

Sometimes, your freedom can deal a real slap to the face to other people who don't understand or agree with your beliefs. You must be careful, because *you cannot antagonize and influence at the same time!* Don't flaunt your freedom.

Regardless of how Ruth dressed, looked, or spoke, the first thing she did upon entering Bethlehem speaks volumes about the internal values she now embraced:

> One day Ruth said to Naomi, "Let *me* go out into the fields to gather leftover grain *behind anyone who will let me do it*." And Naomi said, "All right, my daughter, go ahead."[11]

The ethic of hard work shows up as a value embraced by Ruth. That had to impress the Bethlehemites—regardless of how she dressed! Also, a recognition of kindness shows up. "This doesn't sound like the thinking of a pampered Moabite princess! There have been some internal changes in Ruth!"

Once Naomi and Ruth set foot on the streets of Bethlehem, *it became Naomi's job to provide "an insider's guide" to life in Bethlehem and among the Jews*. However, it seems that Naomi was still in a daze after her disappointing reunion with old friends.

You cannot antagonize and influence at the same time!

When Ruth offered her proposal to glean among the fields for food, it was all that Naomi could do to simply say yes. According to rabbinic and historical sources, Ruth faced considerable risk as a beautiful young woman wandering into the fields alone; still, Naomi didn't offer a word of warning or advice at that point.[12]

Even though the Law of Moses that Bethlehem lived by provided *some* protection to foreigners and women, there were still some loopholes in the law, and evidently there were serious lapses in the social conscience of some. It appears that Ruth was in some danger of "being taken advantage of." We take our cue from the comments Boaz himself made to Ruth.[13]

> Then Boaz said to Ruth, "Let me give you some advice. Don't gather grain anywhere except in this field. Work with the women here; *watch them to see where they are reaping and stay with*

them. I have ordered my men not to molest you. *And whenever you are thirsty, go and* drink from the water jars that they have filled."[14]

Boaz was the first to take an active role as protector and guide to Ruth, who had been a total stranger and foreigner only minutes earlier. In Ruth's mind, this must have been a refreshing value change from the apparently misogynistic Moab! I wonder how she would have felt viewing modern music videos. Safe? Protected?

Who to Ask Directions from in a Rough Part of Town

We live in a modern society in which most cities, towns, and counties have established police departments and laws on the books that protect us from harm in most cases. But anyone who has wandered off main thoroughfares into a potentially dangerous zone understands what a relief it is to find an ally or a friend in such a place.

Areas that are safe *to a local* can be terrifying or even fatal *to a stranger* unfamiliar with the "ins" and "outs" of a neighborhood. Perhaps you know how it feels to find a friendly clerk at a convenience store in an unfamiliar and obviously rough neighborhood who shows you how to make your way safely back to the main road or the highway home.

Have you ever found yourself on the receiving end of undeserved kindness? Perhaps you've received an unexpected raise, or enjoyed a five-star meal with the boss at an elite restaurant—walking right past the large sign at the elegant entrance that says, "For Members Only."

This must have been how Ruth felt as Boaz publically offered her his personal protection and special treatment. In fact, she said so:

At this, *she bowed down with her face to the ground. She exclaimed,* "Why have I found such favor in your eyes *that you notice me*—a foreigner?"[15]

There was a connection to Boaz. Unsolicited destiny had intervened. Ruth caught Boaz's eye. And Boaz welcomed Ruth to his value system. She felt undeservedly protected and valued.

How many of us long for a Boaz to extend the umbrella of protection around us? *Boaz* is often only found in Bethlehem, the place that *values* values.

We know, by virtue of hindsight and the detailed historical and biblical account, that Ruth would ultimately give birth to a son by Boaz. That son would become the grandfather of David, and a direct forebear in the lineage of the Messiah.

These events taking place on a partially harvested field between these two strangers from two opposing cultures were literally forming the framework of a miracle. This miracle would preserve the family line of Elimelech, Mahlon, and Boaz. It would make possible the fulfillment of God's promise to send a Savior into the earth.

Somewhere in the dormant DNA of Ruth was the genetic link to Abraham the father of the Jews. Her ancestor Lot was Abraham's nephew. That tenuous link is made even weaker by its incestual parentage. But there was in this woman the DNA of the Father of Faith. When exposed to the soil of the Promised Land, something began to germinate. Sometimes what is in you only begins to grow when exposed to the right environment.

Moabites were not to enter the congregation of the Lord "even to the tenth generation."[16] Yet, something about Ruth—about her tutelage from Naomi and her connection to a pillar of the community, Boaz—so broke the bondage of legalism, that grace birthed David, "a man after God's own heart," was born a mere three generations later.

Are you aware that you, too, can be a Ruth? Or a Naomi? You can change the future of your friends and your family just by embracing the values of Bethlehem.

But the creation of a family with a great future—especially an impossible blended family like this—*is not a do-it-yourself project.*

Our Western culture, with its mobile lifestyles and U-Haul mentality, has done its part to rip the very fabric of extended family stability and structure. We've gained choices, opportunities, freedoms, and financial increase, but at what cost? In the end, all of this seems to have left us feeling more isolated than ever before. Sometimes, in moving closer to a job, we move further from family. Be careful with your "connections"—they are easier to break than to make.

Sometimes, society seems to value isolation more than relationship. We are able to educate ourselves, entertain ourselves, work, pay our bills, and even purchase all of our gifts and arrange for their delivery through electronic means—without ever leaving our homes if desired.

Ruth's single-minded devotion to the welfare and care of her mother-in-law stands in stark defiance of our modern trends. We know this much for sure: Boaz is impressed with Ruth, but not just because he noticed her beauty. He also noticed her respect and care for her mother-in-law.

I have a friend who has a very large ministry. He is among the most brilliant and productive human beings I've ever met.

When I find myself in need of wisdom in certain areas, his phone number is the one I call. But the most impressive thing about this man is how he treats his ninety-plus-year-old father.

He takes his father with him often, introduces him, cares for him, and is not even embarrassed by the more frequent acts of senility that I have noticed.

That's his father! He loves him! How much more character does it take to hold the mother-in-law in such high esteem that it is noted by the community? It is a mark of Boaz's wisdom that this is what he noted.

How we treat our "past" family is often an indicator of how we will treat our "future" family. Watch how others honor their heritage, even when it is difficult. Remember, others are watching how you honor your past. Boaz is observing you. Will he see how you value others?

There Is Hope for the "Outsider"

Previous heroes in Israel included Jewish men or women rising to prominent positions in foreign nations. (Moses became a "prince of Egypt," and Joseph followed suit generations later; Daniel rose to the top in Babylon; and Esther as queen saved the Jewish people in Persia.)

This time, the roles would reverse. It would be Ruth the Moabite, *the ultimate "outsider,"* whom God would raise to prominence in Israel with the help of Boaz and Naomi. There *is* hope for the *outsider* wherever and whenever God is involved. While the judgments and limitations of men may push others away, the love and mercy of God continually draw the outsider in. You don't have to be a pedigreed blue blood to rise to prominence in the kingdom of heaven.

Ruth had already experienced the feeling of being an "outsider" during her first few minutes left standing in the "cold" of social indifference—Naomi poured her heart out to her old friends while Ruth practiced her skills as an unseen, immaterial, and unimportant fixture standing right beside or right behind her mother-in-law at the time.

Evidently, Ruth felt Bethlehem's cold shoulder even more when it spread from the street to the fields the very next day. Some experts believe there is enough evidence to say the harvesters in the field of Boaz that first day were "riled up at the presence of a Moabite, that is, according to the stereotype, of a woman with loose morals, in their midst."[17]

Perhaps you've felt the cold chill of life as "the invisible person" standing right in the middle of a group of old friends—all of whom quietly but pointedly ignored your very existence.

In just one paragraph, Boaz overturned generations of curses, animosity, and anti-Moabite sentiment. According to the "norm," Moabites were disdained and avoided by Judeans. The normal course of events featured women drawing water for the men, and for princesses to dine on an abundance of food harvested and prepared by servants.

> There is, in fact, a double reversal in that a Judean [Boaz] serves a Moabite and a woman drinks water drawn by men. [The writer of] Ecclesiastes would not be happy. For him it was outrageous to see slaves on horseback and princes walking.... Starting now, neither Ruth nor Boaz will be the same as before their meeting.[18]

Naomi had offered Ruth no warning or advice about local dangers or social expectations when she asked to go to the nearby fields to search for food. Naomi had simply signaled her approval with little else said, perhaps because she was still deep in despair over her personal loss.

Ruth *did* go to the fields, and she returned with great news that sparked new life into Naomi's heart. It sent a charge into the heart of her hopelessness like a spiritual resuscitator, and new life seemed to explode within her for the first time since she had suffered the loss of her two sons.

It is significant that the return of life in Naomi's heart ignited after Ruth returned home from the fields of Boaz with her amazing report of divine favor:

> *So Ruth told Naomi that she had been working in a field*
> belonging to a man named Boaz.[19]

Just imagine the shock that raced through Naomi's body at the mention of that name! Suddenly a new light came into Naomi's weary eyes that were still bloodshot and swollen from relentless weeping.

Something lit the fire in Naomi's heart because the Bible tells us she started talking to Ruth about God's goodness! This was the same woman who not long before was telling all of her friends on the main street of the city:

> *Do not call me Naomi; call me Mara, for the Almighty has*
> *dealt very bitterly with me. I went out full, and the LORD has*
> *brought me home again empty. Why do you call me Naomi,*
> *since the LORD has testified against me, and the Almighty has*
> *afflicted me?*[20]

Note that Naomi had let present circumstances name her future. She is now "mara" or *bitter*. Don't announce a curse on your future, when you pronounce "bitterness" on your present.

The only time God said He would be a "present help" was in the "time of trouble."[21] That is the only time God stands up and says, "Present."

Name your future according to your faith, not your fears!

You must resist the urge to allow the circumstances you find yourself in to dictate your future. At one point, when the glory of God lifted from

His people, the wife of a priest caught in the depressive moment named her newborn son "Ichabod," meaning "the glory has departed."[22] But that was only partially true! There came a time when the glory returned! But the boy was still stuck with a bad name!

Never memorialize your bad moments by naming them. Keep the name that faith has given you! Name your future according to your faith, not your fears!

Something in Ruth's report revealed the supernatural intervention and provision of God to this desperate widow! Naomi's last-ditch decision to take the road home was beginning to show its first signs of a divine turnaround!

Overjoyed and overwhelmed, Naomi wiped away tears and told her startled Moabite daughter-in-law:

"May the LORD bless him!" *Naomi told her daughter-in-law.* "He is showing his kindness to us as well as to your dead husband. *That man is one of our* closest relatives, *one of our* family redeemers."[23]

Suddenly everything had changed in Naomi's life. She felt new purpose surge through her soul when Ruth reported what had happened in the gleaning fields. Naomi knew her counsel would be vital from this point forward, for Ruth the Moabite was in need of *real advice from her Jewish mentor.*

All this because Ruth brought home an abundant supply of food. People generally don't get this excited over groceries! Something much larger was afoot. It was nothing less than eternal destiny at stake.

Have you ever noticed how God gives you a glimpse at your future without you knowing it? It's a "values" test!

Rebekah watered *all ten camels* of Isaac's before she became his bride.[24] How hard was that? How long did it take? Thirsty Arabian camels can drink as much as twenty-one gallons in ten minutes![25] *That means those ten thirsty camels drank 210 gallons of water that day!*

A gallon of water weighs 8.34 pounds, so it's possible that young Rebekah single-handedly *drew and hand-carried 1,751 pounds of water* to those camels.[26] If her container held ten gallons of water (at

83.4 pounds per trip), then she may have made twenty-one trips to the well and back!

Ruth worked as a gleaner in the fields of Boaz before she married him and became owner of the fields. God will often give you the chance to water and work your own future without you knowing it. Rebekah rode those camels to her destiny. That's the value of hard work!

From the time Ruth returned from the field of Boaz until the day she *owned* that field through marriage, her relationship with Naomi took on an even deeper urgency and closeness.

What began as a covenant commitment through love to endure hardship together in a very uncertain future was now transformed into an adventure of destiny and hope! A new "blended family" was in the making, although the parties involved barely understood what might soon happen—and *none of them* understood its importance to the future of the Jewish people or the world.

Naomi already knew the community strengths and weak spots in her hometown of Bethlehem, but Ruth was in need of a "corporate champion," a local protector who would clear the way of potential dangers. She had "stumbled" upon that champion in a field on the outskirts of Bethlehem.

As a descendant of Moab, a family line marked by violence, incest, betrayal, and child sacrifice, Ruth knew firsthand the cost of broken covenants. She knew that while community exists at many levels, not everyone is a covenant friend.

Most aren't worthy of that level of commitment because they don't comprehend the demands. She had made her covenant with Naomi, and as she began to walk it out, the God of covenant began to create a miracle that would affect the entire world and the generations that would follow. Covenant is obviously one of the values in Bethlehem.

As for Naomi, when she left Bethlehem for Moab, she thought her life was empty. There was no food in Bethlehem.

When Naomi returned on the road home to Bethlehem, as she poured out her sorrows to long-lost friends and renamed herself "Bitterness," she didn't realize that God's provision had followed close at her side. She came back home to Bethlehem from Moab with her answer at her side (and Ruth means "*Satisfaction*"!).

Sometimes you can have *Satisfaction with you* and not be aware of it!

> Not only does Naomi embrace Ruth—the woman who was an *outsider*—but it is Ruth who helps Naomi slowly become whole once again. The stranger, the one who has come the furthest distance, becomes the most intimate, the one who is able to make the most impact on Naomi—once Naomi opens herself up to all that Ruth has to offer.[27]

The miracle beginning to unfold in the book of Ruth speaks of mutual dependence and joint assistance *by choice* between these two remarkable women. Yet there was Another who was at work on their behalf, the one described as "a father of the fatherless, and a judge of the widows...*God in his holy habitation.*"[28]

Two women caught in the backwater of society appeared to have little to offer, and little chance to significantly impact history. Even their ability to touch tomorrow's generations through husbands or children had been taken from them. Greatness is often camouflaged in the torn hearts and tattered garments of everyday men and women.

CHAPTER 10

"I Finally Found It"

Whose Field Is It?

I can't tell you how relieved I was to make the left-hand turn and see the towering hotel in the distance. I knew we had finally found it. "Thank God we made it. I'm tired."

When we arrived at the hotel at 2:00 o'clock in the morning, we learned that they had given our reserved room to someone else. So there we were in Indianapolis in the middle of the night, with the temperature nine degrees outside. As our hearts sank, the clerk said, "Oh, but sir, we have rooms reserved for you at another hotel."

Since I didn't recognize the name of the hotel, I presumed we would find it in some back alley somewhere with sub-par service and less-than-acceptable accommodations. To our surprise, the rooms were not too bad. In fact, they were pretty good. They were *railroad cars* that had been converted into hotel rooms.

I can't say that was one of the most comfortable nights I've ever spent in a hotel, but my daughter who was traveling with me at the time was excited enough to call home the next morning and say, "Mom, you'll never guess. We slept in a railroad car!" That 2:00 a.m. diversion made for some wonderful memories.

Recall the sense of relief you experienced when you could say, "We've finally arrived!" or when you finally found something you had been looking for, perhaps the spouse of your dreams. In the case of this story, Ruth finally found a place of grace.

The Bible states "Noah *found* grace." I don't know if you have ever looked for grace, but the road often takes you through bends and turns in the journey.

When Ruth left Moab, she wasn't certain of what she was looking for. But when Naomi left Moab, she was returning *home* to the values she had lost.

Why have I found *grace in thine eyes...I am a stranger?*[1]

Two marriages, three untimely deaths, and a squandered family fortune left these two living remnants of "the Moab experience" feeling withered and hopeless.

The unyielding glare of searing pain and the ache of permanent loss can weaken the strongest soul given enough time. They left the place of their pain and set their eyes and hopes on the fields of Bethlehem— perhaps here they would find enough provision to live and start over.

Yet, there was something about Bethlehem...something *more* than its fields and hillsides could ever account for. For Naomi remembered times when Bethlehem's fields weren't so productive. In fact, her decision to return was based on rumor. It seems as if she would have come back, even if abundance was not back. What is it about Bethlehem that draws people back? Is it the water? What's the deal with water from the well of Bethlehem? There must have been something very special about that water. Again, it seemed as if everything about Bethlehem— including its well—had more meaning and importance than could be accounted for logically.

The Well of Bethlehem by the Miracle Gate

Generations later, a young Bethlehem shepherd would trade his shepherd's staff for the captured sword of a giant. Then, in a dark moment of separation from his hometown, he would look out from a cave in the wilderness and speak longingly to himself of that beloved well in hushed tones: "Oh that one would give me a drink of the water of the well of Bethlehem, *which is by the gate!*"[2]

A crucial breakthrough would soon occur in Ruth's life at *that same gate* near the same well. That breakthrough at this "miracle gate" would make possible the birth of King David, the young shepherd from Bethlehem, the giant killer, and all of the events in his life. Generations later, *Another* would be born in a humble Bethlehem stable, One who was called "the son of David" and the Bread and the Giver of the Water of Life.[3]

Unfortunately, the reality of life for Naomi and Ruth just didn't ring with prophetic joy the morning Ruth rose early to find a Bethlehem harvest field. Living with "the present problem" while having a prophetic word about the future is the ultimate test of faith.

How many times have you felt as though you were "on top of the world" when someone or something came along to prove that you weren't "king of the hill" any longer? A prettier girl, and better-looking guy, the loan officer with an attitude, or the doctor with a bad report came along to rain on your parade.

Ruth's dependence on the field of God was *real*. She had been raised as a princess in a culture of domination, where bowing before a human ruler and calling him Lord was the norm. Boaz was a judge in a society founded on the Torah, where only God was to be called Lord.

The Jews, historically, bowed to no king unless forced to do so. Generations later, three Hebrew young men in the capital of Babylon would refuse to bow before the image of a human king, and would face the terror of a fiery furnace for their convictions. Mordecai the Jew would barely escape execution (and his people with him) after he refused to bow to the chief confidant of the king of Persia.

(They felt the *same way* about people bowing to *them*—it could take them to the brink of receiving honor due only to God. Many generations later, two men transformed by encounters with God were horrified when a crowd excited about the signs and wonders worked through them wanted to offer sacrifices and bow before them, calling them the Greek deities Jupiter and Mercury.)[4] In short, Jews historically did not bow or allow themselves to be bowed to!

Her Ignorance of Custom Was Covered by Her Purity of Heart

That this unlearned Moabite princess bowed in humility before Boaz speaks volumes. Her ignorance of custom was covered by her purity of heart, and her devotion to kindness and faithfulness.

Boaz may have been embarrassed by Ruth's over-the-top demonstration of humility and gratitude, but I have a feeling that Boaz was doing some "over-the-top" acting of his own.

According to Hebrew scholars and rabbis, Boaz was using some very pompous and stiff language in his reply to Ruth's sincere question.[5] Perhaps we're seeing a normally confident single "alpha male's" self-conscious response to a startlingly beautiful young woman.

> *"Why are you being so kind to me?" [Ruth] asked. "I am only a foreigner."*
>
> *"Yes,* I know," *Boaz replied. "But* I also know about *the love and kindness you have shown your mother-in-law since the death of your husband. I have heard how you left your father and mother and your own land to live here among complete strangers.*
>
> *"May* the LORD, the God of Israel, *under whose wings you have come to take refuge, reward you fully."*[6]

Whether a modern president, ancient king, or adolescent boy, all have been known to wilt or grow tongue-tied in the presence of a beautiful young lady; surely there is room for a mature village official to be affected by the beautiful Moabite widow, Ruth. She now had an advocate.

For someone who entered a foreign harvest field powerless and seemingly without connections, Ruth was now doing pretty well. Ruth (and Naomi as well) had unknowingly engaged the services of another heavenly advocate. As we noted earlier,

> *His name is the LORD . . .*
> *Father to the fatherless, defender of widows—*
> this is God, *whose dwelling is holy.*
> God places the lonely in families.[7]

Perhaps what we are observing is God "placing" in a family. Despite his stiff, formal, and awkward response, the message had gotten through to Boaz. Somebody had "showed" him or told him of Ruth's character-revealing care of her mother-in-law, and her abandonment of Moab's values and her full embrace of Judaic values.

Then it got awkward with "the Lord reward you fully." Boaz was about to be the Lord's hand!

Corporate Champions Can Make Good Things Happen on Your Behalf

Many people have seen their prospects rise and their upward movement in a corporation accelerate significantly through the friendship of a "corporate champion." When a person who is well placed and very influential in an organization sees your potential or "takes a liking" to you, he or she has the ability to make good things happen on your behalf, to "champion" your cause.

While I don't necessary encourage you to seek out or cultivate a "corporate champion," I would say that God is the ultimate corporate champion. It is *wise* to receive *God's* favor when it comes your way!

A young Christian evangelist held a tent crusade in Los Angeles in 1949, and a local underworld figure and a prominent disc jockey walked forward to receive Christ along with many others. The evangelist's ministry took off after newspaper magnate William Randolph Hearst ("for reasons unknown") ordered his publications to "Puff Graham" and other newspapers picked up the story. Then, at publisher Henry Luce's request for some "reason," articles appeared in *Time* and *Life* magazines favoring his ministry.[8] (We know the "reason"—it was the Heavenly Advocate's work on Billy Graham's behalf.)

Ruth had the same "corporate champion," the backer who excels and exceeds all others. Perhaps Ruth didn't realize it, but her "good luck" or "unexplained favor" didn't come her way just because her good gene pool had given her phenomenal beauty. She hadn't even received such favor because she had journeyed to the fields of Bethlehem. Her provision came from the *field of God*. Man can be a resource, but God is "*the Source*."

Take note! She didn't just parade down the catwalk in the field! She *worked* in the field! She scavenged for food, despite how backbreaking and humiliating the work was. No arrogance here, no "don't you know who I am?" attitude. No princess pouting. Ruth, with all of her well-documented outer beauty, embraced the work ethic of Bethlehem and shined the spotlight on her true inner beauty.

This was no Paris Hilton putting in a public relations spin of the TV hit *The Simple Life* on a farm. This was no "photo op"—this was reality.

A Work of God in the Field of God

Perhaps Naomi was still battling depression in her empty house when all of this took place. Her "insider insights" and inborn accumulation of Jewish traditions didn't come into play during the miracle in the field. Ruth's stunning beauty played a part in God's plan, but we have already seen how her looks could just as easily work against her. This was a work of God in the field of God.

Again, if Boaz hadn't been moved beyond his natural caution and legal instincts to offer a stranger his personal protection, then Ruth would have been in very real danger. She was in a unique situation as a *Moabite* woman. She might be viewed as technically exempt from the protections offered foreigners, and she was working in an open field without visible or clearly established protection in the Jewish community.

According to the guidelines of that era she could have been forced into sexual relations by men in the field without any real fear of being accused of adultery or seduction![9] The prevailing stereotype of Moabite women seems to have been that "all of them were promiscuous," and little better than temple prostitutes![10]

Ruth obviously didn't have all of the "Jewish rules of the road" down pat, and she just didn't fit into the usual stereotypes. She was a princess from Moab, and evidently she was strong and self-assured enough to challenge the stuffy but *uncommitted* statements by Boaz about God blessing her. Ruth had submitted herself to God, but she skillfully placed the responsibility for action back on Boaz, which was right where it belonged:

> "May I continue to find favor in your eyes, my lord," she said. "You have given me comfort and [you] have spoken kindly to your servant—though I do not have the standing of one of your servant girls."[11]

Whether Boaz liked it or not, he represented the hands, heart, and resources of God sent to Ruth and Naomi. It seems our invisible God *always* uses human instruments to do heaven's business on earth.

Only transparency can reveal inner beauty.

At the same time, Ruth evidently hadn't heard the career advice that says you don't "get ahead" by pointing out all of your differences or shortcomings to others. Most Moabite strangers would try to tone down their differences from the Jewish "locals." Instead, this woman made a point of highlighting them. If Ruth was out to impress, she sure went about it in an odd way. *She became transparently honest.* She pointed out, "*I do not have the standing of one of your servant girls.* I'm not a Jew. I am not one of your workers."

One scholar said it well, noting that Ruth "knows that *pious words do not replace a personal commitment.*"[12] She thanked him for his kind words but left a question dangling in the air. If the question had not gone unsaid, it would have probably sounded like this:

> You say you know all about me and how I've cared for Naomi. Well then, you also know how desperate our situation is. You said "the Lord" was going to take care of me. Is that your way of dodging responsibility? You know my needs. What are you going to do about it?

The wisdom of Ruth to imply this question without asking it is still the playbook for wise women today.

How many times have you had to wait on something you really needed, earned, or were promised because someone else hadn't ever "gotten around to it"?

Could It Be That God Is Waiting on You?

Let me ask the question a different way: How many times do we say each week, "I wish *somebody* would *do something* about that problem" or "Why doesn't somebody minister to all of those messed-up people?" Could it be that God is waiting on *you*?

By law, Boaz could have thrown out Ruth. After all, she was a Moabite. But instead, he rose to the challenge and immediately put action behind his words.

> *At mealtime Boaz said to her, "Come over here. Have some bread and dip it in the wine vinegar."*
>
> *When she sat down with the harvesters, he offered her some roasted grain. She ate all she wanted and had some left over.*
>
> *As she got up to glean, Boaz gave orders to his men, "Even if she gathers among the sheaves, don't embarrass her. Rather, pull out some stalks for her from the bundles and leave them for her* [handfuls on purpose[13]] *to pick up, and don't rebuke her."*[14]

Only as the leftover grain passed through (not into!) the hands of men did it have purpose! Otherwise it was just an accident!

Boaz had "field values." The things that mattered to him and worked in his life were just as visible and effective in the marketplace as they were in a religious setting. He was conservative, but he also had the backbone to take a risk.

This man had a lot to lose and seemingly very little to gain by getting involved with the young widow from the forbidden nation of Moab. His first step into God's adventure was to *bless Ruth in the field* with protection. Now he had taken the second step to *bless Ruth the Moabite at his table*—and he did it right in front of his field workers. The rumor mills of Bethlehem had fresh news to grind and process.

Boaz invited Ruth *out* of the field and up to his table. In a scene that reminds me of the many meals Christ shared with His disciples, Ruth was invited to eat the bread and dip it in the vinegar, a highly valued condiment in that day. Yet, Boaz would take another step that spoke of the future. Ruth took her seat beside the reapers, but it was *Boaz* who personally served her.

Ruth was surrounded by fellow workers, any one of whom could have handed her the things she needed from that table. But it was the owner of the field, the great leader and judge of the community, who personally "reached her parched corn." One translation said Boaz served Ruth "more than she could eat."[15] Everybody else had to notice, but sometimes those smitten by the love bug are the last to see these things!

Orders from the Boss: Leave Her "Handfuls *on Purpose*"

Once he'd taken those steps, Boaz took another. It was almost as if he couldn't help himself! As soon as Ruth excused herself from the table to return to her work in the fields, Boaz called his male field hands together for a private conference with management. It is safe to say they had *never* had a conference like this one. Their orders from the boss were simple:

"Leave her 'handfuls *on purpose*.' Whatever we have to do, make sure she gets more than enough." Where did the workers drop all of those blessings? Not in the parking lot and not at the shopping mall. Your provision is always connected to the field of God. Ruth had to stay on task to be blessed.

Boaz also warned the men directly and personally: "And *don't rebuke her*." The Berkeley translation puts it this way: "Don't be hard on her, don't embarrass her."[16]

Your provision is always connected to the field of God.

You and I can be harassed in the harvest field—even though we may be working in the fields for heaven. In fact, it is very possible that you may be harassed or hurt by *other workers* who are jealous or don't understand you! This is the value of Bethlehem being highlighted.

Long before any government on earth defined "harassment" as a crime, or "sexual harassment" as unacceptable, the heavenly government adopted this position.

Boaz verbalized it in one translation when he told his workers to not *molest* Ruth. Another value of Bethlehem highlighted! What young lady or child wouldn't want to live in a place where the orders were stated, "No molesting!"

One of the definitions of *molest* in my thinking is "to take away innocence." It seems as if there is a concentrated effort "to take away innocence" in modern society. We need more men like Boaz who will issue strong edicts to protect the innocents!

Protection of the innocent must be restored!

As the secular culture relentlessly invades the sacred *values* upon which our culture was built, we often pay a terrible price. The first to fall victim to the loss of values in a society are the innocents and the pure.

Those involved would do well to heed the warning of Jesus:

> *Therefore, whoever humbles himself like this child is the greatest in the kingdom of heaven.*
>
> *And whoever welcomes a little child like this in my name welcomes me.*
>
> *But if anyone causes one of these little ones who believe in me to sin,* it would be better for him to have a large millstone hung around his neck and to be drowned in the depths of the sea.[17]

With pedophilia seemingly an epidemic, no wonder there is the sense of a migration from Moab. (Remember, Moab practiced child sacrifice to Molech.)

Unfortunately, "home" for some children is not the place of safety and security we've talked about. Of all the places a baby should be safest, the mother's womb should be *the safest*. Yet in a Moab-like society, it is the most dangerous place for a baby to be.

With nearly four out of every ten babies born in America being born out of wedlock[18] and millions of unborn children lost to legalized abortion, it seems there are a large number of men and women trying to enjoy all of the benefits of marriage without the commitment and responsibilities attached to it by a society *of values*.

In the end, it is the children—the "innocents"—who pay the price for yesterday's pleasures enjoyed and forgotten by their uncommitted parents. After a baby is born, the place they have every expectation to feel safe and unmolested is at home and among extended family. Yet, the highest percentage of molestations take place in that very environment. May the values of the sanctity of childhood be restored. May there be more Boazes in Bethlehem.

It's ironic that other workers in the field are the very ones that Boaz warned against robbing the innocence of Ruth. This should be a warning to every jaded "worker in the field"—don't spoil the innocence of a new worker. Don't let your difficulties and disappointments steal their joy at being in the field.

Every parent and every adult given the opportunity to influence the young should ask themselves, "Are we robbing our children of their innocence by what we say, by what we do, or by what we expose them to?" We should also ask, "Are we contributing to the loss of their innocence by what we *do not* say, by what we *do not* do, or by what we *do not* expose them to?"

Naomi not only "revived" when she heard Ruth's report of what happened in the harvest fields, but she also began to gently correct and guide Ruth, her daughter-in-law.

> *"The LORD bless him!" Naomi said to her daughter-in-law. "He has not stopped showing his kindness to the living and the dead." She added, "That man is our close relative; he is one of our kinsman-redeemers."*
>
> *Then Ruth the Moabitess said, "He even said to me, 'Stay with my [male] workers until they finish harvesting all my grain.'"*
>
> *Naomi said to Ruth her daughter-in-law, "It will be good for you, my daughter, to go with his girls, because in someone else's field you might be harmed."*
>
> *So Ruth stayed close to the servant girls of Boaz to glean until the barley and wheat harvests were finished. And she lived with her mother-in-law.*[19]

Naomi is revived and remembering the protocols of the field. She is refreshing herself on Bethlehem's value system and fine-tuning Ruth's new knowledge.

Ruth Wasn't Entirely Accurate in Her Account

Ruth wasn't entirely accurate in her account of what Boaz had told her, and small differences can create great misunderstandings or calamities. Ruth said Boaz told her to stick close by his *male* field hands until the end of the harvest.

The fact is that Boaz specifically told her, "My daughter, listen to me. Don't go and glean in another field and don't go away from here. Stay here *with my servant girls*. Watch the field where the men are harvesting, and *follow along after the girls*. I have told the *men* not to touch you."[20]

Taking into account Ruth's Moabite background, she probably didn't realize that in polite Israelite society, men and women just didn't mix freely outside of the marriage relationship or close family. This is still true in many Middle Eastern cultures.

Naomi wasn't in the field when Boaz gave his instructions to Ruth, but Naomi knew her culture and she knew the Judaic principles that honored and elevated the values of modesty and purity. She knew exactly what values Boaz would deliver in that situation, because she *shared the same values* Boaz did.

To Ruth's credit, she listened to Naomi's counsel and spent the rest of the harvest season working side-by-side with the maidens in the fields of Boaz. Another value of Bethlehem highlighted: *Stay in the field!* Not until everything is harvested and gathered are we done. What a testimony of faithfulness.

There was a time in the history of Israel that we've named *Icha-bod*—literally "the glory has departed." Enemies had stolen the ark of the covenant. When it was restored, the Scriptures say that the men of Bethshemesh were "in the field" working, when they looked up and saw the glory (the ark of the covenant) coming back on a new cart.[21]

What do you do when the glory is gone? Just keep doing what you know to do. Stay in the field, keep working, and you'll be among the first to see it come back.

As for Ruth and Naomi, this seemed to place their lives on "autopilot" until the end of the dual harvest season marked by two great Jewish feasts. Put your life on autopilot—predetermine your faithfulness. *I will not quit!* Commit to the field.

First, the locals harvested the barley crop, marked by the celebration of the great Passover Feast. Seven weeks later, they would complete their harvesting labor for the winter wheat crop which ends with Shavuot, or the "Giving of the Torah" to Israel.[22]

The end of the harvest seasons also marked the "closing" of the "community food bank" since there would no longer be any grain to glean in the open fields. Although the end of a chapter *seems* to speak of a happy ending, it actually forebodes a pending deadline for action. As one scholar puts it, "The end of the harvest acts *as an "ominous counterpoint."*[23]

What do we do next?

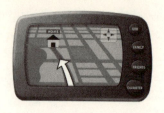

CHAPTER 11

The Road to Redemption

Whatever Did She See in Him?

Have you ever seen a couple that seemed to be so obviously mismatched, that the phrase "Whatever does she see in him?" was at the forefront of your mind? Obviously, something led her to choose him, or him to choose her. It is always interesting when the "beautiful" wind up being married to the "not so beautiful." They seem to not be obsessed with the glitterati and the glamour.

Sometimes I wish I had attended my ten-year high school reunion.

First of all, I'd like to know how everybody is doing. And secondly, I'd like to show off my beautiful wife to all of the girls who wouldn't have anything to do with me. I feel great knowing that *she* chose me, regardless of all the foolish ones who didn't.

That is why the lyrics of the song "Beauty and the Beast"—a "tale as old as time" and "true as it can be"—have come to mean so much to me.[1]

I have always been fascinated by the fairy tale of *Beauty and the Beast*. I often read the Disney version to my daughters, saw the video with them countless times, and even saw the stage play with them.

I guess what fascinates me is also what I identify with. I never considered myself to be good-looking. As I said, I never dated the "pretty girls" while growing up in high school. That's why I was so shocked when my wife (to be!) fell in love with me! She was beauty, and could have chosen others; I was the beast!

She is the kindest person I've ever met, I have never known her to do anything wrong on purpose. Just being with her has made me a better person. She has tamed my beast within. But never mistake her meekness for weakness!

The Power of Kindness

The power of kindness lies in its choice. You choose to be kind. Even when circumstances would justify your actions otherwise. What changed the beast in the fairy tale? What value made him choose to be kind? It was the knowledge that "Beauty" chose him.

In our story, Boaz is obviously the "Beast" (at what some say is approximately eighty years of age!) and Ruth is his "Beauty." Long before my own stunned reaction over the choice of my own "Beauty," Boaz expressed his surprise and delight over the choice of lovely Ruth:

> *"The LORD bless you, my daughter!" Boaz exclaimed.* "You are showing more family loyalty [kindness[2]] *now than ever by not running after a younger man, whether rich or poor."*[3]

Did you note that word, "kindness"? Did you read that phrase, "family loyalty"? Kindness may be a serious candidate for the endangered virtues list.

This staple of civilized human society has largely been replaced by modern "anti-values" such as a "dog eat dog" success mentality coupled with freestyle "get ahead" tactics and "anything goes until you get caught" ethics. Top off the concoction with liberal doses of old-fashioned selfishness and you are headed for "success" on the so-called American plan.

Popular prime-time television dramas, situation comedies, and big-screen releases, as well as the lifestyles of the stars and top musicians they feature, seem to trumpet these anti-values as the new norm for Western society. If it was a campaign, then we might say it is working.

It has been said, "Wisdom is justified of all her children."[4] In the same vein, the abundant offspring of the unkind "anti-values" regularly make the evening news, labeled as road rage, spousal rage, "kiddie" rage, "going postal" workplace rage, and even the brutal battering of strangers competing for position at the bargain tables at the beginning of annual Christmas sales!

(Even volunteer Salvation Army "bell-ringers" outside major retail establishments seeking charitable donations have become victims of our vicious society.)

Perhaps that explains why Ruth is such a breath of fresh air to the heart. Her story might be called the parable of overabundance, the tale of "more than enough." She has come to represent the eternal values of the very God she chose to embrace, the same God who is represented by loving-kindness. God's attitude precedes any life-giving action.

Kindness drives Ruth's choice. Not youth, not wealth, but kindness! We are all amazed when we see a youthful young girl attracted to someone with a less-than-awe-inspiring physique or square-jawed good looks. But often, when questioned, the young lady will reply, "He is kind and gentle."

Kindness is often rewarded with kindness.

God never speaks overtly in the book of Ruth, and no one prays directly to Him in the biblical narrative, but His *values* dominate every page of Ruth's story! We see Him revealed throughout her narrative because He is the God who out-gives, out-loves, and out-blesses us all.

Naomi spoke of this rare "over the top" loving-kindness when she looked at everything Ruth brought home and learned it had come from Boaz, and then said, "Blessed be he of the LORD, who hath not left off his *kindness* to the living and to the dead."[5]

Kindness and a Whole Lot More!

The Hebrew word she used, translated as "kindness," is *hesed* (pronounced "huh-said"), which was first mentioned at the end of Chapter 6. But it means a whole lot more than "kindness"! It also means faithfulness to natural obligations, beauty, favor, good deeds, loving-kindness, merciful kindness, and pity.[6] There are a lot of *values* packed into that short word! It's a single Hebrew word for which we have no English equivalent. It takes a paragraph to explain the concept of *hesed*. It makes one wonder, "Have we lost part of our social vocabulary?"

The Lord's command to "love thy neighbour as thyself"[7] may come close to being the New Testament equivalent of the Old Testament *hesed*. Jesus quoted the two greatest commandments of the Torah in that passage, and then He said that "all the law and the prophets" *hang* on them. Picture one nail in a sure place that the entirety of the Bible hangs on. That nail is loving-kindness.

One scholar describes the book of Ruth and its core message this way:

> This is a document for the minorities of every time and every place. Its message is revolutionary because it orients toward solutions marked by *hesed*—that is, generosity, compassion, love. According to the book of Ruth, the center of the Torah is *hesed*, love. Love redeems everything.[8]

In another place, this same writer says, "*Hesed* is the **virtue of excess**,"[9] not the excess of a materialistic Laodicean church that is spoken of as "being rich and increased in goods" yet "poor, blind and naked and don't know it."[10] Laodicea proves you can have almost everything and still not have enough.

Hesed is the widow of Zarephath who had almost nothing, just a handful of flour and some cooking oil.[11] Yet in kindness, she fed the prophet and the Bible says she was awarded with abundance in a time of famine. The oil and flour never ran out. That is the "virtue of excess."

Ruth had no credentials in the Israelite world. She was just a Moabite, a non-Jewish daughter-in-law by marriage to a man who was deceased—but she unleashed what would become a flood of "excessive loving-kindness" beginning with her extravagant commitment of *hesed* to her grieving mother-in-law.

Kindness Was the Key That Unlocked Her Destiny

> *I will go wherever you go and live wherever you live. Your people will be my people, and your God will be my God. I will die where you die and will be buried there.*[12]

Kindness was the key that unlocked the heart of Boaz. He was an expert in the Law, but the Law would offer no key of approval to a Moabite stranger. The first words this powerful landowner uttered about Ruth weren't of the friendly persuasion. He asked his field supervisor, "Whose young woman is that?"[13]

I don't claim to be an expert in Near Eastern biblical languages, but it sure seems to me he was a little upset. It almost sounds as if he was saying, "What is *she* doing here? Isn't it obvious she is a *stranger*? I should have been informed."

Once Boaz heard his hired hand say, "It is the Moabitish damsel that *came back with Naomi* out of the country of Moab,"[14] he instantly updated Ruth's status in his mind from "woman" to "daughter"! He knew of her kindness before he knew her name! He knew her more by reputation than by recognition.

What transformed this man's attitude and actions so dramatically in the space of one sentence? It wasn't the power of the Law; it was the force of *hesed*; it was the history of Ruth's loving-kindness shown toward Naomi.

Boaz explained to Ruth that he had been fully informed about everything she had done for Naomi. He respected the excessive virtue of Ruth's kindness in choosing Naomi over her own Moabite homeland, culture, and close family ties. He knew that after Ruth's husband died, all of her obligations to her mother-in-law had ended. Anything done after that was done through pure *hesed*, or loving-kindness.[15]

Ruth also leveraged her loving-kindness with the virtue of diligence, and diligence can create destiny. Ruth went to work early and stopped late. In the course of a single workday her work ethic had already won notice. By the time Boaz appeared, he had already heard the news. In essence, he told Ruth, "Everybody brags on you *and* your incredible work!"

Are you noticing Ruth's embrace of Bethlehem's values beginning to make a difference? In a few short sentences, kindness, hard work, and prioritizing family began to work on Ruth's destiny!

If we take a backward glance at *hesed* in motion, we see it grow in importance—moving aside legal boundaries and making possible the impossible. Remember, kindness begets kindness. Passion may ignite marriage, but kindness can keep it burning.

Boaz Ordered His Men to Get in on the *Hesed* Act

Boaz, himself, demonstrated the "virtue of excess" to Ruth when he invited her to lunch at his table, personally served her portions of his own food, extended to her select privileges, and gave her *more than she could eat*.[16] In fact, Ruth had enough "extra" to take a meal home for Naomi at the end of the day.

Then Boaz ordered his men to get in the *hesed* act three ways:

1. Let her move right up among the *unharvested* stalks of grain.
2. Pull out some of the barley heads for her. (In other words, Boaz was saying, "I'll pay you to harvest *for Ruth* today.")
3. Drop some of the grain you harvest for her *on purpose* to make it easy for her to pick up, but do it secretly so she won't realize you are helping her.[17]

Remember that I said, "Kindness is often rewarded with kindness"? It may take some time but your kindness will catch up to you. Imagine, having someone else pay to reap your harvest! All because you "came home" to a place you'd never been! You embraced the values God embraces! Is Bethlehem beginning to feel like home?

When the loving-kindness of God begins to flood through your life, His influence even begins to move those around you to leave unexpected raises, blessings, and provision for you. This is the value of *relationship* at work.

All of this happened in Ruth's life once Boaz realized she was *connected* to Naomi, and that she had faithfully shown her mother-in-law extravagant loving-kindness for years. Your loving connections can open doors for you that your lifetime of accumulated skills can never open.

Once Naomi heard about the *excessive* favor shown to Ruth by her near male relative, her hopes rose. Perhaps she could encourage Boaz to show kindness (*hesed*) to her daughter-in-law and somehow broker a marriage. (Ironically, the greatest act of supernatural kindness in his mind by the end of this story would come from Ruth, not Boaz!)

Relationships can open doors that knowledge could never unlock.

It is during the seven weeks of harvest routine between the wheat harvest and the barley harvest that Naomi the mother-in-law becomes Naomi the matchmaker and Ruth's life coach for matters of the heart.

Naomi Offers the Strangest "Motherly Advice" Ever Given

On the final night of the final harvest feast of the year, Naomi unveiled her plan. Ruth, her young Moabite daughter-in-law, was about to receive some of the strangest "motherly advice" ever given.

> One day Naomi her mother-in-law said to her, "My daughter, should I not try to find a home for you, where you will be well provided for?
>
> "Is not Boaz, with whose servant girls you have been, a kinsman of ours? Tonight he will be winnowing barley on the threshing floor.
>
> "Wash and perfume yourself, and put on your best clothes. Then go down to the threshing floor, but don't let him know you are there until he has finished eating and drinking.
>
> "When he lies down, note the place where he is lying. Then go and uncover his feet and lie down. He will tell you what to do."
>
> "I will do whatever you say," Ruth answered.[18]

When Your Mother-in-Law Is Your Matchmaker

Naomi evidently felt the pain of Ruth's loneliness herself. It is almost as if she was saying to her daughter-in-law, "I feel your pain. I may never marry again, but I want to see you have that dream."

I can say one thing about Naomi: she understood the importance of timing. And however you look at it, Ruth's mother-in-law was actually schooling her in the art of wooing a man!

Some have wondered why a previously married Moabite woman would need coaching in the art of attracting a man and seduction, but Ruth was not pursuing a Moabite; she was wooing an upright man—a Jew who followed the value code of Bethlehem. The natural attraction of her body would not be the primary asset, because *she wanted more than a one-night stand under the stars!*

Ruth is seeking for connection, for comfort, for protection. She wants a home, not a sexual thrill. Ruth is thinking legacy and a redeemer for Naomi. She wanted a husband to father a son who would rescue and carry on the family heritage of her beloved adopted family.

Meet Him Just over the Fence

For Naomi's long-shot scheme to succeed, she would have to send her beloved Moabite daughter-in-law *over the boundary fence of the Law* and into the cultural and religious minefield of Israelite courtship.

I don't know about salvage yards where you live, but the scrapyards in Louisiana boast some of the hungriest, meanest, and scariest-looking junkyard dogs in the world. Those dogs are kept inside the fenced enclosure for one reason: to keep the salvage parts inside, and thieves outside. Once you cross the boundary fence, you are fair game for those snapping sets of teeth mounted on those muscular bodies that are equipped with very small brains.

Ruth was about to cross the line into a no-man's zone guarded by vigilant religious watchdogs known for their zeal and devotion to every little section of the Torah "fence."[19] Their job can be simply stated: Only keepers of the letter of the Torah were to come into the covenant fold of God. *All* others were to be kept *out* of the family compound (congregation) of Abraham, Isaac, and Jacob.

When Naomi shared her plan with her daughter-in-law, she knew that *everything would hinge on two things*:

1. The power of *Ruth's loving-kindness (hesed)*
2. The *virtuous character* of Boaz

Would the man's appreciation for Ruth's faithful love lift him past the razor wire of legalism to see God's bigger plan to bring "outsiders" back "inside" His house through love? Beauty had made her choice; would the Beast look past the problems and embrace the divine potential at his feet?

Naomi had no thoughts of saving her nation—she didn't have the benefit of looking backward over thousands of years of history as we do. But she *did* care about the future of her faithful daughter-in-law, and she still had a faint hope of seeing her family's name preserved in the future of Israel.

> So [Ruth] went down to the threshing floor and did everything her mother-in-law told her to do.
>
> When Boaz had finished eating and drinking and was in good spirits, he went over to lie down at the far end of the grain pile. Ruth approached quietly, uncovered his feet and lay down.
>
> In the middle of the night something startled the man, and he turned and discovered a woman lying at his feet.[20]

The *first* problem Ruth faced was a very important one. Her violation of this regulation immediately put her at serious risk. Before she could take even one step onto the threshing floor, she faced a permanent decision point from which there could be no turning back!

She Would Venture onto the Forbidden Threshing Floor

Ruth made up her mind the moment Naomi finished sharing her plan. She announced she would do everything Naomi suggested, and then she followed through with her commitment. She would venture onto the forbidden threshing floor in the dark of night, *dressed for a wedding rather than a harvest*. On a different mission!

The threshing floor was an open-air location, perhaps with a tent erected over it to offer some protection to the grain from morning dew.[21] The open access to the breeze was needed to "winnow" the grain, and the process went on into the night hours. This part of the harvest was so important that it was common for the owner himself to oversee the operation.[22]

No decent woman was allowed on a threshing floor in those days. Those who did come were considered prostitutes, who always came under cover of darkness and disappeared before sunrise.

> So [Ruth] went down to the threshing floor and did everything her mother-in-law told her to do.
> When Boaz had finished eating and drinking and was in good spirits, he went over to lie down at the far end of the grain pile. Ruth approached quietly, uncovered his feet and lay down.[23]

This is one of the most hotly contested Old Testament passages among rabbinical and Christian scholars. It concerns the mystery of "the way a man loves a woman" mentioned in Proverbs.[24] This passage has been "read quickly" and quietly bypassed by teachers of the Scriptures from generation to generation because of its "difficult" implications.

"Messy" Deliverances and "Complicated" Testimonies

The easy interpretation is to say that Ruth lifted a corner of Boaz's blanket and somehow discreetly curled up at his feet like a compliant pet. The original Hebrew doesn't let us off so easily, just as the realities of life often confront us with "messy" deliverances and "complicated" testimonies of how God blesses despite our messes.

One writer summarized the views of many different scholars when she examined the double meanings of the original Hebrew phrases and explained:

> Ruth is to "uncover"—what?...so that Ruth would uncover his legs, and euphemistically, even his [private parts]....
>
> There are only two possibilities: she is uncovering him, or herself....
>
> But it is clear that Naomi is sending Ruth to do something which is totally inappropriate behavior for a woman, and which can lead to scandal and even to abuse.[25]

The Scriptures say Ruth "came softly" to Boaz. If the rumors and stereotypes about Moabite women were true, then this transformed woman was far different from the princess of Moab who worshiped the false fertility gods with promiscuous rites at every harvest feast.

At the very least, it seems clear from the original Hebrew—when free of "religious retouching" and religiously correct reinterpretation—that Ruth would "uncover the lower part of Boaz's body, and stretch out by his side.... The scene is scandalous."[26]

Risky Is an Understatement

Ruth literally put herself in harm's way armed only with "the virtue of *hesed*." Should she be seen, or rejected, or abused and discarded, then any charge of adultery leveled against Ruth *the Moabitess* would almost certainly result in a quick guilty verdict and an even quicker execution of the sentence—death by stoning.

To call this "risky" is an understatement.

> *There is a total wager, a dangerous double or nothing.* One may lose her reputation or her life. In any case, *the faint heart will never be able to understand such risks....*
>
> Naomi was possibly sending her daughter-in-law to her destruction.[27]

Can you picture the scene in the dusky darkness of that night? It was hard enough to slip surreptitiously through the slumbering workers and under the makeshift tent covering the threshing floor with its large pile of winnowed grain at one end. And then can you imagine how Ruth's heart raced the moment she lifted the covers over the sleeping form of Boaz and settled in at his feet?

Naomi had some uncommon courage to hatch such a bold plot to "help" Boaz, her near relative, cross the great divide from interest to action. But she had no idea that Ruth had her own brand of raw courage.

Somehow, some way, she had to advertise her choice to Boaz: that she had not chosen youth, whether rich or poor; that Beauty had chosen the old Beast. In fairy tale or children's stories, this is usually implied by a well-timed public kiss.

Ruth's discretion wanted Boaz to know her feelings, but *privately*, so that if he chose, he could reject her.

The most difficult moment was yet to come.

We don't know exactly when Boaz went to sleep beside the winnowed grain, but we know when he woke up!

> *Around midnight, Boaz suddenly woke up and turned over. He was surprised to find a woman lying at his feet!*
> *"Who are you?" he demanded.*
> *"I am your servant Ruth," she replied.* "Spread the corner of your covering over me, for you are my family redeemer."[28]

Ruth took the situation in her own hands and put her reputation, her future, and her very life on the line by proposing to Boaz herself!

Ruth Risked All During One Night with the *Judge*

Another Bible heroine, Esther, unknowingly carried the future of her nation with her as she risked all to burst in unasked, and walk across the forbidden throne room floor in front of many witnesses to petition for the continuation of her race before the king of Persia.

Now this Moabite princess from a doomed race unknowingly carried the future of Israel and the Messianic line with her as she risked all to enter the forbidden threshing floor with no witnesses present but Boaz and God. Ruth risked all during one night with Boaz the *judge* to make a proposal to save her mother-in-law's family name and property. This was a man trained in the law and trusted to interpret, defend, and enforce it.

Keep in mind this was a patriarchal society centered around the male leader. A woman simply didn't propose to or betroth herself to a man. It simply wasn't done—even if she had all of the necessary credentials plus a lot of money or family prestige backing her in the process. Ruth had none of that. Her mother-in-law had some family property she had evidently pawned to another simply to survive. Ruth had only her Moabite ancestry with poverty and a previous marriage added in for good measure.

This was nothing less than a raw, risky, high-stakes appeal to a righteous man through seemingly unrighteous means!

The Letter Would Condemn Her or the Spirit Would Restore Her

To use the example provided by Paul the former Pharisee generations later, either the letter of the law would condemn Ruth, or the Spirit of the law would restore life to a lost family legacy in this risky maneuver at the threshing floor of Boaz.

> *"The LORD bless you, my daughter!"* Boaz exclaimed. "You are showing more family loyalty *[hesed] now than ever* by not running after a younger man, *whether rich or poor.*
>
> *"Now don't worry about a thing, my daughter. I will do what is necessary, for everyone in town knows you are an honorable woman."*[29]

We can only imagine how Boaz felt when Ruth made her unexpected and unorthodox proposal. This righteous man had spent most of his life as a bachelor grappling with the dynamic tension between the power of *hesed*—of loving-kindness—and the letter of the Law of Moses.

And then you add the emotional tension of who Boaz's mother was. Perhaps you don't really know why this was such an emotional minefield to Boaz.

Boaz had often heard and perhaps retold the legendary story of his mother, the Canaanite woman from Jericho originally called "Rahab the harlot." She and her family members were spared when Jericho fell, and she ultimately married Salmon, a prince of Israel.[30] Salmon begat Boaz.

Perhaps Boaz knew as none other could ever know that "you can't judge a book by its cover." His own mother had been labeled a harlot, but all he knew of her was a faithful wife and a loving mother.

Boaz knew better than most not to judge a woman by her past. Perhaps that's why Naomi and Ruth so trusted his kindness.

By the letter of the law, Rahab's heritage disqualified her, but her *hesed*—the *loving-kindness* she extended to the two spies Joshua sent to Jericho—made her a heroine to the Israelites.

As for Boaz, pressed to make a decision in the twilight hours on a Bethlehem threshing floor, his decision was decisive and almost instantaneous. Ruth chose wisdom over beauty, and he chose *love* over legalism. It didn't matter to him that he would face possible persecution, loss of reputation, and legal battles over his decision to redeem and marry this Moabite woman—it was the right thing to do. It was *hesed*—the one-word concept that takes pages to explain.

Ruth's act and Boaz's reaction released God's grace to *supersede rigid religious boundaries and create the new realities* in line with God's purposes. Her choice, combined with Boaz's agreement and participation, opened the door of possibility for the future birth of David and "the son of David" who would set us all free.

This is the ultimate value of God, to "so love the world that He gave."[31] This is the reason you *go home*, and this is the way you *get home*.

Love is the ultimate value!

Boaz told Ruth, "You are showing even greater family loyalty in what you are doing now than in what you did for your mother-in-law."[32]

If you love somebody, never let it be unsaid. If you want to connect with someone, never miss the opportunity. Pursue relationships. In the natural realm, sons and daughters have no say about the identity of their fathers and mothers. However, according to the law of adoption in the spirit realm, we may "choose" or recognize our spiritual fathers. Those who are wise instinctively observe the principle of mentoring by seeking out and connecting with people who improve their destiny.

The power of loving-kindness (*hesed*) seems able to make a way where there is no way. It often seems to bypass the limits of the law through the heart and values of God. It calls out the greatness in people while rejecting every form of prejudice. As the apostle Paul would say many generations later, love "beareth all things, believeth all things, hopeth all things, endureth all things."[33]

Only the hidden hand of God could orchestrate the birth of something so holy, pure, and sacred in the middle of a situation that appeared to be so profane, impure, and unrighteous. One of the most remarkable things about this verbal enchange between Boaz and Ruth was their mutual submission to one another on the threshing floor when compared to "earlier questionable unions" in the history of the Israelites.[34]

One scholar comparing the two brief meetings between Ruth and Boaz writes:

> The first meeting was by chance; the second is by choice. The first was in the fields; the second at the threshing floor. The first was public; the second private. The first was work; the second play. The first was by day; the second by night. Yet both of them hold the potential for life and death.[35]

What happens next puts the two on the "road of no return" leading to a new beginning, a restoration of lost legacy, and a door of destiny that would shake eternity. But first, Ruth and Boaz must endure the longest night in their lives, waiting for the fulfillment of their desire in the painful vacuum of uncertainty and helplessness.

CHAPTER 12

Sometimes You Have to Wait for Direction

Traveling in the Dark

Have you ever seen somebody pulled off the road just before an intersection who seemed to be studying a map or perhaps calling someone on a cell phone while gesturing wildly? That was probably me with one of my travel assistants.

Sometimes you just have to pull off the side of the road and wait until you get direction instead of speeding off and not knowing where you are going. It is hard to sit still and wait for those instructions, but it's better than flying off in the wrong direction.

Direction is more important than speed.

We often feel as though we are traveling in the dark and the signs are hard to see. If the road of life had clearly lit signs that said, "Turn here, do this, say that, go there," it would be a lot easier. But it's not that way.

I can hardly find my way down the dark hallways of my home without stubbing my toe on some furniture sticking out, much less when stumbling my way through life. There is one hallway in the house that you have to go halfway down before you can get to the light switch.

It always feels strange to make your way down that hallway, because you have to feel your way as you go, making sure the terrain hasn't changed since the last time you passed that way. An easy passage in daylight can become a difficult challenge in darkness. The goal of the darkened hallway is to proceed with caution until the switch is found to bring light for the rest of the journey. Impatience in that corridor can be painful.

If "the trek to Bethlehem" in *our* lives is an embracing of mature values, then one of the most difficult values to master has to be *patience*.

Especially in our society of instant gratification.

Where problems are presented, examined, and resolved, all in a twenty-eight-minute TV-mandated time frame.

What if you had to wait for directions, for your promise to come true?

All night?

There is a literary phrase that is overused: "the dark night of the soul." Perhaps it's overused because it's "over-true"!

We've all been there. Holding on to hope, waiting out the darkness of not knowing. This is where patience and faith combine to help you make it through the night.

It's time to add another value to our Bethlehem collection. *Patience*. Ruth embraced the waiting. The waiting in uncertainty.

The waiting in the emergency room of life, waiting for the doctor to step out and give us some information on how things are going.

The waiting is worse when the problem is out of our hands, or out of our sight.

Then, along with patience, trust is deposited into the bag of Bethlehem values.

If we trust, then we can be patient.

But there is one problem. While it is true that I am one of your family redeemers, there is another man who is more closely related to you than I am.

Stay here tonight, and in the morning...*if he is not willing, then as surely as the LORD lives, I will marry you!* Now lie down here until morning.[1]

What could be harder than to "lie down and wait until the morning" when everything in you wants to know *now* in the heart of your darkest night? Especially when you are lying next to your promise!

This was Ruth's dark night of the soul, when her emotional state must have alternated between waves of excitement and riveting fear colored by vivid remembrance of the past. With faith in the middle along with resignation to the will of God.

The search for home and what really matters wouldn't be so challenging if God would "take plastic" at the "miracle register." It seems that faith is the only currency accepted at His house.[2]

Most of us seem determined to live on "plastic"; in this case, I'm referring to the synthetic mixture of religion, self-powered good works, and personal agendas that often seems to pass for "the Christian life."

Have you noticed that difficult delays, personal struggles, and faith-stretching sacrifices seem to be "required" after the delivery of great promises in the Bible? This can't be good for popularity polls, because this kind of thing has never gone over well with the impatient masses. Yet, every serious God chaser will tell you it *is* God's way. To procure the *promise*, you must possess patience.

The line of people who "waited" for their promise seems to dominate the pages of history and the Bible.

God Makes a Course Correction
Through Ruth's Life

God's promise to Abraham and Sarah didn't come through until they were in their nineties. Not to mention the two-thousand-year-old promise that his descendants would be as plenteous as stars and sand.

The Lord's promise of the throne of Israel to young David the shepherd boy took about twenty-two years to come to pass. While he waited, he had to avoid being hunted down as a traitor by King Saul his father-in-law, and Israel's armies and allies. Once he was crowned, King David ruled Israel for another thirty-three years, and his influence still continues today.[3]

The moral of the story is this: *Just because God seemingly has stopped His provision does not mean He has lost your address!*

One of the greatest of the ancient prophets was sent into hiding by the Lord after pronouncing a famine in the land. He was sent into a wilderness area far from food and the basic necessities of life. God told him to hide by a brook with abundant running water, and supernaturally supplied him with bread and meat delivered by ravens. Then the brook dried up due to the famine, and the ravens (and the bread and meat) stopped coming.[4]

The prophet was probably wondering, "What next?" until the Lord announced it was time for a change of address and methodology. Again, just because God has seemingly stopped His provision does *not* mean He has lost your address!

Sometimes God will use the discomfort of present circumstance to move us onto the premises of our promise.

God knows where you are even when you don't!

Ruth had just been given a covenant promise by Boaz: "*As surely as the LORD lives, I will marry you! Now lie down here until morning.*"[5] This vow, based on the *life of God Himself*, was a promise Boaz would risk his life to keep!

Now the longest night of Ruth's life was about to begin, and the stress point came with an announcement that was probably a *surprise* to Ruth, and would *become* a surprise to Naomi.

It began with a big "but": "**But** there is *one problem*. While it is true that I am one of your family redeemers, *there is another* man who is *more closely related to you than I am.*"[6]

Boaz recognizes that Ruth's approach to him arises from her loyalty to Elimelech's family, which goes far beyond any possible
expectation. It is a true *hesed* and he blesses her for it.[7]

This is "theological speak" for: "Boaz realizes that part of Ruth's interest in him is to help preserve the legacy of Naomi—but he loves her all
the more for it."

So valuable was the life of a family that the *extreme emergency* of
a family line fading from history through lack of male heirs warranted
extreme measures. The use of a surrogate mother and donor banks
for the father have become an accepted practice in the twenty-first
century. The ancient world had its own surrogacy plan, or what I call
"The Brother Clause."

I don't exactly know what it costs a couple to undergo fertility
treatments, to attempt in vitro pregnancy, or to have a child through a
surrogacy, but the costs must go to the tens of thousands of dollars at
least. That tells us the value of a lineage in modern times. Again, the
ancients did not have access to modern technology.

When Boaz spoke of "doing the kinsman's part," he spoke specifically of what I've called "The Brother Clause," better known in Jewish
history as the "levirate law."[8,9] This concept sounds totally foreign to
modern ears.

The ancient world didn't have the medical knowledge or technology
we have today, so many societies—including Naomi's Judean society—
relied on "The Brother Clause," in which a deceased man's brother
would become a "surrogate" husband to help a widow conceive a son,
and so carry on a deceased husband's family line. It seems this could be
in marriage, or simply be a "legal one-night stand" just long enough to
preserve the family bloodline.

Boaz was willing to become *more* than a temporary surrogate. But
he revealed what neither Ruth nor Naomi knew—unfortunately, he
wasn't the only possible surrogate in the family lineup. The legalities
of "The Brother Clause" stipulated that the closest willing kinsman
should become the surrogate husband of the widow.

There were "pros and cons" of this arrangement. One of the

inducements to the brother is that any property belonging to the deceased brother would transfer with the widow to him. The detriment is that *all* property would now be shared with all children. Even his previous children. Their inheritance could be diluted.

There is one major drawback to Naomi's plan: there is another kinsman....

Boaz must eliminate him from the picture before he can join himself and the land to Ruth and Naomi. But in the meantime, he asks her to stay the night. Does he sleep with her? The text does not tell us, but it does indicate that the answer is important.[10]

It Shall Be in the Morning...

Naomi never mentioned the problem of *another and closer kinsman* when she shared her plan. It seems she didn't know about him, and about the technicality he would pose. But Boaz the judge would know! It was a *big* technicality. The next thing Boaz says poses yet *another* problem (for us):

Tarry this night, *and* it shall be in the morning, *that if he will perform unto thee the part of a kinsman, well; let him do the kinsman's part: but if he will not do the part of a kinsman to thee, then will I do the part of a kinsman to thee, as the LORD liveth:* lie down until the morning.[11]

When he said, "Tarry this night," Boaz instantly committed himself as a "party to the plot." He *knew* Naomi had sent Ruth to him as the *only* "betrothal bid" a widow could make lawfully.[12] He could have jumped up, alerted the guards, and unraveled the plot to restore Naomi and connect Ruth. If he had cried out in alarm, Ruth could have been stoned. But he said, "Spend the night"!

Perhaps Boaz felt that to send Ruth back to her mother-in-law at midnight would be viewed as an outright rejection of Ruth's generous offer and an insult to both women—especially given their unique circumstances as widows without land, money, or position.

By this point in the book of Ruth, our "delicate" modern sensibilities are reeling from the possibility that God's plan might possibly include an unmarried man telling a beautiful young widow to spend the night with him! Our sanitized sensibilities react to many things found in the Bible.

What is reeling in our mind is the big question: "Did they or didn't they?" We simply aren't told! How frustrating of God to not fill in the down-and-dirty details. They obviously are not as important to the story as they are to our inquisitive minds. What was important was Boaz's commitment to work out the problem. His invitation to Ruth to stay implicates him in the whole plot!

The Bible is embarrassingly blunt and honest at times, and we are constantly discovering that God is truly "greater than His Law."[13] Everything in the Word is true, and everything revealed in the Word lines up with God's character, but we are told something surprising in the Gospel of John:

> *And there are also many other things which Jesus did, the which,* if they should be written every one, *I suppose that even the world itself could not contain the books that should be written. Amen.*[14]

Some things are just not written!

Still Reeling from the Truth

God is also greater than any cultural idea of what is acceptable. For instance, the world is still reeling from the truth that Jesus had to suffer and die physically to restore us to God. Crosses have been removed from public display by congregations embarrassed by accusations of following a "bloody religion."

One scholar tells us, "There is undeniably a succession of improper events in salvation history."[15] A simple glance at the lineage of the "pure one," the Messiah, gives us a glance at the inclusionary and redemptive tactics of God.

Rahab the harlot and Ruth the Moabite are in the direct lineage of Jesus. If they are there with all of their improprieties, so can you be included in the heritage of destiny.

The Lord always seems to see to it that *faith* is required to move forward—and He often seems to throw in a few "backward" steps just to keep the journey interesting (and *faith-building*)!

"Tradition prescribes one path to the goal, the straight path of observance; yet, the same tradition attests historically to the fact that *the goal is achieved through a crooked, twisted path*, where observance of the law seems to play a minor role."[16]

One writer puts it this way: "The Torah loves the breaking of barriers."[17]

So what does all of that mean? It means when you can't account for all of the details and logic of a situation, trust God's character until you are able to grasp God's methods.

Look at the "big picture" and trust God in your situation. This is the same One who *demonstrated* His love for you by taking your place and by paying the price for your sins.

When you can't track God, just trust God!

In Ruth's situation, we shouldn't get too caught up in the details of the situation on the threshing floor.[18]

Everything on the threshing floor hinges on the godly character of Boaz. One scholar puts it this way: "*Remove the sacred and everything becomes suspect or otherwise despicable.*"[19]

Viewed through the strict lens of the law (without the side issues of Ruth being a Moabite and therefore a supposed "loose woman"), Boaz could have been accused as a co-participant in adultery that night whether he slept with Ruth or not *unless* he followed through in marriage.

However, Boaz knew he couldn't proceed with marriage until the problem of the nearer kinsman was resolved. He called Ruth an honest woman, and Boaz is clearly a good man according to the Scriptures.

Boaz made a commitment that night that he intended to keep. His future was bound to Ruth's future from that moment forward, and I suspect that is *exactly* why Boaz asked Ruth to remain at the threshing floor. Perhaps this was his way of demonstrating commitment to Ruth and to Naomi to become their kinsman-redeemer. He forever linked their future (bad or good) by his invitation to "stay the night."

How strange it is that we are reading—in a book on the return to values—of two unmarried adults spending the night! (Under the covers, at that!)

Just what "value" are we discovering now?

In my mind it's pretty simple: commitment!

Regardless of the mistakes we (or Boaz) may make, if we are committed to do what's right, destiny will be preserved.

Commitment may be the rarest value in our throwaway society. We discard babies like garbage, marriages like old clothes. Everything is disposable. Commitment is rare because commitment is hard.

Taking on Responsibility as a Token of Commitment

Some men immediately take on their fiancees' debts once their proposals are accepted. By their choice, they are taking on responsibility as a token of their commitment to their future covenant relationship in marriage.

In an obvious New Testament example of this, Jesus Christ stepped away from His exalted position in heaven and willingly limited Himself to the physical body of a human being (with all of its experiences, good and bad). By doing this, He *committed* Himself to our future.[20]

He would experience betrayal, pain, suffering, and the sorrow of condemnation, and then He would die in our place so that we could walk with God in His garden once again.

Boaz had taken the step Naomi and Ruth (and the future of Israel itself) desperately needed. Everything hinged on the rare *value of trust*.

Prostitutes might come to the threshing floor in the middle of the night, but not proper women, and if Ruth were to be seen, the gossips would be busy. Moreover, if Boaz took advantage of her, what recourse would she have? Who would believe that a woman who came to the threshing floor was raped? Naomi's plan **presumes that Boaz will prove trustworthy** and will continue to act in the spirit of benevolent *hesed* that he has shown so far. And her plan **demands enormous trust from Ruth**, who must truly believe that Naomi wants only good for her, and is not using her for prostitution; and she must also **share Naomi's faith in Boaz.**[21]

Various experts in the Hebrew language claim on linguistic grounds that the term used in Ruth and elsewhere in the Old Testament, "spread the corner of your covering over me," is meant to have double meanings. In fact, the *same phrase* appears in the Lord's expression of His betrothal of Israel to Himself:

> *And when I passed by and saw you again, you were old enough to be married. So* I wrapped my cloak around you to cover your nakedness *and* declared my marriage vows. *I made a covenant with you, says the Sovereign LORD, and you became mine.*[22]

Nearly all of the sources I consulted agree that Ruth's request amounted to a classic marriage proposal by the standards of the day (with the exception that Ruth was proposing rather than Boaz).[23]

Boaz and Ruth are presented from beginning to end as honorable people based on their deeds and treatment of others. Boaz was a lawgiver, judge, and "chief of the Hezronite clan" in Bethlehem.[24] It seems out of step for him to deviate from perhaps eighty years of godly behavior for one night of illicit passion.

But to redeem Ruth, Boaz was willing to have his reputation questioned. Does God do this? Ask Hosea, who was instructed to wed a prostitute in order to become a living example of how much God loved Israel—despite her unfaithfulness! (That could put a damper on a prophet or a preacher's reputation!) Ask Jesus. For our sake He was willing to have His reputation tarnished. "He made himself of no reputation."[25] Boaz teaches us that we must value the redeemed more than our own reputation.

The scriptural record has distinguished itself as one of the most bluntly transparent narratives in human history. The Bible makes it a point to tell us that Boaz and Ruth married, that Boaz had relations with Ruth, and that *then* she became pregnant.[26]

Boaz was obviously concerned about Ruth's reputation, and he knew what she had already been through in Moab. Perception is often more important than reality—whether you are guilty or not.

It seems God was even interested in how everyone else perceived His heroine and her hero. Is it possible that He chose to hide and shelter this couple from public disdain and shame? (We have a precedent for this: Joseph was careful to protect the reputation of his mysteriously pregnant fiancée, Mary[27].)

Ruth lay at Boaz's feet until morning. She was watching for any sign of sunlight as a signal it was time to move.

My good friend Randy Phillips is known by many as a recording artist and member of Phillips, Craig & Dean. Others know him as a pastor and Christian television host. His little girl simply calls him "Daddy."

I recall his story of the night she just could not, or *would not*, go to sleep. Randy had already exhausted all of the usual parental ploys to induce sleep in his precocious little prodigy, but he put her back in her room once more and then staggered back to his own room at the point of exhaustion.

Sure enough, a little bundle of energy showed up at his bedside once again, and this time he personally walked her back to her room at the other end of the house. Then he firmly told her not to leave her bed until she saw the light of morning coming through her windows.

He was sound asleep when he heard the familiar little voice once more. Try as hard as he could, he didn't see any evidence of morning light in the room, but when he asked his little girl why she had disobeyed him, she had an explanation.

"Daddy, it *is* morning outside. I can see it." It was obvious to Randy that it was pitch-black in his room, but when he walked his daughter back to her room, she went over to her bedroom window which faced the east and said, "See, Daddy? Can you see it? There's just *a little bit of morning* outside."

When he peered toward the horizon, sure enough he could see just the faintest evidence of a "bit" of dawning light beginning to brighten the horizon dividing the earth from the sky.

So it might be for you, my friend. The "dark night of the soul" is almost over. Patience is about to be rewarded. There's a little bit of morning outside.

In the twilight, things are still murky. That's when Ruth rose up.

A man in that time period and culture did not drop to one knee and offer his fiancée an engagement ring. He did things such as *"cover her" with his outer robe* and offer her father a "bride-price" or dowry.

There were no fathers or males available to receive a formal bride-price for Ruth, but we have both the "covering of Ruth" and the offering of a "gift" to Naomi, Ruth's mother-in-law.

> So Ruth lay at Boaz's feet until the morning, *but she got up before it was light enough for people to recognize each other. For Boaz said, "No one must know that a woman was here at the threshing floor."*
>
> Boaz also said to her, *"Bring your cloak and spread it out." He measured out six scoops of barley into the cloak and helped her put it on her back. Then Boaz returned to the town.*[28]

The rewards of honesty, faith, and trustworthiness are not always immediate. Ruth had suffered "a long streak of bad luck," and we can assume she prayed that it wouldn't last. Ruth had endured yet another *long night of waiting.*

And then Boaz said, "Bring your cloak and spread it out." He filled it with grain and sent her back to Naomi with a "full measure, pressed down, running over" blessing. This was not payment for an illicit night; this was provision until the promise would come. This was to carry Naomi's faith through the uncertainty of "What will happen next?"

When Naomi saw what Ruth brought back from her threshing floor date, and heard the message Boaz sent to her, Naomi could finally "sit at peace." She had held on to the hope of the promise all night long, while no word came from the threshing floor. Did Boaz accept her? Did he reject her?

Naomi had trusted in Boaz's goodness. "He will do the right thing," she said. Now faced with an overflowing cloak of food and a direct personal message from Boaz, "Go not empty to your mother-in-law,"

Naomi can rest! And she tells Ruth to rest. Because *Boaz* won't rest until he finishes doing the right thing!

Can I encourage you? Trying times come to those attempting to find their way back to what really matters.

Sometimes you *must just trust*. Trust your Boaz, trust God! He will "do the right thing"!

When a matter is out of your hands, it takes a certain level of trust to carry you through.

> *And when she came to her mother in law, she said,* Who art thou, my daughter? *And she told her all that the man had done to her.*
>
> *And she said, These six measures of barley gave he me; for he said to me,* Go not empty unto thy mother in law.
>
> *Then said she, Sit still, my daughter, until thou know how the matter will fall: for the man will not be in rest, until he have* finished *the thing this day.*[29]

Even while you are waiting for your harvest, you need provisions to hold until the promise comes. Perhaps the extra measures of grain were given to reassure Ruth and Naomi, and to help boost their trust level for the last hurdle before them.

Dare Ruth hope that *this is the last night she would sneak out as if she were a mistress?* If all goes well, she will be a wife from here on out.

Then Boaz measures out the barley and pours it into her cloak!

This is the last time Ruth only takes a piece of the farm home.

After this, she owns the whole thing.

It seems that something dramatic happened to Ruth between the time she left Naomi's house at dusk the night before and when she returned as the sun rose. Something about her countenance had changed—and Naomi was *hoping and looking* for evidence that it had happened.

Every true mentor, teacher, or leader looks for the moment of transformation, illumination, and comprehension that signals a permanent change for the future.

When Naomi sees Ruth, she asks, **"Who are you?"**[30]

*   *   *

The potential of the promise has so changed Ruth that Naomi scarcely recognizes her. After your night at the threshing floor, when you have linked your future to who Boaz of Bethlehem really is, your countenance will shine too!

And note Naomi calls her "my daughter," not "my daughter-in-law" as before. Relationships are shifting closer. May that happen to you, also, my friend.

CHAPTER 13

Reverse Is a Good Gear to Have

I Know It's Around Here Somewhere...

Do you know why men don't stop to ask for directions? Often, the women in our lives are giving us directions from inside the car. Even the GPS navigation systems in my car speaks in a woman's voice!

My grandfather told me a story about an old car he once had with no reverse gear. He had to be very careful where he parked it so that whenever he left he could always pull forward, because there was no way to back up.

If you are not sure how to find a particular location, but you are thinking, *I know it's around here somewhere*, then *reverse is a good gear to have*. If you don't have it, you'll do a lot of driving "around."

I have circled the same block several times saying, "I know it's here somewhere." Maybe you've circled life when what you really needed to do was to just back up and find the right place to turn. It is interesting that sometimes you have to back up to go forward. But that's life.

Some of the most humiliating and often-repeated moments in my life are when my wife—and now my daughters—say, "Dad, you just passed the place." I have to stop the car, put it in reverse, and back it up; all the while mumbling, "I knew it was around here somewhere."

Let's back up a bit in Ruth's story to an obscure reference:

And may the LORD give you descendants by this young
woman who will be like those of our ancestor Perez, the son of
Tamar and Judah.[1]

As the last shadows of the night gave way to a new day, Boaz the clan
chieftan and judge hurried to prepare himself for the legal sparring
that would soon take place at the city gate.

Ruth, the beautiful Moabite widow, had slipped away from the
threshing floor before first light, taking his heart with her. Boaz
couldn't shake her memory from his racing thoughts, even though he
was about to initiate the most important and risky legal proceeding of
his life.

The logical pathways of legal presentation and argument for that
confrontation were clearly laid out in his trained mind, but there was
no guarantee things would go his way.

It didn't matter. He didn't require a guarantee. His course was set,
his commitment made. He would risk everything for this "treasure in
the field" the Lord had brought into his life from the fields of Moab.

The possibility was so outrageous to his mind that it hadn't
occurred to him until Ruth appeared at the threshing floor, just before
she delivered her shocking proposal. She freely offered to Boaz what
was most valuable to a man—especially to a widower of his advanced
age—when she said, in essence, "I *choose* you."

Her beauty was breathtaking, and the thought that she had chosen him over all of the eligible young and willing men in Moab just
astounded him. He had been told she was of royal blood, a princess of
Moab—what man in her country would bypass such a prize?

Of course it was absurd. Ruth wasn't even half his age! Yet, here
she was, choosing him above all others. Many generations later, a Man
whose family line would descend from that treasure found in the field
of Boaz would teach the multitudes:

The Kingdom of Heaven is like a treasure *that a man discov-*
ered hidden in a field. In his excitement, he hid it again and sold
everything he owned to get enough money to buy the field—and to
get the treasure, too![2]

Boaz Knew He Had Found a *True* Pearl of Great Price

What appeared to be a calm legal transaction between two powerful, wealthy, and landed brothers[3] in the public gate of Bethlehem was, in reality, an epic confrontation. There was more at stake than either could know.

The prize *appeared* to be the considerable landholdings of their deceased brother, Elimelech. For there would be a legal decision, a "reading of the will" so to speak, to see who would inherit the property.

Yet, Boaz knew he had found a *true* pearl of great price hidden in the heart of Elimelech's Moabite daughter-in-law, a woman who had left all for the love of her mother-in-law and her God.

The decisions made that morning would be every bit as significant (and more) as any contemporary U.S. Supreme Court proceeding on First Amendment rights, Civil Rights reform, or the rights of the unborn.

The Talmud speaks of this moment in the same tone as is used to describe Queen Esther's fateful intervention to save her people from certain destruction. It seems that from the Talmudic perspective, Ruth had literally been born for such a time as this.

One rabbi stated that the only reason the nation of Moab had been spared was because God was waiting for Ruth to be born.[4]

Noting that God specifically told Moses *not* to provoke or go to war with Moab, one rabbinic authority cited a biblical passage *encouraging* military action against the Midianites. Then the rabbi cites what the Talmud provides as the explanation given to Moses for this apparent injustice:

> "Surely the same policy should be applied against the Moabites who were the instigators[?]" But God told Moses, *"I think differently! I still have a wonderful treasure to pull out, Ruth the Moabite."*[5]

Once again, we see Ruth described as "treasure" to be pulled out of the field of Moab. The rabbis did with Ruth and Boaz what writers and thinkers have done with the lives of their central characters and philosophies for multiple generations.

How to Measure a Person's Impact on People and Nations

They *worked backwards* through history to measure their impact on people and nations. (In other words, they "put the car in reverse" to arrive at the right conclusions.) Then they estimate the possible consequences if that person's life was cut short or aborted altogether. Rabbi Noson Weisz said:

> Not only was Ruth David's great-grandmother. It was specifically she that was required to be able to bring David into the world. *The need for her was so great that the entire Moabite nation was sustained for several hundred years in her merit while the world waited for Ruth to be born.*[6]

Boaz left the threshing floor at morning light and walked past the fields toward Bethlehem, stopping at the city gate (Moses had instructed the Israelites to establish a court of judges and officers in every gate the Lord gave them).[7]

After locating and mentally marking the location of the other elders and city leaders at the gate, he sat down and waited. Everyone had to pass by or go through the city gate on their way to work or do business.

It wasn't long before Boaz saw his relative, identified only as *Ploniy Almoniy,* the Hebrew version of "John Doe," and calls to him.[8]

In the days before lawyers and seemingly endless court litigation, the legal process was simple and decisions immediate. When someone called you to the city gate, you answered by pulling aside and taking a seat for the meeting that was just about to convene.

After Boaz called Ploniy over, he asked a legal quorum of ten elders of the city to establish an on-the-spot municipal court bench before launching his historic legal proceeding.

> So Boaz went to the town gate and took a seat there. When the family redeemer he had mentioned came by, Boaz called out to him, "Come over here, friend. I want to talk to you." So they sat down together.

> *Then Boaz called ten leaders from the town and asked them to sit as witnesses.*
> *And Boaz said to the family redeemer, "You know Naomi, who came back from Moab. She is selling the land that belonged to our relative Elimelech."*[9]

Some Things Are Worth Advertising!

Naomi was right—Boaz was a man on a mission that morning. After that short introduction to the elders and the near kinsman, he got down to business. Two major legal issues would arise before everything was said and done, but Boaz wisely began with the "carrot" while counting on—and praying for—a distasteful reaction to "the stick" in the deal.

First, Boaz announced Naomi's intention to release the family property for sale—everyone there knew the basics of her problem, and that the harvest season was over. She needed quick money to live on.

> *And I thought to* advertise *thee, saying, Buy it before the inhabitants, and before the elders of my people.*[10]

Boaz was openly dangling the property of their deceased brother in front of the eyes of Ploniy Almoniy (also called "So-and-so"), who had first option to buy that property.

> *If you want the land, then buy it here in the presence of these witnesses. But if you don't want it, let me know right away, because I am next in line to redeem it after you.*[11]

Some things are *worth advertising!* The original meaning of this phrase was to "reveal, disclose, publish, and tell," but Boaz fully intended to *advertise* his intentions toward Ruth and Naomi in the open and in public—but at the right time.[12]

Even the Elders at the Gate Didn't Realize All of the Implications

It is ironic that the "nearer kinsmen" and perhaps even the elders at the gate didn't realize all of the implications or issues at stake. Perhaps a veil had been placed over their eyes to accomplish a purpose greater than any they had seen before.

Don't be surprised if other people in your community or even in your family fail to understand what God is doing in your life. It seemed to be a major theme in the lives of those who preceded Boaz and Ruth in their respective family lines.

Boaz Mentioned Naomi by Name and Invoked the Law of Redemption

How many American farmers would have rejoiced to see a "near kinsman" show up ready to redeem their property at the thousands of forced farm sales and bank default sales across the Midwest over the last hundred years?

Countless farming families watched generations of family farming heritage pass into dusty history during the Dust Bowl crisis of the 1920s, and in subsequent economic downturns ever since. Today, corporate farming megaplexes dominate the agricultural sector and farming families have been forced to migrate away from the soil to larger cities or to simply work for farming "companies" today.

Boaz launched the legal hearing with what appeared to be a plain business deal, but he actually baited the hook with a juicy morsel that Ploniy Almoniy evidently found impossible to ignore.

In our day, so-called corporate raiders specialize in the aggressive art of buying up struggling companies with their seemingly overwhelming financial resources. They sell off the choice parts of the companies before liquidating the rest—much as a salvage yard buys up damaged vehicles and makes a profit "parting out" the undamaged pieces before melting down the unsold "remains." Unfortunately, there are thousands of jobs and family income sources at stake in each of these business deals.

It's Not a Business Decision

Boaz already knew what Ploniy Almoniy was about to find out concerning these two widows: "It's not a business decision."

Too many people try to analyze and make crucial decisions about things that cannot be framed or understood outside the realm of the heart or the spirit. One factor that no one can afford to overlook when dealing with widows is the overwhelming power of their legal advocate. (It seems God Himself personally litigates their cases and advocates for their causes!)[13]

Judging from the skilled timing and case presentation of Boaz, it is likely he waited until the last possible minute before "dropping the other shoe," to use a calculated pun. We can almost imagine him waiting until Ploniy Almoniy gets to his feet and begins to turn back toward the open street.

He was nearly gone by the time Boaz reached out for his brother's arm and gently recaptured his attention, already fixed on the potential profits to be made from such a lucrative business acquisition. "Oh, by the way . . ."

"Of course, your purchase of the land from Naomi also requires that you marry Ruth, the Moabite widow. That way, she can have children who will carry on her husband's name and keep the land in the family."[14]

With one sentence, Boaz turned over Ploniy Almoniy's applecart by invoking the rarely used obligation of *levirate marriage*. He cheerfully added that along with the land comes the requirement that he marry the Moabite widow of childless Mahlon. "That way" she could *bear children* and carry on the family name of their deceased brother, Elimelech. That was the final straw.

He Could See Himself Losing Four Different Ways

Suddenly, even Ploniy Almoniy realized this was *more* than a business decision. It was a people decision requiring supernatural kindness and selflessness. He could see himself losing four different ways in this deal suddenly gone sour!

Unlike Boaz, Ploniy Almoniy was married and with kids. The scenario of adding Ruth to that mix set up a potential catastrophe of biblical proportions in his mind.

Second, with the *levirate* law in effect, he would simply be buying property to turn it over to any heir who might be born. He wasn't interested in carrying on his deceased brother's heritage; he was only interested in *his own*.

Thirdly, this woman was a *Moabite!* What would that do to his reputation and business standing? And finally, the relative who married the Moabite woman had died in Moab for a *good reason*, acccording to what he had heard (and so did the man's father, Elimelech). He probably thought to himself, *Why should I take on my dead brother's family problems? I have a family of my own to look out for.*

> "Then I can't redeem it," *the family redeemer replied*, "because this might endanger my own estate. *You redeem the land; I cannot do it.*"
>
> *In those days it was the custom in Israel for anyone transferring a right of purchase to remove his sandal and hand it to the other party. This publicly validated the transaction. So the other family redeemer drew off his sandal as he said to Boaz, "You buy the land."*[15]

Mr. Good Had Some Bad Consequences to Process

Evidently, *hesed* and family obligation weren't key priorities in this man's life, a person later called *Tob* by rabbis—or "Mr. Good." In the vernacular, our modern version might be "Mr. Goody Two-Shoes." According to the Scriptures, Mr. Goody Two-Shoes had some bad consequences to process (and he was going to "lose a shoe" in the process and become "Mr. Goody One-Shoe").

> If the surviving brother does not want to marry his deceased brother's widow, then the ceremony of *chalitzah*, as described in Deuteronomy 25:7–10, must be performed. The ceremony is to be performed in front of five rabbinic judges. The passage from Deuteronomy is read by the widow. She removes a shoe, specially made for this purpose, from the surviving brother. Then she spits on the ground in front of him. This is a symbolic sign of rebuke and contempt for his shirking of responsibility.[16]

Boaz Was Ready to Take up the Slack for the Shirker

Fortunately for "Mr. Good," tradition allowed a modification of the most unpleasant portion of the official ceremony. Since Boaz was ready to take up the slack for the shirker, "the usual ignominy was spared, and the plucking off the shoe the only ceremony observed, as a pledge of the transaction being completed."[17]

While I'm not prepared to push for levirate marriage to be preached from modern church pulpits, I do advocate the *principle* Boaz acted upon. He sought to preserve past heritage and create a new heritage based on *hesed,* the loving-kindness of God and His people. We don't live in the past, but we *do* honor the past.

Have you noticed that no one seemed to be crying about "Mr. Good's" refusal to marry Ruth? You get the feeling that more people were "exhaling in relief" than reaching for tissues! A respected female Jewish scholar and writer says:

> The closer relative, Ploni Almoni (curious how the text refuses him a real name of his own, as if it couldn't be bothered, as if it were all at once impatient with averageness), is willing enough to buy the land: *John Doe always understands money and property. But he is not at all willing to accept Ruth....*
>
> If he has missed his chance to become the great-grandfather of the Psalmist, he is probably, like Ploni Almoni everywhere, a philistine scorner of poetry anyhow.
>
> And we are glad to see him go...let him go in peace—*he is too ordinary* to be the husband of Ruth.[18]

We can understand the man's family complications, but along with his boring, unadventurous, and money-obsessive qualities, Ploniy Almoniy also seems to have a racial prejudice problem. It caused him to miss out on the greatest "investment" he would ever encounter in his life.

Another value is set in place in Boaz's Bethlehem. No prejudice! No racial prejudice and no gender prejudice.

Love, and not rejection, is the great truth of Ruth. Forget "Mr.

Good's" opinion of rejection. God says, "You are My treasure. I choose *you*, and I am your Kinsman-Redeemer. Will you trust Me?"

Jesus came to free *all*, not just a privileged few. He values people over things, and love over misplaced religious rules. He once described two religious Jews who refused to help a wounded and downtrodden Jew because it was such a "nuisance." It took an *outsider*, a hated Samaritan, to show love (true *hesed*) to the wounded man.[19]

Now it was Ruth the *outsider* who was showing God's love to Boaz! He understood the deeper meaning in Ruth's unusual proposal of marriage. She was saying, "If you get me, you get the field and more!"

Mr. Good *wanted the field, but not the Moabite.* (It is possible he had lusted over Elimelech's abandoned fields ever since his flight to Moab.)

Boaz had a different set of values. Mr. Good, afraid of sullying his reputation by marrying a Moabite, prioritized a field; but Boaz prioritized *Ruth* over the field.[20]

> *Then Boaz said to the leaders and to the crowd standing around, "You are witnesses that today I have bought from Naomi all the property of Elimelech, Kilion, and Mahlon.*
>
> *"And with the land I have acquired Ruth, the Moabite widow of Mahlon, to be my wife. This way she can have a son to carry on the family name of her dead husband and to inherit the family property here in his hometown. You are all witnesses today."*[21]

The Least Romantic Wedding Vow in History?

This may qualify as one of the least romantic wedding vows in history, but Boaz had a pure heart. A man who knew what it was like to grow up in a "racially mixed" home with his Canaanite mother, Rahab, was willing to risk everything to marry his "socially unacceptable" Moabite bride. This was a matter of values, love, loyalty, and courage in the face of opposition.

The moment Mr. Goody Two-Shoes took off one shoe, he signaled the purpose for which Boaz was born. It was his time, it was his day to step up and make a difference in the future of the human race through one bold public declaration.

There are also such things as "values in the negative." That is why Jesus gave us the privilege of binding *and* loosing. Some values you hold high (such as Boaz's choice to love Ruth), and some values you hold low (it was *good* for Mr. Good to walk home with a limp, one shoe on and one shoe forever *off*).

The kingdom of heaven says, "The way up is down"; man's kingdom says, "The way down is up." These "anti-values" are a natural by-product of the return to true values.

Ceremonies sometimes may have obscure meanings or seem irrelevant to the uninformed, but they are important. For instance, the gift of barley that Boaz sent home with Ruth for Naomi amounted to a silent but rock-solid engagement commitment that was about to be made very public.

Public Affirmations of Privately Held Values

The exchange of the sandal at Bethlehem's city gate, the exchange of rings at a twenty-first-century church on the hill, the sharing of communion in a living room or large church gathering—they all point to the importance of symbols and ceremonies in life. They are public affirmations of privately held values, commitments, and shared identity.

These may include virtually anything that serves as an important milestone in life including public confessions of faith, vows of marriage, graduation ceremonies, funerals, or baptisms. Ancient Israel used to set up stones of remembrance, and modern societies often place cornerstone plaques or time capsules in the foundations of new buildings.

Nearly all ceremonies or important events call for *witnesses*. The unsuspecting citizens and leaders of Bethlehem found themselves pulled personally into the miracle marriage of Boaz and Ruth. They became *witnesses* to a union that would transform the destiny of their descendants.

From Witnesses to Proclaimers in a Heartbeat

In fact, those witnesses moved beyond the passive act of "watching" to the prophetic act of *declaring God's blessing* upon the unlikely couple, and with amazing accuracy!

> *Then the leaders and all the people standing there replied, "We are*
> *witnesses! May the LORD make the woman who is now coming into*
> *your home like Rachel and Leah, from whom all the nation of Israel*
> *descended! May you be great in Ephrathah and famous in Bethlehem.*
>
> *And may the LORD **give you descendants by this young***
> ***woman** who will be like those of our ancestor Perez, the son of*
> *Tamar and Judah."*
>
> *So Boaz married Ruth and took her home to live with him.*
> *When he slept with her, the LORD enabled her to become preg-*
> *nant, and she gave birth to a son.*[22]

There was a day when anyone using the name of Tamar in an oath or proclamation over your marriage would be *cursing* you and all of your descendants! After all, she was the frustrated daughter-in-law of the Jewish patriarch Judah who disguised herself as a prostitute to trick Judah into impregnating her![23]

There may have been a time when invoking Ruth's name as a bless-ing *also* would have amounted to a curse. (Perhaps this helps to explain why, generations later, King David's jealous enemies would cry "foul" and attempt to disqualify him on the basis of racial purity.)[24]

But not any longer.

Under normal circumstances, no one would ever consider linking a Moabite woman with the revered matriarchs of the twelve princes of Israel (Jacob), Rachel, and Leah. Yet, in one brief public prophecy in Bethle-hem, we saw all of these things happen with God's blessing upon it!

Perhaps this explains why:

In one birth, Ruth has provided Boaz with a descendant, Elim-elech with a memory, Naomi with renewal, and Israel with the grandfather of kings. But then, like Tamar, the mother of Perez, Ruth disappears: all the women name the child, and Ruth ascends into the pantheon of throne mother.[25]

It appears that God's purposes can spring from man's failures. Solo-mon's wisdom bloomed despite a bad heritage rooted in David's adul-tery with Bathsheba. What or *who* will spring from *your* heritage?

Most people would try to hide a family tree populated by prostitutes, schemers, adulterers, and murderers. The Bible openly displays *all of these* in the Lord's earthly "family tree" and encourages us to publicly read from its pages at every meeting![26]

It is good that God has a "reverse gear." He can back up and rewrite the history of your life. He can literally "reverse the curse." No matter what has happened, God can restore the destiny that was always yours. (He can take the curse off of your life.)

Having scrolled through a lengthy sample of the unusual gallery of chosen sinners and unlikely saints God used to bring the Savior to our rescue, one scholar writes:

> As for the son and heir of David, the glorious King Solomon, he is born of "Uriah's wife," that is, of an adulteress and a murderer... *the Messiah would have a loaded ancestry![27]*

That proves it doesn't matter where you've *come from* as long as you know where you are *going to*. It is a process of finding your way to move on and make progress. Understand that making good decisions was never about making easy decisions.

It would be nice if life was really as easy as the phrase displayed on one church marquee I passed. It said, "Directions to Heaven: Turn Right and Go Straight." Honestly, I wanted to stop and throw a rock through that sign *because it simply isn't that easy*. I know by experience.

Sometimes I've turned "left." And heaven knows I have not always gone straight. I was more likely to "stray" than go straight! Thank God there is a reverse.

> *Matthew 1:3, 5–6, 16, NLT*
> *Judah was the father of Perez and Zerah (their mother was* **Tamar***)....*
> *Salmon was the father of Boaz (his mother was* **Rahab***). Boaz was the father of Obed (his mother was* **Ruth***). Obed was the father of Jesse.*
> *Jesse was the father of King David. David was the father of Solomon (his mother was* **Bathsheba***)....*

*Jacob was the father of Joseph, the husband of Mary. **Mary** was the mother of Jesus, who is called the Messiah.*

Tamar the disguised prostitute, Rahab the undisguised prostitute, Ruth the despised Moabite, Bathsheba the adultress, and Mary the teenage girl with an incredible, almost unbelievable, story—society permanently put a question mark over their names.

It makes one wonder why these, and only these, specific women's names were mentioned in the Holy Bible. Except that God wanted to prove that He could totally reverse the curse.

CHAPTER 14

The Value of Values

The Road Map to What Really Matters

Once we have determined the true values of life, making the right choices or the correct turn must follow. Once you've discovered that some choices are more important than others, you are on your way.

One time in our young marriage, I spied an imported automobile that I knew I just had to have. I talked my reluctant wife into buying a beautiful green Jaguar, telling her it was a "good value."

My wise old dad said, "Son, it doesn't matter how cheap it is to buy—*how expensive is it to maintain?*" I insisted that I knew what I was doing and proceeded to buy the car—only to have the engine blow up. I can't tell you how painful it was to call my dad.

"Dad, I'm stuck on the side of the road!"

"What's the matter, Son?"

"Well, I overheated the engine in my car and I need a ride home."

"Son, I told you you're going to find it is more expensive to fix that than fix a Ford."

Several thousand dollars and a couple servings of humble pie later, that car was back for sale. My stomach turns over every time I see a Jaguar now because I remember how much my experience cost me. Sometimes the beauty of something is not its true value. It may be beautiful, but not very valuable. We will discover that things such as faithfulness, loyalty, family, friends, character, and God are more valuable than other flashy or starry substitutes offered in their place.

Our story ends with Naomi being proclaimed as a woman of value:

> *And the women of the town said to Naomi, "Praise the LORD who has given you a family redeemer today! May he be famous in Israel.... And they named him Obed. He became the father of Jesse and the grandfather of David."*[1]

"May he be famous." Did you read that? "The grandfather of David." Naomi's claim to fame was that she was the great-great-grandmother of David the giant-killer, the great king and psalmist of Israel. That reminds me of another David, one who isn't quite so spiritual. David Letterman—the nationally known comedian and host of *The Late Show* on CBS—made his mother famous simply because she is the mother of David Letterman.

Sometimes it's not about *your* destiny. Sometimes the road of your destiny has more to do with the future. Could it be that your claim to fame could be rooted in your child or in the life of that young man or woman who has entered your life? Why do they have to relearn all of the things we've paid so dearly to learn? Maybe one of the keys to David's greatness is the story handed down through Ruth and Naomi.

That verse we just read, "May he be famous..." is *not* the big thing in this story. The big thing is, "The Lord has given you *a family*." Both Naomi and Ruth came from Moab, were given a family, and were placed in the lineage of the Messiah.

Moving from famine of the soul to a life that is whole. These are the lessons I learned from Ruth.

One lesson that you learn is the prodigal's advantage—"he knows the way back." Naomi knew the way back, and because she knew the way back Ruth could find the way out! For some of us, it is the way *back*. For others, it is the way *out*. But all of us need a road map, a way to determine what is really valuable.

If it were land, or property, or jewelry, we could get it appraised to determine its real value. But how do you put a price on what Ruth received—a family? And what are friends—*real friends*—worth? Can an appraiser set the value of strong character? Scripture says the wealth of the world does not equal the value of even one human soul that has found God.[2]

Just determining that family is vital, friends are valuable, character is crucial, and God is essential, *puts you on your way.*

Boaz knew the legal paper trail that could restore and redeem a family fortune. All of these characteristics were valuable to the future of the nation and the world.

David knew "the way back" home was really the way back to God's own heart. He learned how to negotiate his way through his fractured family history, angry giants, jealous kings, adulterous failures, and even his own ambitious family members—all to find his way back home to the values that caused God to say, "David son of Jesse is a man after my own heart."[3]

A Poverty of the Soul and Famine of the Family

We live in a land of plenty where we are bombarded with choices—relentless vendors, manufacturers, advertisers, marketers, entrepreneurs offer us something in return for our money. Unfortunately, in the midst of our freedoms and diversity we *have* descended into *a poverty of the soul* and *famine of the family.*

On one particular night, my middle daughter was enduring "one of those days." I have no idea whether the difficulty was hormonally induced or adolescence induced, but regardless of the source, my daughter's day was not a happy one.

She really didn't want me to "do" anything about the problem. We just sat and watched a TV show together—one that made us laugh. Before it was over, my twenty-something daughter was resting her head in my lap, and we were being Daddy and daughter again.

It's memories like that one that will get her through tough times when she feels tempted to let strangers run their fingers through her hair. And while we were making that memory, I didn't take phone calls or do anything remotely work related. I, too, am bombarded by a downpour of distracting choices in my life, but that day I made a choice for one I really value. And I encourage *you* to make those choices too.

It seems to me that our need for a Redeemer to restore our family fortunes is more critical *in our affluence than in our lack!* When we are hungry or hurting, at least we *know* we need God's help. Abundance lulls us into a false security and pleasure-induced sleep from which we may never awake.

This isn't a rant against financial success, the accumulation of wealth, or the ownership of nice homes, vehicles, and personal possessions. None of these things is wrong or evil in and of itself. The question is, "Do we possess our possessions, or does our 'need' to possess possessions *actually possess us*?" It is a warning and a reminder that we *all* need the anchor of true values in our lives.

Famine can drive us far from home in search of food. However, the overabundance of choices can become a deadly distraction from what matters the most! The danger of an "unexamined life" in a culture consumed with pleasure-seeking is the recipe for shipwreck. The overwhelming drive to work long hours to finance the illusion of affluence—this deadly cocktail will begin to take a toll.

You can only refinance your future so many times before the mortgage comes due.

At one point long ago in my family history, I assume around the turn of the century or before, a member of our family owned a huge plantation on the banks of the Mississippi River. But when my dad's great-great-grandfather passed away, his widow remarried. Through what I have been told was a pattern of chronic gambling and mismanagement, the entire plantation was lost.

I've often wondered what it would be like to still have thousands of acres (with the oil rights), along with the heritage of the genteel farmer connected to it. But I wouldn't trade the ability to inherit a multimillion-dollar farming operation with an antebellum home for the family heritage that I *have* inherited.

Losing the farm did not destroy our family. In fact, it may have made the family into the tough, resilient group of people we have become. I traced my family heritage "down the bayou" (as it's called here in Louisiana) south of New Orleans all the way to where the Mississippi Delta meets the Gulf of Mexico. It is a hardy group of people.

And from that, mingled with East Texas sawmill town values from my mother's side of the family, I can say that I've been babysat by my great-grandmother.

I have stories of my Cajun uncle Dunand and aunt Bert, not just stories that I was told, but things that I lived. Because buried within our family is an innate tendency to stay close, to know one another, to defend one another. For some reason, we've not allowed modern conveniences to completely tear the fabric of our family. I don't say that to make you jealous; I only say that to let you know what I have discovered to be really valuable.

It's not the farm or the plantation that was lost, but the family that we kept. You may have your own sad story of losing a house, a car, a relationship, or a job. But whatever happens, you can keep your connections. Or, create new ones. You can return to your values. Or you can find them for the first time. What *is* really important? Your work, your bank account, your toys, or your loved ones?

You may have to make hard choices about living with less money to invest in more time with those you love. When kids grow up, they rarely remember all of the *things* you gave them fifteen years earlier, but they will *never* forget the times they spent making memories with *you*.

Stranded in a "Moab" of Our Own Making

We pay dearly for lives built around frantic activities and the endless acquisition of things. Our long hours of labor away from home leave us with little energy or opportunity for rest, reconnection, and the nurture of life-building values. It leaves our children essentially parentless, and our marriages without true intimacy or unity. *It leaves us stranded in a "Moab" of our own making.*

For this reason, that vague ache to return to "the good ol' days" may be deeper than you realize. And your longing to "go home" really goes much deeper than a physical return to the single-story New Mexico ranch house, the Brooklyn brownstone, or the two-story Cape Cod home where you grew up. The depth of it cannot be contained in the city limits of the place on the map that marks the geographic location of your birth.

Although the familiar faces and warm voices of the people populating our memories may resurrect a faint image of what we feel—the true Source of the longing far surpasses them, as wonderful as they are.

Naomi literally experienced all of these things. She took a physical journey from her residence of pain to the place of her longing—she took the road back home hoping to find what she had lost. She had to find her way back to the things that really mattered.

She knew she couldn't resurrect her dead husband, but it seems Naomi was shocked to find she couldn't even resurrect her "old feelings" with her friends immediately upon her return. Too much time and pain had passed under the bridge of her life.

Naomi managed to make her way back home across great distances and difficulties. She finally reached the familiar "city limits sign" of Bethlehem and reentered the place she had long called home. She reached what she thought was her final destination, only to discover that her feelings had betrayed her. Naomi's initial feelings of excitement and the eager anticipation of her reunion with loved ones suffered a head-on collision with her crushing feelings of loss and hopelessness.

Inner Pain Contaminated Her Hope with Sorrow

Naomi's inner pain had accompanied her on the nostalgic journey to "what once was." Then it contaminated her hope with sorrow. She even tried changing her name to "Mara," because everything seemed "bitter."

Left to its own devices, the bitterness you've carefully disguised may drive you to change your name from a blessing to a curse too. All of us have hidden baggage and issues from the past that demand attention. They cry out for a Boaz. "Can *somebody* give me a break, bring relief, and resurrect hope?"

We often look for "good breaks" in bad neighborhoods. It doesn't matter whether you are a fourth-generation local looking for a "break" to somehow escape the self-fueling cycle of bad schools, bad gangs, bad friends, no jobs, and no opportunities; or if you are the absent-minded *outsider* who was unfortunate enough to find yourself dodging burned-out cars and shredded furniture on the Street Leading to Nowhere in "the 'hood."

Or perhaps the unfortunate product of a broken home, complete with all of the accompanying broken promises and broken dreams.

You strain your eyes looking for *any sign* of a break in the frightening scenery...a friendly face, a likely road, a police substation, an on-ramp to heaven (or *anywhere* but *here*!). Give me a *break!* Please?

In her despair, Naomi in effect shook her fist at God and told those who whispered her name in tearful reunion, "Don't call me Pleasant. Call me Bitter."

Don't rename yourself in mid-crisis. The tendency will be to depress your destiny. Naomi's first name, "Pleasant," was right; she had just not made it to her destination.

Keep traveling! Keep walking the road that leads to that place where you are valued. Even if you stumble, or momentarily get lost. Get up, keep moving forward, and find your way!

What happened to redeem her crisis and transform it into a triumph so remarkable that it spans the centuries and eternity itself? Ruth and Naomi *decided* to go back home and to trust God for the rest.

Naomi didn't have all of the details figured out, and neither did Ruth! They didn't *know* they would find a rescuing kinsman-redeemer in Bethlehem—Naomi was fighting total despair, and Ruth was walking into the great unknown as a stranger in a new land.

Their new life literally began months before the vow at the city gate, beginning with their decision to go back to what matters the most. *Our promise for a better tomorrow often begins with a dose of "divine discontent" with today.*

Even when your "better tomorrows" come, not everyone will celebrate your success and acceptance.

Even David Dealt with Racial Prejudice and Family History

David the psalmist of Israel had to deal with brutal rejection of his leadership based on racial prejudice and his family history! The way he was treated by his father and brothers deserves suspicion. In the Scriptures that list David's lineage, the father of his two sisters *is not Jesse.*

David's mother was not Jesse's wife. Jesse was not married to David's mother when she conceived him....

If this is indeed the case, as some Jewish commentators believe, if David was the product of a secret affair of his father with Nahash's wife [the man listed in 1 Chronicles 2:16 as the father of David's two sisters, Zeruiah and Abigail], then he would have been considered a shame to his family and kept out of sight as much as possible. David was the one who said, "When my father and mother forsake me, then the Lord will take care of me" (Psalm 27:10) and "In sin my mother conceived me." (51:5)[4]

David survived his childhood rejection, and then King Saul's demented persecution throughout early adulthood, only to face the adult scorn of Doeg, the Edomite, who "repeatedly attacked David's reputation on the grounds that *he was of Moabite ancestry....* [He] claimed that since David's great-grandmother [Ruth] was a Moabite, her marriage to Boaz was a forbidden union and therefore David was a *mamzer,* or bastard."[5] Therefore, he was not worthy to be a king.

Don't allow your past to abort your future.

Your past cannot abort your future, except in the minds of the jealous. Wherever you came from, be it ancient Moab or a modern mess, is less important than where you are headed. Which direction is your path taking you? May you find your way to the place God is sending you.

The Women of Bethlehem *Accepted* Ruth on a Grand Scale

When Ruth gave birth to Obed, the Jewish women of Bethlehem *accepted* Ruth on a grand scale. They offered unequaled words of praise to the Moabite princess who had embraced Naomi's God and married the son of Rahab, the Canaanite prostitute:

May this child [Obed] restore your youth and care for you in your old age. For he is the son of your daughter-in-law who loves you so much and who has been better to you than seven sons![6]

As it was with the stranger and foreigner, Ruth, so it is with us. We all have a deep need to return to and be accepted by our Creator and be restored to His family.

Ruth was accepted in ancient Judah because she was accepted *in* Boaz. Her name became synonymous with his. You and I are accepted in Jesus Christ, or as the Bible says, He adopted us as His children by grace and made us *"accepted in the Beloved"* (the "Beloved" is Jesus Christ).[7]

This doesn't happen because we come from the right family, because we deserve it or earn it, or even because we *desperately need it*. It happens through a combination of God's *hesed*, or loving-kindness, and through our acceptance of His free gift in Christ. And it happens because we make a decision to find our way home.

"Home" is not a house.

"Home" is not a house. Nor is it a city of origin, or the neighborhood you grew up in. Neither is home a collection of people from your childhood. The home that I'm talking about and the home that I think you are seeking is that place where *things that really matter* take priority and precedent. Find your way there and you'll feel at home. Set your compass by the values of home and friends, strength of character, and God.

Habitual Picture-Straighteners Have Some Issues with Ruth

The habitual picture-straighteners among us have some issues with Ruth because there seem to be some untidy loose ends in her rapid rise from outcast to honored mother in Israel.

The truth is they are right! It seems the Creator plants a chasm in the middle of our path back home that only *faith* can bridge. Perhaps many are unwilling to take hope for the brokenness and longing in their own lives because *the bridge* appears to be so shaky to the legalistic mind.

God seems unwilling to give us steel-clad guarantees in formulas, mantras, or even rituals *apart* from direct and personal trust in *Him*.[8] Even prayer becomes powerless when reduced to repetitive but empty religious formula![9] Prayer without faith is just words.

I can't promise you anything but a good GPS in God's Word. The journey is up to you. Finding your way back sometimes feels like "fighting your way back." Some common things that people confess is, "I'm so messed up" or "Things are *so* bad..." That's like saying, "The journey is too far, so I'll never even begin."

David could have said the same thing, that the journey to the throne that was prophesied was too far, too unbelievable. For a multi-ethnic, possibly illegitimate outcast to make it all the way seemed impossible. But his values carried him all the way to the throne. He embraced the pain. The stories of his journey, even his family fights, were legendary.

But most of all, what made David great was that he loved God. If God exalted David even though "the Messianic lineage" wasn't pure by human standards, then I believe there is hope for you and me.

> If scribes of Davidic times had wanted to invent a perfect lineage
> for the Messiah, they certainly could have done so, but they did
> not. And why not? One answer is that the questions in them-
> selves are valuable: *they leave room for mystery; and therefore
> for faith*.[10]

---

*If there is room for Ruth in the grand scheme of
God, there is room for you.*

We've already agreed that sometimes God achieves His goals through "a crooked, twisted path, where observance of the law seems to play a minor role."[11] When we look at the amazing assortment of flawed and "unqualified" people God chooses along the way, that path almost seems to turn into a series of "mountain switchbacks" en route to the Messiah and the Cross.

How many of us understand why God chose to deliver not only David the royal king but also His perfect Son to this world *through the courageous choices of such desperate women in such precarious circumstances?*

If the letter of the Law had ruled in their lives, then most of them would have been put to death. Instead, they are considered heroines and saints of the faith worthy of recognition and honor. They found a "place." Take hope, so can *you.*

> *Now these are the generations of Pharez: Pharez begat Hezron,*
> *And Hezron begat Ram, and Ram begat Amminadab,*
> *And Amminadab begat Nahshon, and Nahshon begat Salmon,*
> *And Salmon begat Boaz, and Boaz begat Obed,*
> *And Obed begat Jesse, and Jesse begat David.*[12]

This list of names is really a family tree of miracles, of divine intervention, and of journeys from disappointment and rejection to a place called home.

Why should we be shocked to learn that the Lord used extraordinary means and very ordinary people to bring about a supernatural salvation to us on the earth?

And why should *you* be shocked that God would use extraordinary means to help you take your *own* journey back to what really matters? He really *doesn't* "play favorites."[13]

What He did for Naomi or Ruth, He is just as ready to do for you! But the decision to close the door of yesterday's house and step on the road to your Bethlehem is completely up to *you!*

If you take that step, look for these familiar landmarks of the journey. They may help you find your way back home:

- Leave your Moab behind... it should mark only "where you have been," but have no influence on where you are going. This is the place where you existed but never really *lived.*

- Expect some difficult partings. Be a "clinger" and not just a "kisser." Not everyone you love will take the journey with you, and some may do everything they can to draw you back to their familiar places. If all you can offer your Naomi or your Lord is a kiss, then you aren't ready. (Even an Orpah or a Judas can do that.) If you can't help but *cling* to the dream and adopt your Guide's values as your own, then you are ready. Start walking and don't look back.

- Declare your intention to find your way back home at all cost. Anything less than total commitment always produces less-than-acceptable results.

- Reorder your values to match those of your new home and family.

- Be prepared for culture shock. "We aren't in Moab anymore, Toto." Adjustments are part of the journey.

- Expect to discover your true Boaz in the field of God. (His name is Jesus.) He has *already completed* His business in the gate of eternity, so He has already redeemed you, given you a new name, and provided for your future.

- Expect new birth experiences that will produce even more "journeys home" in the lives of others. (That means your new and transplanted family tree is producing "good fruit" again.) And treasure your relationships. They are part of the values that make God's house a home.

Start walking forward and don't look back.

We *began* our journey with Naomi and Ruth *"remembering"* the past.

Have you noticed that once you "get past" the hard times, once you've reached a safe place and healing comes to your woundedness—that even your painful memories seem to lose their power to hurt you anymore?

Instead, they may actually become trophies of God's ability to see you through. Those without your memories can't understand your pain or healing.

This is how the *process* of remembering is transformed into God's *miracle* of remembering, of resetting the dislocated parts of your life and reattaching what has been lost.

Then we followed Naomi and Ruth as in their *"returning"* to Bethlehem, the "house of bread." The road of return can often push you to your limits and beyond. As Naomi discovered to her dismay, once she reached the destination that dominated her dreams for a decade, she was overcome by the very same grief that had haunted her before she began her journey of return! But the pain did not last because God had a Boaz waiting for her and for Ruth.

From a Place Apart to a Place in God's Heart

Finally, we saw the *"redeeming"* of Ruth and Naomi. The journey to what really matters isn't the cure, the goal, or the end in and of itself. The journey is your personal passage from *where you are to where God has called you to be.*

It is the *process* that moves you step by step, one day at a time, from *a place apart* to *a place in God's heart.*

Remember Rebekah? Another woman stranded without a husband showed kindness to a simple servant, and provided gallons of water to thirsty camels of a stranger. What kindness. What *hesed!*

One day she watered the camels on which she would ride to meet the husband of her dreams the next.[14] She didn't realize she would have to ride on those camels to her destiny tomorrow.

As far as Rebekah knew, she was just watering another stranger's camels that day as she had done many other times in her life. *But God* had other plans, and as usual, when He unleashes destiny in your life, things change. Water somebody else's dreams, provide comfort for a vision.

There is a safety net of provision in our lifelong network of relationships. Your kindness, diligence, virtue, and values demonstrated today may well produce your provision tomorrow! In Ruth's case, it could be said that she worked on the farm one day, and *owned* the farm the next!

Whose Mother or Father Will You Become?

It has been said that "success has many fathers, but failure is often an orphan." I suspect that Ruth looked backward in time and occasionally thought to herself, *Everybody likes me now, but I can remember what it felt like to be an outsider.* She entered Bethlehem with the shadow of failure all over her, and she knew what it was like to be treated like an orphan. When her risky gamble of faith succeeded, and her son, Obed, was rocking in Naomi's arms, she became the heroine of the neighborhood.

When Ruth is first mentioned, she is in wicked Moab. The last mention of her is in the genealogy of Jesus. I don't know the first mention of your failure or despair, but I *do* know that the last of *your* story has yet to be written. May you "find your way" onto the pages of destiny by discovering what really matters!

ENDNOTES

Chapter 2: How Did I Get Here?

1. Ruth 1:1.
2. This true story formed the basis and fueled the motivation for my book *God's Favorite House: If You Build It, He Will Come* (Shippensburg, PA: Destiny Image Publishers, 1999). In this book, I more fully develop the true role of worship in preparing a "house" or dwelling place for God's abiding presence.
3. See Galatians 4:26.
4. Ecclesiastes 12:5b.
5. Some theological eagles may read this and cry, "Foul! No one can be saved their conduct on earth!" That is correct. The Bible makes it clear we are saved by faith in Christ Jesus, and not by our "works" or deeds on earth (see Titus 3:5). However, as I said in the text, our deeds may help indicate or *point to* the One in whom we have believed! It was Jesus who said "... by their fruits—*the good things you see in their lives*—you shall know them" (Matthew 7:16a NKJV, emphasis mine). This is exactly what happened in Ruth's life—she was the "ultimate outsider" who saw something in Naomi's *conduct* that ignited holy hunger in her heart. It was God speaking *through* Naomi's life and loving ways, drawing the "outsider" to come "inside" His family.
6. See Psalm 68:5.

Chapter 3: How Do I Get Back on the Road?

1. Ruth 1:1 *The Message*, emphasis mine.
2. See Jeremiah 17:9.
3. Ruth 1:2 *The Message*, emphasis mine.
4. Biblesoft's *New Exhaustive Strong's Numbers and Concordance with Expanded Greek-Hebrew Dictionary.* Copyright © 1994, 2003 Biblesoft, Inc. and International Bible Translators, Inc., Elimelech—OT:458 'Eliymelek (el-ee-meh'-lek); from OT:410 and OT:4428; God of (the) king; Elimelek, an Israelite.

5. André LaCocque, trans. K. C. Hanson, *RUTH: A Continental Commentary* (Minneapolis, MN: Fortress Press, 2004), p. 39.

6. Biblesoft's Strongs, Naomi—OT:5281 No 'omiy (no-om-ee'); from OT:5278; pleasant; Noomi, an Israelitess.

7. LaCocque, *RUTH*, pp. 40–41; italic emphasis on names mine.

8. Midian, whose name means "strife," was the fourth son born to Abraham in his old age through Keturah, whom he married after Sarah's death. So Abraham was also the father of the Midianites (see Genesis 25:2; 1 Chronicles 1:32).

9. C. F. Keil & F. Delitzsch, *Commentary on the Old Testament*, 10 volumes, New Updated Ed. Reprinted from the English edition originally published by T & T Clark, Edinburgh, 1866-91. Electronic Database. (Peabody, MA: Hendrickson Publishers, Inc., 1996. All rights reserved.) On Ruth 1:1–5: "Now the Midianites oppressed Israel for seven years, and their invasions were generally attended by a *destruction of the produce* of the soil (Judg 6:3–4), *from which famine must necessarily have ensued.* Moreover, they extended their devastations as far as Gaza (Judg 6:4)." *Through Abraham's last wife, Keturah (emphasis mine)*.

10. Ibid. "From this at any rate so much may be concluded with certainty, that Boaz was a contemporary of Gideon, and *the emigration of Elimelech into the land of Moab* may have taken place in the time of the Midianitish oppression. 'To sojourn in the fields of Moab,' i.e., to live as a stranger there" (emphasis mine).

11. LaCocque, *RUTH,* p. 39.

12. Isaiah 58:7 NLT, emphasis mine.

13. See Genesis 25:29–34.

14. "Brass ring," Wikipedia, the free encyclopedia. Accessed 1/30/2007 at http://en.wikipedia.org/wiki/Brass_ring. This two-page article includes color photographs of Brass Ring dispensers.

15. Genesis 19:36–38 summarizes the origin of Moab and his brother, Ammon: "Thus were both *the daughters of Lot* with child *by their father.* And *the first born bare a son, and called his name Moab:* the same is the father of the Moabites unto this day. And the younger, she also bare a son, and called his name Benammi: the same is the father of the children of Ammon unto this day" (emphasis mine).

16. Deuteronomy 23:3–4 *The Message.*

17. See Judges 3:12–14.

18. *Fausset's Bible Dictionary*, Electronic Database Copyright (c)1998, 2003 by Biblesoft. The Scriptures cited as mentioning the resources of Moab are Isaiah 15–16 and Jeremiah 48:1.

19. *McClintock and Strong Encyclopedia*, Electronic Database. Copyright © 2000, 2003 by Biblesoft, Inc. All rights reserved. On Moab: "It occupied the southern half of the high tablelands which rise above the eastern side of the Dead Sea. On every side it was strongly fortified by nature. On the north was the tremendous chasm of the Arnon. On the west it was limited by the precipices, or more accurately the cliffs, which descend almost perpendicularly to the shore of the lake, and are intersected only by one or two steep and narrow passes. Lastly, on the

south and east it was protected by a halfcircle of hills, which open only to allow the passage of a branch of the Arnon and another of the torrents which descend to the Dead Sea."

20. See Deuteronomy 32:48–52; 34:1–9.
21. Ruth 1:4 *The Message*, emphasis mine.
22. See Judges 3:12–31.
23. Leonard S. Kravitz and Kerry M. Olitzky, *RUTH: A Modern Commentary* (Tel Aviv, Israel: URJ Press, 2005), p. 3, "Rashi finds proof in the Talmud that the men from Ephrat, now settled in Moab, were important people. He cites *Nazir* 23b, which posits that Eglon, king of Moab, gave his daughter Ruth in marriage to Mahlon."
24. Cynthia Ozick, "Ruth," a chapter appearing in Judith A. Kates and Gail Twersky Reimer, ed., *Reading Ruth: Contemporary Women Reclaim a Sacred Story* (New York: Ballantine Books, 1994), pp. 215–16.
25. See Judges 3:22.
26. Bling-bling is a reference to elaborate jewelry and clothing and the appreciation of it. "Oxford dictionary shows off new 'bling-bling' per the Oxford Dictionary," *St. Petersburg* (FL) *Times*, from the article attributed to the Associated Press, according to the Associated Press, June 8, 2003. Accessed via Internet at http://www.sptimes.com/2003/06/08/Worldandnation/Oxford_dictionary_ sho.shtml.
27. LaCocque, *RUTH*, p. 42, citing Numbers 25.
28. Ibid.
29. J. P. Lange, *A Commentary*, cited in a footnote to Ruth 1:16b in *The Amplified Bible*, p. 316.
30. LaCocque, *RUTH*, p. 122, emphasis mine.
31. Psalm 37:23a.

Chapter 4: Past Loss Magnifies Present Pain

1. Ruth 1:3, 5.
2. *Adam Clarke's Commentary*, Electronic Database (Copyright © 1996, 2003 by Biblesoft, Inc. All rights reserved.), notes, "It is imagined, and not without probability, that *Mahlon and Chilion are the same with Joash and Saraph, mentioned 1 Chron 4:22*, where the Hebrew should be thus translated, and Joash and Saraph, *who married in Moab*, and dwelt in Lehem. See the Hebrew" (italic emphasis mine).
3. Clarke cites this direct quote from the *Targum* (a Chaldee version or paraphrase of the Old Testament dating back to Ezra the Scribe during the Captivity) on the phrase, "And Joash, and Saraph" as it appears in 1 Chronicles 4:22: "And the prophets and scribes which sprang from the seed of Joshua, and the Gibeonites, whose office it was to serve in the house of the sanctuary because they had lied to the princes of Israel; also *Joash, who is the same as Mahlon*; and *Saraph, who is the same as Chilion*, who took *wives of the daughters of Moab* and *Boaz, the chief of the wise men of the college of Beth-lehem*, and of those who existed in former days" (emphasis mine).
4. *Keil and Delitzsch Commentary on the Old Testament* (New Updated Edition, Electronic Database. Copyright © 1996 by Hendrickson Publishers, Inc.

All rights reserved). The authors of this commentary note that Jerome the early church father agreed that this passage in 1 Chronicles 4 actually referred to the sons of Elimelech in Moab, offering this citation: "Note: Jerome has given a curious translation of [1 Chronicles 4] v. 22, 'et qui stare fecit solem, virique mendacii et securus et incendens, qui principes fuerunt in Moab et qui reversi sunt in Lahem: haec autem verba vetera,' - according to the Jewish Midrash, in which lᵃmow'aab baa 'aluw 'asher was connected with the narrative in the book of Ruth. For yowqiym, qui stare fecit solem, is supposed to be Elimelech, and the viri mendacii Mahlon and Chilion, so well known from the book of Ruth, who went with their father into the land of Moab and married Moabitesses."

5. "Verse by Verse: A Modern Commentary" by Rabbi Ruth H. Sohn, a contributor to Kates and Reimer, *Reading Ruth*, p. 15. "Why does not this verse say Naomi was left *with* her two sons? Because at the time of Elimelech's death, Naomi and her sons were not of one mind."

6. Mona DeKoven Fishbane, "Ruth: Dilemmas of Loyalty and Connection," a contributor to Judith A. Kates and Gail Twersky Reimer, ed., *Reading Ruth: Contemporary Women Reclaim a Sacred Story* (New York: Ballantine Books, 1994), "Notes" from *Reading Ruth*, p. 376, emphasis mine.

7. This is implied in Nehemiah 13:24, although the Moabites are "near kin" to the Israelites.

8. See Exodus 31:14.

9. Fishbane, *Reading Ruth*, p. 304.

10. Sohn, *Reading Ruth*, p. 15: "Rashi [Rabbi Shlomo Yitzchaki (1040–1105)] is the best known of the medieval commentators. Rashi's commentary includes both his own interpretations of the text as well as his frequent citation of classic midrashim of the earlier rabbinic period, which he feels shed light on the true meaning of the biblical text."

11. Ibid., p. 17: "Why does the verse [Ruth 1:6] say then those two—Mahlon and Chilion (**Vayamutu gam shneihem Mahlon v' Chilion**)? Isn't this repetitious? This is to teach us that they died together on the same day. And how did they die? They died as a result of a fall, when the roof they were building for their new house collapsed" [*boldface* emphasis in the original].

12. Leonard S. Kravitz and Kerry M. Olitzky, *RUTH: A Modern Commentary* (Tel Aviv, Israel: URJ Press, 2005), p. 4. The authors quote the *Targum,* an explanatory Chaldee or Western Aramaic paraphrase of the Old Testament provided for Jews from the Captivity with little or no knowledge of written Hebrew. The rabbis who translated the *Targum* often added their own explanations or interpretations of the original passages, which came to be viewed and taught as if they had the same authority as the original Scriptures.

13. Ruth Rabbah 2:10 (as cited in original document noted below).

14. Rabbi Arie Strikovsky, an excerpt from "Ruth," an online article. © Pardes Institute of Jewish Studies in Jerusalem. All rights reserved (italic emphasis mine). Accessed at http://www.pardes.org.il/online_learning/holidays/ruth.

15. Biblesoft's *New Exhaustive Strong's Numbers and Concordance with Expanded Greek-Hebrew Dictionary.* (Copyright © 1994, 2003 Biblesoft, Inc. and International Bible Translators, Inc.)—Ephrata: OT:672 'Ephraath (ef-rawth'); or

'Ephrathah (ef-raw'-thaw); from OT:6509; fruitfulness; Ephrath, another name for Bethlehem.

16. Clarke, commenting on opinions offered in the *Targum* linking a passage in 1 Chronicles 4:23 to the book of Ruth: "[These were the potters] 'These are the disciples of the law, for whose sake the world was created: who preside in judgment; and establish the world; and they build and perfect the fallen down house of Israel: they dwelt there with the Shechinah of the King of the world, in the study of the law and the intercalation or months, and determining the commencement of years and festivals: and they computed the times from heaven in the days of Ruth, the mother of kingdoms, to the days of Solomon the king.'-*Targum*."

17. Strikovsky, "Ruth."

18. Ruth 1:6–9.

Chapter 5: Stumbling onto the Right Road

1. This miraculous restoration of bread after famine in the book of Ruth forms the exciting foundation for the first book I ever wrote, which also became my first best-selling book, *The GodChasers* (Shippensburg, PA: Destiny Image Publishers, 1998), see especially Chapter 1.

2. Jesus told the story of the prodigal son in Luke 15:11–32.

3. See Exodus 16:31; 25:30.

4. Leonard S. Kravitz and Kerry M. Olitzky, *RUTH: A Modern Commentary* (Tel Aviv, Israel: URJ Press, 2005); this Hebrew idiom was quoted by the authors in reference to Naomi's decision to return home, p. 5.

5. Ruth 1:10–14 NASB, emphasis mine.

6. It will become clear in this chapter and in later chapters of this book that the future of the Jewish people, the fulfillment of Messianic prophecy, and even the future of Israel's most memorable enemies hung in the balance that day.

7. Matthew 26:31–35 NLT, emphasis mine.

8. Ruth 1:14 NASB, emphasis mine.

9. Kravitz and Olitzky, *RUTH*, p. xi.

10. Ruth 1:13b NKJV, emphasis mine.

11. "How many part with Christ at this crossway? Like Orpah they go a furlong or two with Christ, till He goes to take them off from their worldly hopes *and bids them prepare for hardship,* and *then they fairly kiss and leave Him.*" (William Gurnall, cited by James C. Gray and George M. Adams, *Bible Commentary*.) AMP, p. 316, footnote to Ruth 1:14b, emphasis mine.

12. Excerpt from the JewishEncyclopedia.com article concerning Orpah: "In rabbinical literature Orpah is identified with Harafa, the mother of the four Philistine giants (comp. II Sam. xxi. 22); and these four sons were said to have been given her for the four tears which she shed at parting with her mother-in-law (Sohah 42b). She was a sister of Ruth; and both were daughters of the Moabite king Eglon (Ruth R. ii. 9). Her name was changed to 'Orpah' because she turned her back on her mother-in-law (*ib.*; comp. Sohah *l.c.*). She was killed by David's general Abishai, the son of Zeruiah (Sanh. 95a). E.C.J.Z.L." JewishEncyclopedia.com. By: Executive Committee of the Editorial Board. Jacob Zallel Lauterbach. Copyright 2002 JewishEncyclopedia.com. All rights

reserved. Accessed 10-21-06 at http://www.jewishencyclopedia.com/view_friendly.jsp?artid=141&letter=0.

13. Cynthia Ozick, "Ruth," a chapter appearing in Judith A. Kates and Gail Twersky Reimer, ed., *Reading Ruth: Contemporary Women Reclaim a Sacred Story* (New York: Ballantine Books, 1994), p. 224.

14. See Luke 24:13–32.

15. See Acts 9:1–7.

16. See Matthew 2:1. NOTE: We understand that nowhere in the Scriptures are we told there were *three* wise men, thus our term, the "*proverbial* three."

17. Ruth 1:15 NKJV.

18. Ruth 1:16–18 NKJV, parenthetical inserts mine.

19. See Genesis 2:24 to compare Ruth's covenant with Adam's ancient covenant pronouncement over Eve.

20. See 2 Timothy 1:14.

21. Kravitz and Olitzky, *RUTH*, p. xi. "The mutually supportive and accepting relationship that developed between Naomi and Ruth is perhaps unparalleled in the Bible. *But it was not until the deaths of her sons* that Naomi was able to open her heart and welcome Ruth" (emphasis mine).

22. Ibid. "Today, many relate the Book of Ruth to the positive experience of contemporary Jews-by-choice, who have embraced Judaism in their own lives, as well as those who have chosen to cast their lot with the Jewish people by living in its midst without the benefit of conversion. . . . Since Shavuot marks the giving of the Torah to the Jewish people—and their acceptance of it—it is appropriate to link Ruth to the holiday."

23. Gloria Goldreich, "Ruth, Naomi, and Orpah: A Parable of Friendship," a contributor to Judith A. Kates and Gail Twersky Reimer, ed., *Reading Ruth: Contemporary Women Reclaim a Sacred Story* (New York: Ballantine Books, 1994), p. 37.

24. J. P. Lange, *A Commentary*, AMP, p. 316, footnote to Ruth 1:16b, emphasis mine.

25. See Matthew 9:20–22.

Chapter 6: The Journey Back

1. Ruth 1:18–19a NKJV.

2. See Matthew 17:20; 21:21.

3. "Verse by Verse: A Modern Commentary" by Rabbi Ruth H. Sohn, a chapter appearing in Judith A. Kates and Gail Twersky Reimer, ed., *Reading Ruth: Contemporary Women Reclaim a Sacred Story* (New York: Ballantine Books, 1994), p. 19.

4. See Matthew 26:48–54.

5. Ruth 1:19b NKJV.

6. Ruth 1:19–21, emphasis mine.

7. Sohn, *Reading Ruth*, p. 21.

8. Ibid.

9. Ruth 1:22—2:2 NIV, emphasis mine.

10. Sohn, *Reading Ruth*, p. 19, bold emphasis mine.

11. See Ezekiel 34:17.

12. In Luke 6:45, Jesus said, "A good man out of the good treasure of his heart bring-eth forth that which is good; and an evil man out of the evil treasure of his heart bringeth forth that which is evil: for of the abundance of the heart his mouth speaketh."
13. Ruth 2:1–2 NIV, emphasis mine.
14. See Deuteronomy 19:14; 27:17.

Chapter 7: Coming Home to a Place You've Never Been
1. Ruth 1:22a, emphasis mine.
2. These quotes have been attributed to Blasé Pascal and Augustine of Hippo, respectively. The first quote by Pascal, in particular, has been used and quoted extensively by many, including the Reverend Billy Graham and the late Dr. Francis Schaeffer.
3. See Matthew 11:28; John 7:37
4. Jesus said, "*I am the way*, the truth, and the life: no man cometh unto the Father, but by me" (John 14:6, emphasis mine).
5. Genesis 3:6 records the *last* walk the first father and mother ever enjoyed with their Creator. We can assume this was a daily experience for Adam and Eve prior to their fall under the shadow of the "tree of the knowledge of good and evil." The Bible says in Genesis 1:26, "And God said, Let us make man *in our image, after our likeness*" (emphasis mine).
6. Biblesoft's *New Exhaustive Strong's Numbers and Concordance with Expanded Greek-Hebrew Dictionary.* Copyright © 1994, 2003 Biblesoft, Inc. and International Bible Translators, Inc., kindness, OT:2617 checed (kheh'-sed); from OT:2616; kindness; by implication (toward God) piety: rarely (by opposition) reproof, or (subject.) beauty: KJV—hesed, favour, good deed (-liness, -ness), kindly, (loving-) kindness, merciful (kindness), mercy, pity, reproach, wicked thing.
7. Tamar Frankiel, author of "Ruth and the Messiah," a chapter appearing in *Reading Ruth*, writes on p. 327: "We know that *chesed* has always been con-sidered a primary Jewish virtue, and not only because of Abraham: the sages said that kindness, mercy, and modesty are characteristics of the entire Jewish people. We are reminded repeatedly in the Torah that we should be kind to the stranger because you were strangers in the land of Egypt" (Exodus 22:20; 23:9; Leviticus 19:33–34; Deuteronomy 24:17–18).
8. Ibid. NOTE: Ruth is called an "orphan" here because it is possible she and her sister fled to the fields of Moab as orphans after their tyrant father was killed. It was there, according to some rabbinic traditions, that they met and married the sons of Naomi.
9. Sohn, *Reading Ruth*, p. 21 (emphasis mine).
10. Ruth 2:1–3, emphasis mine.
11. Ruth 2:4–7 NLT, emphasis mine.
12. Rabbi Arie Strikovsky, an excerpt from "Ruth," an online article. © Pardes Institute of Jewish Studies in Jerusalem. All rights reserved. [Italic emphasis mine.] Accessed at http://www.pardes.org.il/online_learning/holidays/ruth.
13. According to the Targum, the words describing Boaz as a "very important

person" actually mean "a powerful person, strong in Torah" (or God's Word). From Leonard S. Kravitz and Kerry M. Olitzky, *RUTH: A Modern Commentary* (Tel Aviv, Israel: URJ Press, 2005), p. 23.

14. Ibid., p. 25. See Numbers 6:24.
15. Ruth 2:5–6 NLT, emphasis mine.
16. Andre LaCocque, trans. K. C. Hanson, *RUTH: A Continental Commentary* (Minneapolis, MN: Fortress Press, 2004), p. 66.
17. Ruth 2:7 NLT, emphasis mine.
18. Tommy Tenney, *Finding Favor with the King: Preparing for Your Moment in His Presence* (Minneapolis: Bethany House Publishers, a division of Baker Book House Company, 2003), pp. 157, 205. This phrase was adapted from a principle and a similar "Protocol of the Palace" in this book based on the life of Esther, who found favor with the king and saved her people: "Favor is what happens when preparation meets opportunity. Success is what happens when preparation meets potential."
19. Kravitz and Olitzky, *RUTH*, p. 26.
20. Mona DeKoven Fishbane, "Ruth: Dilemmas of Loyalty and Connection," a contributor to Kates and Reimer, *Reading Ruth: Contemporary Women Reclaim a Sacred Story*, notes on page 301: "The rabbis suggest that Ruth was so beautiful that men had seminal emissions when they looked at her."
21. Ruth 2:8–9 NLT, emphasis mine.
22. "It was only when Moab seduced Israel to idolatry and impurity (Num 25), and hired Balaam to curse them, that they were excluded from Jehovah's congregation to the tenth generation (Deut 23:3–4)." (From Fausset's Bible Dictionary, Electronic Database Copyright (c)1998, 2003 by Biblesoft.)
23. Kravitz and Olitzky, *RUTH*, p. 28.
24. Frankiel, *Reading Ruth*, p. 329.
25. It takes more than a formula to reverse the curse of death and punishment for us—it takes a Savior. Jesus went to the root of our bitter contention with God in the garden, and then *reversed the curse* by taking all of the blame and just punishment upon Himself (who knew no sin).
26. Frankiel, *Reading Ruth*, pp. 328–29.

Chapter 8: Finding Your Way to Things That Really Matter
1. If you noticed there should not be a hyphen in *reconnection*, congratulations, you are correct. Please pardon the breach of punctuation etiquette—I am determined to emphasize this crucial point!
2. Ruth 1:16b NLT.
3. Ruth 1:16–17 NASB.
4. The Amish are a Christian religious community whose roots trace back to the Reformation in Europe in the early 1500s, when a young Catholic priest from Holland named Menno Simons joined the Anabaptist movement (advocating salvation by faith and baptism as an adult rather than through child baptism). The like-minded groups who united under his leadership were later called "Mennonites." The group practiced "the ban" or "shunning" based on the New Testament command not to associate with an unrepentant church member involved in sinful conduct. Followers of Jacob Amman felt the unrepentant individual should be completely shunned or avoided rather than merely refused

communion. The group split with the Mennonites in 1693 and were later called Amish. Both groups accepted William Penn's offer of religious freedom as part of Penn's "holy experiment" of religious tolerance and settled in what later became known as Pennsylvania. Today, Amish communities are located in twenty-three states, with some of the largest communities located in Pennsylvania and Ohio.

5. Joann Loviglio, "Amish Men Sentenced for Drug Roles," The Associated Press, June 30, 1999.

6. Michael Janofsky, "Amish Are Facing Modern Vice in a Drug Case," *The New York Times*, July 3, 1998.

7. Current tourism figures courtesy of the Pennsylvania Dutch Country Visitor Center, at Internet site http://www.800padutch.com/reasons.shtml. The author did research onsite for this book, and for its fiction counterpart, also based on the book of Ruth.

8. Lucy Walker, "The Devil's Playground," *21C magazine*, 2002. Lucy Walker wrote this article about her film by the same name, describing her lengthy documentary endeavor among the Amish youth of Ohio. NOTE: Amish women are not permitted to cut their hair, or to wear "English" style clothing because it is considered vain.

9. *Merriam Webster's Collegiate Dictionary, 10th* Edition (Springfield, MA: Merriam-Webster, Incorporated, 1994), p. 1305.

10. Ruth 2:11 NIV, emphasis mine.

11. "The Book of Ruth: A Mystery Unraveled," Rabbi Noson Weisz, aish.com, One Western Wall Plaza, POB 14149, Old City, Jerusalem 91141, Israel. Accessed via Internet at http://www.aish.com/holidays/shavuot/The_Book_of_Ruth_A_Mystery_Unraveled_p.asp on 10/21/06.

12. French mathematician and philosopher Blaise Pascal (1623–1662) may have been the earliest writer credited with this quote (Pensees 6.425), but he never specifically wrote anything describing "a God-shaped hole." Then came the French existentialist, Jean-Paul Sartre who wrote "...*Our existential dilemma would leave humanity conscious of a hole the size of God.*" But he wasn't writing about our need of salvation through Christ—his official Nobel Peace Prize biography says his official philosophical position was that *atheism was taken for granted.* It seems that modern evangelical writers and speakers refined the phrase to describe humanity's need for God and Christ as the only Savior to meet that need.

13. See Micah 5:2; Matthew 2:1–6. Micah prophesied in the middle of the Assyrian siege of Judah, predicting the birth of a deliverer in Bethlehem. This occurred somewhere between 722 and 701 B.C. according to *Eerdmans' Handbook to the Bible*, David Alexander and Pat Alexander, eds. (Grand Rapids: William B. Eerdmans Publishing Company, 1973), "Micah," pp. 449–50.

14. See Jeremiah 31:15; Matthew 2:18.

15. See Matthew 2:19–21. It is interesting to see what happens to those who murder innocents or agree with such acts. Verse 20 includes the phrase "they are dead." Adam Clarke note that "Herod's son Antipater was at this time heir apparent to the throne, and he had cleared his way to it by procuring the death of both his elder brothers, he is probably alluded to here, as doubtless he entered into his father's designs. 'THEY are dead'—Antipater was put to death by his father's command, five days before this execrable tyrant went to his own place.

See Josephus, Antiq. 16:11; 17:9." (From Adam Clarke's Commentary, Electronic Database. Copyright © 1996, 2003 by Biblesoft, Inc. All rights reserved.)

16. See 1 Chronicles 11:16–18.
17. Ruth 1:20–21 NLT.
18. See Genesis 37:33.
19. Mark 8:36.
20. Jesus cited two core values of God from the Old Testament as the two most important values of all: "Thou shalt love the Lord thy God with all thy heart, and with all thy soul, and with all thy mind. This is the first and great commandment. And the second is like unto it, Thou shalt love thy neighbour as thyself. On these two commandments hang all the law and the prophets" (Matthew 22:37–40; see also Deuteronomy 6:5 and Leviticus 19:18).
21. Amos 8:11.

Chapter 9: Family Is Not a Do-It-Yourself Project

1. Ruth 2:19–20 NLT.
2. See Titus 2:3–4. This process of older women training the younger women continues into the New Testament (and is *supposed* to continue even now). The only group Paul did not specifically tell *Titus* to teach was younger women. Here again, the apostle instructs Titus, "Let the older women teach them."
3. Luke 9:62 NKJV, emphasis mine.
4. See 3 John 2.
5. Deuteronomy 23:3 NLT.
6. Deuteronomy 23:4–6 NLT.
7. Deuteronomy 23:7–8 NLT.
8. Ruth 1:19b, emphasis mine.
9. Biblesoft's *New Exhaustive Strong's Numbers and Concordance with Expanded Greek-Hebrew Dictionary.* Copyright © 1994, 2003 Biblesoft, Inc. and International Bible Translators, Inc.: OT:1949 *huwm* (hoom); a primitive root [cp. OT:2000]; to make an uproar, or agitate greatly.
10. Andre LaCocque, trans. K. C. Hanson, *RUTH: A Continental Commentary* (Minneapolis, MN: Fortress Press, 2004), p. 65. Commenting on Ruth 2:5, the author notes that Boaz's question "Who does this woman belong to?" was so blunt that it made some rabbis wonder if he was correcting his servant for allowing gleaning. Something triggered that intense interest and LaCocque names three possible reasons Ruth stood out to Boaz when he approached his field (and these may well have applied in the streets of Bethlehem as well). First, his servant told him about Ruth's relationship to his relative, Naomi; second, he noticed she didn't fit in with the regular workers because her ethnic characteristics made her stand out; and third, Ruth was naturally beautiful.
11. Ruth 2:2 NLT, emphasis mine.
12. Mona DeKoven Fishbane, "Ruth: Dilemmas of Loyalty and Connection," a contributor to Judith A. Kates and Gail Twersky Reimer, ed., *Reading Ruth: Contemporary Women Reclaim a Sacred Story* (New York: Ballantine Books, 1994), p. 301: "The rabbis suggest that Ruth was so beautiful that men had seminal emissions when they looked at her."

13. We examined these scriptural comments in Chapter 5 as well, but from a different angle.
14. Ruth 2:8–9 TEV, emphasis mine.
15. Ruth 2:10 NIV, emphasis mine.
16. See Deuteronomy 23:3–8.
17. LaCocque, *RUTH*, p. 27.
18. Ibid., p. 69 (parenthetical insertion mine).
19. Ruth 2:19 TEV, emphasis mine.
20. Ruth 1:20–21 NKJV.
21. See Psalm 46:1.
22. See 1 Samuel 4:19–22; 7:1; 2 Samuel 6:12–16.
23. Ruth 2:20 NLT, emphasis mine.
24. See Genesis 24.
25. "The A-to-Z of Camels," by Arab.net. Accessed via Internet at http://www.arab.net/camels/.
26. "How Much Does a Gallon of Water Weigh?" accessed via Internet at http://www.aacounty.org/News/Current/WaterCompetition.cfm.
27. Leonard S. Kravitz and Kerry M. Olitzky, *RUTH: A Modern Commentary* (Tel Aviv, Israel: URJ Press, 2005), pp. xii–xiii.
28. Psalm 68:5, emphasis mine.

Chapter 10: "I Finally Found It"
1. Ruth 2:10b.
2. 2 Samuel 23:15, emphasis mine.
3. See where Jesus *is* the Bread of Life in Luke 2:4–21, John 6:35–41; and He is the *Giver and Source* of the water of life in John 4:10–14 and Revelation 21:6; 22:1.
4. See Acts 14:11–18.
5. Andre LaCocque, trans. K. C. Hanson, *RUTH: A Continental Commentary* (Minneapolis, MN: Fortress Press, 2004), p. 71: "It is clear that the arrival of the two women at Bethlehem was a sensation. On 'has been fully told me' [vs. 11a]...*Boaz continues to speak in a bombastic stream*, employing here a double Hophal (passive casual form; something like, 'It was told me saying,' or 'It was made to be told to me')." Emphasis in quote is mine.
6. Ruth 2:10b–12 NLT, emphasis mine.
7. Psalm 68:4–6 NLT, emphasis mine.
8. Excerpt from the article "Billy Graham and the Billy Graham Evangelistic Association—Historical Background" prepared and posted 11/11/04 by the Billy Graham Center Archives at Wheaton College, Chicago, Illinois: "At the end of 1949, he suddenly came into national prominence. An evangelistic campaign Graham was leading in Los Angeles resulted in the dramatic conversion of a local underworld figure and a prominent disc jockey, among others. The newspaper magnate, William Randolph Hearst, for reasons unknown, ordered his publications to 'puff Graham' and other newspapers around the country followed suit. The campaign, planned for three weeks, lasted seven. Next, Graham went to Boston for a scheduled series of campaigns and again the results were spectacular. He then went on to Columbia, South Carolina, where he met publisher Henry Luce, who was impressed with the evangelist and had

articles about him written for his publications, *Time* and *Life* magazines."
Accessed via the Internet at http://www.wheaton.edu/bgc/archives/bio.html
on 11/24/06.

9. LaCocque, *RUTH,* p. 68: "The young men could be attracted to this young
   woman *with whom a sexual relation would not be considered as adulterous*
   (Lev 20:10; Deut 22:22) or as *reprehensible seduction* (Exod 22:16 [MT 15];
   Deut 22:28–29)." [Emphasis mine.]

10. Ibid., p. 79—"Ruth is clearly living dangerously.... We saw above that a
    young widow could constitute an even stronger temptation, since having inter-
    course with her was not punishable by any legal means"; and p. 83, where the
    author notes: "One can expect nothing more than promiscuity from a Moabite."

11. Ruth 2:13 NIV, emphasis and parenthetical insertion mine.

12. LaCocque, *RUTH,* p. 72.

13. The King James Version offers this colorful translation.

14. Ruth 2:14–16 NIV, emphasis and parenthetical insertion mine.

15. Ruth 2:14b NLT.

16. *The Modern Bible: The Berkeley Version* (Peabody, MA: Hendrickson
    Publishers, 2005). Used by permission. All rights reserved.

17. Matthew 18:4–6 NIV, emphasis mine.

18. "Nearly 4 in 10 U.S. babies born out of wedlock," The Associated Press, Novem-
    ber 21, 2006, as reported by MSNBC.com. Accessed 11-27-2006 via the Internet
    at http://www.msnbc.msn.com/id/15835429/.

19. Ruth 2:20–23 NIV, emphasis mine.

20. Ruth 2:8–9 NIV, emphasis mine.

21. See 1 Samuel 6:13.

22. LaCocque, *RUTH,* p. 80, "Ruth is sheltered in two places: the field of Boaz and
    the house of Naomi (v. 23). This situation can only be provisional. It will last
    just through the time of the two harvests, barley and wheat. This is the reason,
    as we will see, that at the end of the chapter, when she 'attached herself to Boaz's
    servants' and 'lived with her mother-in-law,' this does not constitute a 'happy
    ending,' but is the expression of a malaise."

23. Ibid., "But here the end of the harvest acts as an "ominous counterpoint....
    Their sources of sustenance are depleted, the two widows remain alone
    together."

Chapter 11: The Road to Redemption

1. A portion of the lyrics for the Oscar-winning title song written by the late
   Howard Ashman for Disney's animated feature movie, *Beauty and the Beast*
   (1991). Source: "IMDb, The Earth's Biggest Movie Database," via Internet at
   http://www.imdb.com/name/nm0039141/bio.

2. The King James Version translation of the word.

3. Ruth 3:10 NLT, emphasis mine.

4. Luke 7:35.

5. Ruth 2:20b, emphasis mine.

6. Word definition for "kindness" derived from Biblesoft's *New Exhaustive
   Strong's Numbers and Concordance with Expanded Greek-Hebrew
   Dictionary* (Biblesoft, Inc. and International Bible Translators, Inc.,
   Copyright © 1994, 2003): OT:2617 *checed* (kheh'-sed); from OT:2616; kind-

ness; by implication (toward God) piety: rarely (by opposition) reproof, or (subject.) beauty: KJV - favour, good deed (-liness, -ness), kindly, (loving-) kindness, merciful (kindness), mercy, pity, reproach, wicked thing. OT:2618 *Checed* (kheh'-sed); the same as OT:2617: favor; *Chesed*, an Israelite: KJV - *Hesed*.

7. Jesus said, "Thou shalt love the Lord thy God with all thy heart, and with all thy soul, and with all thy mind. This is the first and great commandment. And the second is like unto it, Thou shalt love thy neighbour as thyself. On these two commandments hang all the law and the prophets" (Matthew 22:37–40).

8. Andre LaCocque, trans. K. C. Hanson, *RUTH: A Continental Commentary* (Minneapolis, MN: Fortress Press, 2004), p. 27.

9. Ibid., p. 28, bold emphasis mine.

10. See Revelation 3:17.

11. See 1 Kings 17:8–15.

12. Ruth 1:16–17 NLT.

13. Ruth 2:5 NIV.

14. Ruth 2:6, emphasis mine.

15. See Ruth 2:13.

16. See Ruth 2:14.

17. See Ruth 2:16.

18. Ruth 3:1–5 NIV, emphasis mine.

19. Please understand that I mean no disrespect toward the descendants of Abraham, Isaac, and Jacob in my use of a salvage yard for this example. From a messianic point of view, the very mission of the Abrahamic covenant (and specifically of Ruth's mission) was to *salvage* and *restore* what had been wrecked or set aside by human weakness, error, or sin. It will quickly be shown that classic rabbinic teachings support the concept that the Almighty has often redeemed or preserved families, tribes, or nations using what seems to be "questionable" methods or individuals such as Tamar, the daughters of Lot, and Ruth.

20. Ruth 3:6–8 NIV, emphasis mine.

21. *Adam Clarke's Commentary*, Electronic Database. (Copyright © 1996, 2003 by Biblesoft, Inc. All rights reserved.) Commentary on Ruth 3:7—"[Went to lie down] As the threshing-floors of the Eastern nations are in general in the open air, it is very likely that the owner or some confidential person continued in the fields till the grain was secured, *having a tent in the place* where the grain was threshed and winnowed. Boaz seems to have acted thus" (emphasis mine).

22. *Jamieson, Fausset, and Brown Commentary*, Electronic Database (Copyright © 1997, 2003 by Biblesoft, Inc. All rights reserved.) Commentary on Ruth 3:2— "'He winnoweth barley to-night in the threshing-floor.' The winnowing process is performed by throwing up the grain, after being trodden down, against the wind with a shovel. The threshing-floor, which was commonly on the harvest-field, was carefully leveled with a large cylindric roller, and consolidated with chalk, that weeds might not spring up, and that it might not chop with drought. *The farmer usually remained all night in harvest-time on the threshing-floor, not only for the protection of his valuable grain, but for the winnowing.* That operation was performed in the evening, to catch the breezes which blow after the close of a hot day, and which continue for the most part of the night. *This duty at so important a season the master undertakes himself:* and accordingly

of ancient manners, Boaz, a person of considerable wealth and high rank, laid himself down to sleep on the barn floor, at the end of the heap of barley that he had been winnowing" (emphasis mine).

23. Ruth 3:6–7 NIV, emphasis mine.

24. Proverbs 30:19b NLT.

25. Tikva Frymer-Kensky, *Reading the Women of the Bible: A New Interpretation of Their Stories* (New York: Schocken Books, a division of Random House, Inc., 2002), pp. 247–48 (parenthetical insertion mine).

26. LaCocque, *RUTH,* p. 86.

27. Ibid., p. 83, emphasis mine.

28. Ruth 3:8–9 NLT, emphasis mine.

29. Ruth 3:10-11 NLT, emphasis and parenthetical insertion mine.

30. *McClintock and Strong Encyclopedia*, Electronic Database. (Copyright © 2000, 2003 by Biblesoft, Inc. All rights reserved.), from the article on Rahab: "As regards Rahab herself, we learn from Matt 1:5 that she became the wife of Salmon, the son of Nahshon, and the ancestress of Boaz, Jesse's grandfather. The suspicion naturally arises that Salmon may have been one of the spies whose life she saved, and that gratitude for so great a benefit led, in his case, to a more tender passion, and obliterated the memory of any past Disgrace attaching to her name. We are expressly told that the spies were 'young men' (Josh 6:23)...and the example of the former spies who were sent from Kadesh-Barnea, who were all '*heads of Israel*' (Num 13:3), as well as the importance of the service to be performed, would lead one to expect that they would be *persons of high station.* But, however this may be, it is certain, on the authority of Matthew, that Rahab became the mother of the line from which sprang David, and, eventually, Christ" (emphasis mine).

31. See John 3:16.

32. Ruth 3:10b TEV.

33. 1 Corinthians 13:7.

34. Tamar Frankiel, author of "Ruth and the Messiah," a chapter appearing in *Reading Ruth: Contemporary Women Reclaim a Sacred Story* (New York: Ballantine Books, 1994), pp. 330–31: "Each person completely yields to the authority of the other. It is as if each one, even though faced with an unusual suggestion or surprising turn of events, recognizes in it the will of God, and accepts it with utter egolessness."

35. LaCocque, *RUTH,* p. 92, citing Phyllis Trible, *God and the Rhetoric of Sexuality* (OBT. Philadelphia: Fortress Press, 1978), p. 183.

Chapter 12: Sometimes You Have to Wait For Direction

1. Ruth 3:12–13 NLT, emphasis mine.

2. See Hebrews 11:10.

3. *McClintock and Strong Encyclopedia* (Electronic Database. Copyright © 2000, 2003 by Biblesoft, Inc. All rights reserved.); dates drawn from the detailed article on "David," specifically the authors' placement of David's early anointing by Samuel the prophet in 1068 B.C., and his anointing as the king of Israel by consensus in 1046 B.C.

4. See the story of Elijah the prophet in 1 Kings 17:1–9.

5. Ruth 3:13b NLT, emphasis mine.

6. Ruth 3:12 NLT, emphasis mine.

7. Tikva Frymer-Kensky, *Reading the Women of the Bible: A New Interpretation of Their Stories* (New York: Schocken Books, a division of Random House, Inc., 2002), pp. 248–49.

8. "Whereas the law merely imposed the obligation of marrying the childless widow upon the brother, and even allowed him to renounce the obligation if he would take upon himself the disgrace connected with such a refusal (see Deut 25:7–10); according to Ruth 4:5 of this book it had become a traditional custom to require the Levirate marriage of the redeemer of the portion of the deceased relative, not only that the landed possession might be permanently retained in the family, but also that the family itself might not be suffered to die out." *Keil and Delitzsch Commentary on the Old Testament: New Updated Edition* (Electronic Database. Copyright © 1996 by Hendrickson Publishers, Inc. All rights reserved).

9. Andre LaCocque, trans. K. C. Hanson, *RUTH: A Continental Commentary* (Minneapolis, MN: Fortress Press, 2004), p. 47: "The issue of the levirate is at stake from the outset in the book of Ruth.... The term...designates a brother-in-law (Latin *levir*) in the law of the levirate (Deuteronomy 25:5–10)."

10. Frymer-Kensky, *Reading the Women of the Bible*, pp. 248–49.

11. Ruth 3:13, emphasis mine.

12. Frymer-Kensky, *Reading the Women of the Bible*, p. 247: The author says, "[Naomi] does not feel she can approach Boaz directly. Perhaps widows did not have the right to negotiate marriage contracts; or perhaps Israel had a dowry system in addition to bride-price, and being destitute, she could not provide it."

13. LaCocque, *RUTH*, p. 28: "The book of Ruth as hermeneutical method—in other words, according to an expansive interpretation of the Law—comports with a theological insight of the first order that one can summarize briefly: *God is greater than his Law*...regarding the central issue in Ruth of *hesed*, for the word is an opening on an interpretation of the Law that surpasses the letter. One could believe that this view is more Christian than Jewish; but, significantly, this is a virtue that the early rabbis recognized within earlier Hasidim. They proceeded 'beyond what the Law asks,' a technical expression applied in the Talmud to charismatic individuals whose interpretation of the texts through *hesed* brought them to accomplish commandments beyond the letter. *Hesed* is the virtue of excess."

14. John 21:25, emphasis mine.

15. LaCocque, *RUTH*, p. 84. The writer adds, "This is a case of what Soren Kierkegaard called a 'teleological suspension of the ethical.'"

16. Tamar Frankiel, author of "Ruth and the Messiah," a chapter appearing in *Reading Ruth: Contemporary Women Reclaim a Sacred Story* (New York: Ballantine Books, 1994), p. 323.

17. LaCocque, *RUTH*, p. 70. The author's footnote cites, "Ostriker, 'Redeeming Ruth,' 175 n. 1." The full bibliographical reference reads: Alicia S. Ostriker, "The Redeeming of Ruth." In idem [meaning 'in something previously

mentioned'], *The Nakedness of the Fathers: Biblical Visions and Revisions*, 169-75 (New Brunswick, NJ: Rutgers Univ. Press, 1994).

18. Ibid., p. 84. "The issue is returning life to an Israelite clan obliterated by the death of its progenitors. Only a combination of the laws on redemption and on the levirate is able to revive the clan of Naomi from the dead."

19. Ibid., p. 87.

20. See Philippians 2:5–11.

21. Frymer-Kensky, *Reading the Women of the Bible*, p. 248, boldface emphasis mine.

22. Ezekiel 16:8 NLT, emphasis mine.

23. Four different commentators offer the following views on the "cover" phrase in Ezekiel 16:8 and reference Ruth in their comments: Adam Clarke said that to say, "I spread my skirt over thee" means "'I espoused thee.' This was one of their initiatory marriage ceremonies." *Adam Clarke's Commentary* (Electronic Database. Copyright © 1996, 2003 by Biblesoft, Inc. All rights reserved). Another commentary notes, "The cloak is often used as a bed coverlet in the East." *Jamieson, Fausset, and Brown Commentary* (Electronic Database. Copyright © 1997, 2003 by Biblesoft, Inc. All rights reserved). Keil and Delitzsch wrote, "'I spread my wing over thee,' [means] the lappet of my garment, which also served as a *counterpane* [an embroidered quilt, bedspread]; in other words, I married thee (cf. Ruth. Ezek 3:9), and thereby covered thy nakedness." *Keil and Delitzsch Commentary on the Old Testament: New Updated Edition* (Electronic Database. Copyright © 1996 by Hendrickson Publishers, Inc. All rights reserved). Matthew Henry, referring to God's adoption of the children of Israel and their passage in the wilderness, writes, "When God led them under the convoy of the pillar of cloud and fire *he spread his skirt over them.*" *Matthew Henry's Commentary on the Whole Bible: New Modern Edition* (Electronic Database. Copyright © 1991 by Hendrickson Publishers, Inc.), emphasis mine.

24. *International Standard Bible Encyclopedia* (Electronic Database Copyright © 1996, 2003 by Biblesoft, Inc. All rights reserved), from the article on *Boaz*: "1 Chron 2:11–12 makes Boaz a descendant of Hezron, and so probably a chief of the Hezronite clan in Bethlehem. Jewish tradition identifies Boaz with Ibzan (Judg 12:8–10)."

25. Philippians 2:7.

26. See Ruth 4:13.

27. See Matthew 1:18–25.

28. Ruth 3:14–15 NLT, emphasis mine.

29. Ruth 3:16–18, emphasis mine.

30. Frymer-Kensky, *Reading the Women of the Bible*, pp. 248–49.

Chapter 13: Reverse Is a Good Gear to Have

1. Ruth 4:12 NLT.

2. Matthew 13:44 NLT, emphasis mine. Could it be that Jesus had Ruth and Boaz in mind when He shared this parable and its companion tale of "the pearl of great price" in the following verse?

3. Susanne Klingenstein, "Circles of Kinship," a chapter appearing in Judith A. Kates and Gail Twersky Reimer, ed., *Reading Ruth: Contemporary Women*

Reclaim a Sacred Story (New York: Ballantine Books, 1994), p. 204. "The Midrash is more specific than the *megilla* about the nature of Boaz's relationship to Naomi. The majority of the rabbis hold that Naomi's husband Elimelech, Boaz, and another inhabitant of Bethlehem, mentioned briefly in chapter 4 of the *megilla*, are brothers (Ruth Rabba 6:3)."

4. Rabbi Noson Weisz said, "The need for her [Ruth] was so great that the entire Moabite nation was sustained for several hundred years in her merit while the world waited for Ruth to be born." Rabbi Noson Wersz, "The Book of Ruth: A Mystery Unraveled," a featured Shavuot article posted on www.aish.com, a Jewish educational site based in Israel. Accessed 10/21/06 via the Internet at http://www.aish.com/holidays/shavuot/The_Book_of_Ruth_A_Mystery_ Unraveled.asp. (emphasis mine).

5. Ibid., cited from the Talmud (Baba Kama 38a), emphasis mine.

6. Ibid.

7. See Deuteronomy 16:18.

8. *Adam Clarke's Commentary* (Electronic Database. Copyright © 1996, 2003 by Biblesoft, Inc. All rights reserved), on the phrase: *Ho, such a one! turn aside, sit down here* in Ruth 4:1—"This familiar mode of compilation is first used here. The original is sh^abaah poh, p^aloniy 'almoniy! 'Hark ye, Mr. Such-a-one of such a place! come and sit down here.' This is used when the person of the individual is known, and his name and residence unknown. 'Almoniy comes from 'aalam, to be silent or hidden, hence, the Septuagint renders it by kruphe, thou unknown person: p^aloniy comes from paalah, to sever or distinguish; you of such a particular place. Modes of compilation of this kind are common in all languages."

9. Ruth 4:1–3 NLT.

10. Ruth 4:4a, emphasis mine.

11. Ruth 4:4b NLT, emphasis mine.

12. Adapted from Biblesoft's *New Exhaustive Strong's Numbers and Concordance with Expanded Greek-Hebrew Dictionary* (Copyright © 1994, 2003 Biblesoft, Inc. and International Bible Translators, Inc.), definition for "advertise"— OT:1540 *galah* (gaw-law'); a primitive root; to denude (especially in a disgraceful sense); by implication, to exile (captives being usually stripped); figuratively, to reveal: KJV - advertise, appear, bewray, bring, (carry, lead, go) captive (into captivity), depart, disclose, discover, exile, be gone, open, plainly, publish, remove, reveal, shamelessly, shew, surely, tell, uncover.

13. See Deuteronomy 14:29; Proverbs 15:25; Zechariah 7:9–14; and Malachi 3:5.

14. Ruth 4:5 NLT, emphasis mine.

15. Ruth 4:6–8 NLT, emphasis mine.

16. Leonard S. Kravitz and Kerry M. Olitzky, *RUTH: A Modern Commentary* (Tel Aviv, Israel: URJ Press, 2005), p. 17. The author also said, "The chief rabbi of Israel issued a ruling in 1950 that eliminated the requirement of levirate marriage, but it remains an issue in the ultra-Orthodox *chareidi* communities."

17. *Jamieson, Fausset, and Brown Commentary* (Electronic Database. Copyright © 1997, 2003 by Biblesoft, Inc. All rights reserved), from the commentary on Ruth 4:7.

18. Cynthia Ozick, "Ruth," a chapter appearing in *Reading Ruth*, pp. 230–31, emphasis mine.

19. See Luke 10:30–37.

20. André LaCocque, trans. K. C. Hanson, *RUTH: A Continental Commentary* (Minneapolis, MN: Fortress Press, 2004), p. 111.

21. Ruth 4:9–13 NLT.

22. Ruth 4:11–13 NLT, emphasis mine.

23. See Genesis 38.

24. Tamar Frankiel, author of "Ruth and the Messiah," a chapter appearing in *Reading Ruth: Contemporary Women Reclaim a Sacred Story* (New York: Ballantine Books, 1994), p. 323: "One of David's opponents, Doeg, a brilliant man and an adviser to King Saul, repeatedly attacked David's reputation on the grounds that he was of Moabite ancestry, and encouraged Saul to kill David as a rebel (1 Samuel 22). He claimed that since David's great-grandmother was a Moabite, her marriage to Boaz was a forbidden union and therefore David was a *mamzer*, or bastard," p. 323.

25. Tikva Frymer-Kensky, *Reading the Women of the Bible: A New Interpretation of Their Stories* (New York: Schocken Books, a division of Random House, Inc., 2002), p. 253.

26. Paul the apostle said, "Until I come, give attention to the *public reading of Scripture*, to exhortation and teaching" (1 Timothy 4:13 NASB, emphasis mine).

27. LaCocque, *RUTH*, p. 123, emphasis mine.

Chapter 14: The Value of Values

1. Ruth 4:14, 17b NLT.

2. See Matthew 16:26; Mark 8:36.

3. Acts 13:22 NLT.

4. Winkie Pratney, *Fire on the Horizon* (Ventura, CA: Renew Books, a division of Gospel Light, 1999), p. 119.

5. Tamar Frankiel, author of "Ruth and the Messiah," a chapter appearing in *Reading Ruth: Contemporary Women Reclaim a Sacred Story* (New York: Ballantine Books, 1994), p. 323, emphasis and parenthetical insertion mine.

6. Ruth 4:15 NLT, emphasis and parenthetical insertion mine.

7. See Ephesians 1:6.

8. Please understand my purpose in this statement: We seem driven to find "shortcuts" in every area of life, including our salvation. In contrast to God's offer of salvation by grace and faith in Jesus Christ alone, the "other" religions of the world are popular precisely because they offer do-it-yourself work plans, mantras, and how-to kits to some sort of personal higher achievement. God's Word is *better* and more enduring than any "steel-clad" good works contract clause. Yet even Paul the apostle saw a need to clarify the difference between focusing on what he called "the *letter* of the law" and the *spirit* of the law in Romans 2:28–29; 7:6; and 2 Corinthians 3:6. The one produces death-dealing legalism because it seeks a life *separate* from the loving purpose of God who sent His Son to "seek and to save that which was lost." The other, the spirit of the law, acknowledges the need for good deeds and right actions, but places the total power of redemption in the mercy and grace of God Himself.

9. See Matthew 6:7. For in-depth insights into the mission of prayer, see my book

Prayers of a God Chaser: Passionate Prayers of Pursuit (Minneapolis, MN: Bethany House Publishers, a division of Baker Book House Company, 2002).

10. Frankiel, *Reading Ruth*, p. 324 (emphasis mine).
11. Ibid., p. 323. [NOTE: This passage was also cited in Chapter 10.]
12. Ruth 4:18–22.
13. See Galatians 2:6.
14. See Genesis 24–27.

ABOUT THE AUTHOR

Best-selling author of the GodChasers series, Tommy Tenney has ministered in and traveled through more than seventy-two countries. With that much travel he has a great deal of experience in trying to "find his way." He's more than thirty years down the road of ministry and marriage. Tommy and his wife, Jeannie, reside in Louisiana with their three daughters, a son-in-law, three grandchildren and two Yorkies. You can visit him on the Web at www.godchasers.net.

Ruth's Timeless Story–
Now in a Modern Retelling

The Road Home
In this exciting and moving modernization of the book of Ruth, Tenney and Olsen bring Ruth and her mother-in-law, Naomi, to life as they turn Naomi's creaky Impala eastward after hard living claims the men they love. As they journey across America, searching for peace and healing, they find wholeness in the last place they'd expected.

The Road Home by **Tommy Tenney and Mark Andrew Olsen**

More From Tommy Tenney
and Mark Andrew Olsen

Hadassah
Both a Jewish woman's memoir and a palace thriller full of political intrigue and suspense, *Hadassah* brings the age-old story of Esther to life. This historically accurate novel, layered with fresh insights, provides a fascinating twist on a pivotal time in religious history. *Hadassah* is also now a major motion picture, *One Night With the King*, featuring Peter O'Toole and Omar Sharif.

Hadassah by **Tommy Tenney and Mark Andrew Olsen**

The Hadassah Covenant
When an antiquities expert uncovers ancient documents bridging the centuries, he also finds a conspiracy that has tragic implications for modern-day Jews in Iraq and Iran. And Hadassah, the wife of modern-day's Israeli prime minister, may be the only hope her people have. As a history-altering truth thunders across the centuries, can this explosive discovery once again save a people?

The Hadassah Covenant by **Tommy Tenney and Mark Andrew Olsen**

Run With Us

I WOULD LOVE TO CONNECT WITH YOU...

As a GodChasers.network Ministry Partner you will receive –

- A teaching CD every month
- A special letter every month from me to you
- 25% off any product from GodChasers.network

*The ministry I do around the world couldn't happen without people partnering with me. **I** need you, and **they** need God – be the link that brings us together.* Tony Tenney

Become a GodChasers.network Ministry Partner today...

Online:
www.godchasers.net
[click "Ministry Partner" located on the side menu]

By Mail:
P.O. Box 3355 Pineville, LA 71361
[write "Ministry Partner Sign-up" in the memo line of your check]

By Phone:
(318) 442-4273

WHAT YOU CAN DO AT www.godchasers.net
- Order products from our online store
- Check Upcoming Events
- Sign-Up for Daily Devotionals by email or text message
- Sign-Up for Tommy Tenney teachings by PODcast or MP3 Downloads
- Sign-Up to be a Ministry Partner or a Prayer Partner

GodChasers.network
P.O. Box 3355
Pineville, LA 71361, USA
(318) 442-4273

Free Daily Devotions

WOULD YOU LIKE TO RECEIVE A DAILY ENCOURAGING WORD FROM TOMMY TENNEY?

Sign up to receive FREE Daily Devotions straight to your inbox.

Devotions are based on the bestselling books you love and the thought provoking sermons you have listened to. Join up and allow readable revelations to infiltrate your life, one day at a time.

Sign up today and be among the first to read inspiring insight from Tommy's newest book.

Sign up online at: www.godchasers.net
[click the "Daily Devotionals" button on the side menu]

Also...

Sign up for two-line text message devotions for your cell phone. [visit www.godchasers.net for instructions on how you can receive short and sweet inspirational words that pack a punch]
*Standard messaging, data, and other rates may apply

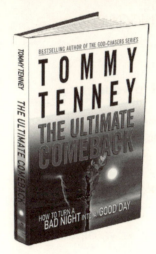

Humanitarian Outreach

GODCHASERS.NETWORK is more than a personality–more than one person–it is all of us working together to make a difference. It is a ministry that enables you to touch those who otherwise you couldn't reach.

With the history of GodChasers.network responding to Hurricane Katrina, a whole new outreach effort was birthed and continues to grow. "I feel like humanitarian outreaches will take a predominant role in the future of our ministry," says Tommy.

Whether distributing GodChasers books to our troops or raising funds to purchase backpacks for foster children, GodChasers and Tommy Tenney are not only pursuing God–but reaching to serve others.

JOIN US IN OUR EFFORT!
www.GodChasers.net